TAKING CHARGE

CHARGE

Volume 2

More Stories on
Aging Boldly

Herb Weiss

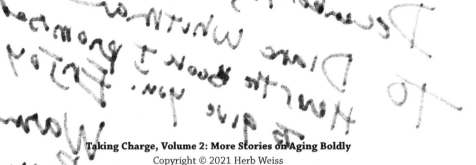

Taking Charge, Volume 2: More Stories on Aging Boldly
Copyright © 2021 Herb Weiss

Produced and printed by Stillwater River Publications.
All rights reserved. Written and produced in the
United States of America. This book may not be reproduced
or sold in any form without the expressed, written
permission of the author(s) and publisher.

Visit our website at
www.StillwaterPress.com
for more information.

First Stillwater River Publications Edition

ISBN: 978-1-955123-13-6

Library of Congress Control Number: 2016938614

1 2 3 4 5 6 7 8 9 10
Written by Herb Weiss
Published by Stillwater River Publications,
Pawtucket, RI, USA.

Publisher's Cataloging-In-Publication Data
(Prepared by The Donohue Group, Inc.)
Names: Weiss, Herbert (Journalist), author.
Title: Taking charge. Volume 2, More stories on aging boldly / Herb Weiss.
Other Titles: More stories on aging boldly
Description: First Stillwater River Publications edition. |
Pawtucket, RI, USA : Stillwater River Publications, [2021] | Volume 1
published 2016 with the title Taking charge : collected stories
on aging boldly, (LCCN: 2016938614).
Identifiers: ISBN 9781955123136
Subjects: LCSH: Aging. | Ageism. | Older people--Social conditions.
Classification: LCC HQ1061 .W3925 2021 | DDC 305.26--dc23

The views and opinions expressed
in this book are solely those of the author(s)
and do not necessarily reflect the views
and opinions of the publisher.

Dedicated to my wife, Patty Zacks,
Samantha and Liliana, Ben, Meralise and Charles,
and Molly, our chocolate Lab.

"Old age ain't no place for sissies."

—Bette Davis

CONTENTS

13. SAGE ADVICE

14. SPIRITUALITY & HELPING OTHERS

15. TRAVEL

16. VETERANS

FOREWORD

By Sarah Lenz Lock

Herb Weiss's collection of 72 essays portrays how we can all age boldly. His book provides a refreshingly positive portrait of living longer. What is striking as you read each of his stories is that despite our culture's general worship of youth, Herb's "age beat" is a place that celebrates the increasing wisdom and experience that comes with longer lives. His writings offer the most human and best way of giving you the advice you need in a way you want: storytelling.

Through *Taking Charge*, Herb intriguingly shows us that aging is an ongoing process, and that it is never too late to move in a better direction. Take his Commencement tips to seniors graduating high school or college. They remind us that every day you wake up is another chance to commence, again. And he provides these insights like a wise friend, suggesting a different approach that might make your life better, richer and just perhaps help avoid some of the pitfalls that may otherwise trip you up.

Herb weaves a story conveying the advice you need to know to age boldly in a way you want to read about it. I lead a distinguished group of neurologists, geriatricians, and psychiatrists from all over the world called the Global Council on Brain Health (GCBH). The GCBH lets people know what works and what doesn't to improve your brain health as you age. After much study over several months these experts produce treatises of helpful information. I am inordinately proud the GCBH distills the science on relevant topics into short, easy to understand, white papers for people to use in their lives. By short, I mean about 25 pages. Long before COVID hit, the GCBH completed our report on how social isolation can harm your brain health. The 2017 Social Engagement report **https:// www.aarp.org/content/dam/aarp/health/brain_health/2017/02/ gcbh-social-engagement-report-english-aarp.doi.10.26419%252F-pia.00015.001.pdf** was only 24 pages long! Herb covered that report, but instead of a dry white paper, he proffers all its wisdom in a delightful one-page story. He shares the charming tale of Nancy and Mark Shorrock coming to a place in Pawtucket called Spumoni's for more than 20 years.

In a piece called, "Where Everybody Knows Your Name," Herb instantly conjures up a place for us we can all recognize and where we all want to be. He feeds us the lessons of how vital social engagement is to our brain health, without us ever having to chew through 24 pages of a white paper, and provides a road map about how to implement it in our own lives with fun. His portrait of community stays with us, and we only have to think of the Shorrocks to know how to live.

I have never met Herb Weiss, but I want to. I have never been to Pawtucket, but I want to do that too. Any place that can inspire a writer like Herb to craft beautiful stories and that provide such a positive perspective on aging must be a nice place to be. So even though you may not be able to go to Pawtucket, or share a meal at Spumoni's right now, you can curl up with this good book. Reading it will help you feel as if you are part of a community of people who choose to take charge of their living, follow their wise friend Herb's advice, and age boldly.

Sarah Lenz Lock is senior vice president for Policy and Brain Health at AARP. Ms. Lock leads AARP's policy initiatives to spark a lifetime of healthier brains and to disrupt dementia. Sarah serves as the executive director of the Global Council on Brain Health, an independent collaborative of scientists, doctors, and policy experts to provide trusted information on brain health.

PREFACE

A growing number of aging baby boomers and senior readers turn to newspapers, electronic media and the internet to investigate issues and identify resources to help them age gracefully.

Over the years, while journalists have made improvements in their reporting, age bias still exists in writing and reporting by reporters immersed in economics or political writing but not familiar with related issues in aging, warns San Francisco-based journalist Paul Kleyman, editor of the e-newsletter, Generations Beat Online (GBONews.org), the Journalists Network on Generations, founded in 1993. The e-newsletter is a great resource for those covering aging. It is distributed to more than 1,000 journalists and authors on aging. Kleyman, a seasoned journalist, covers a wide spectrum of issues the media must spotlight in an aging American society.

Kleyman says: "*The New York Times* has terrific stories, such as Paula Span's "New Old Age" column, or knowledgeable personal finance stories by contributors like Kerry Hannon and Mark Miller in their "Retiring" columns. But then the *Times* will run stories by staff or contributing writers, who fall back into the old conventional folly (no wisdom there) that the aging of the population necessarily will create a burden of illness and weigh down the GDP."

"Illness will always be there with advanced age, but they fail to stop and think at all about the continued contributions of many more who age with greater health and capability," says Kleyman. "Those reporters and their editors somehow fail to consider the substantial gerontological research that for years has contested their underlying assumptions, such as that the only answer to declining birth rates is to incentivize the young to have more babies, not to, for example, look toward today's more educated, healthier older adults for more productivity. That's already the case," he adds.

Kleyman added, "There's always a lag with reporting from conventional and, yes, often distinguished reporters never updating disproven social or scientific views. And that reporting can, unfortunately, reinforce retro policymaking and political decisions."

"The more accurate facts and analyses eventually will lead to smarter understanding and better identification of where to look for the fixes, such as improving policies to combat age discrimination that cuts off older people from being able to contribute to their communities, including through more tax paying," Kleyman says.

He went on, "A positive change, though, has been the influx of very knowledgeable journalists seeding the news media across the web and throughout the country. Herb Weiss has long helped lead the way with richly informed columns."

Through my writings I strive to stand among the more well-informed journalists covering the age beat, who know and write better, and are better able to inform the public about the Longevity Revolution, with all of its challenges and implications, both positive and challenging.

For more than 40 years, with more than 790 published articles (written or co-authored) in newspapers, news blogs and trade publications, this writer has reported on the latest studies and reports on a myriad of aging, medical or health-care issues. Many of these timely articles covered cutting-edge studies and reports released by the Washington, DC-based AARP and other sources, bringing pertinent information to seniors to help their readers better plan for their later years.

The 16 chapters in Vol. 2 of *Taking Charge: More Collected Stories on Aging Boldly,* 75 articles published from 2016 to 2021 were compiled. Each article lists the date and newspaper it was published in.

Like the previous volume, this collection of articles gives the reader insights and practical information about how people in their later years can take charge and enjoy a full and satisfying quality of life, unparalleled in our nation's history. Even if the article was written years ago, and the person quoted is no longer in his or her position, or even deceased, the insight is still factual and valuable to the reader.

While most of my articles cover national research and public policy issues, I localize them by quoting Rhode Islanders. However, their stories are universal and their insights applicable anywhere in the nation.

These articles bring together the expertise and knowledge of experts along with comments of people over age 50 sharing their observations and insights about caregiving, travel, surviving COVID-19, improving health and finances, relationships, retirement and leisure, to their thoughts about mental health, spirituality and death.

Yes, each one of us can tell our own personal stories or even share an experience that just might help others age boldly, live better, and longer.

I will continue to use my weekly columns in the *Pawtucket Times, Woonsocket Call*, RINewsToday and the monthly newspaper, *Senior Digest*, to bring a bully pulpit to advocate for seniors to enhance their quality of life and to bring to them the most informative coverage of aging, medical and health-care issues they need to know.

—Herb Weiss, LRI'12

ACKNOWLEDGEMENTS

I acknowledge and thank my wife, Patty Zacks, for her support and being a sounding board, critiquing my articles penned over 25 years.

To those who encouraged me during my earlier writing years, I acknowledge my parents, Frank and Sally Weiss, my sisters Mickie, Nancy, and my brother Jim, his wife, Jennifer, my brother-in-law, Justin Aurbach, and family friends Fred Levy and Myron Ball.

To Sarah Lenz Lock, Senior Vice President, Policy & Brain Health, Policy, Research and International, AARP and Executive Director, Global Council on Brain Health, who wrote the foreword of my book, and to my reviewers former AARP Rhode Island Director Kathleen S. Connell, Robyn Spizman, a *New York Times* best-selling author, UCLA Professor Dr. Fernando Torres-Gil, Max Richtman, President and CEO of the National Committee to Preserve Social Security and Medicare, and Nurse Educator and Clinician Dr. Janet Cogliano, I am honored by your participation on my book project. My appreciation to Lauren Long for copy editing the final draft of my second book, Taking Charge, Volume 2: More Stories on Aging Boldly.

I would like to express my gratitude to Publishers Steve and Dawn Porter of Stillwater River Publications, who provided guidance to me on editorial content and graphic design during this book project and the completion of *Vol. 1*.

Thank you to Keri Ambrosino of Designs by Keri for assisting me in bringing my social marketing materials to life.

I would like to take this opportunity to express my thanks to Regional Publisher Jody Boucher and Executive Editor Seth Bromley, of Rhode Island Suburban Newspapers, publishers of the daily newspapers, *Pawtucket Times* and *Woonsocket Call*, Editor Nancy Thomas of **www.RINewsToday.com**, a statewide news blog, and TCI Press, Inc., publisher of *Senior Digest*, a monthly publication for seniors, for giving me a bully pulpit to advocate for America's seniors.

Almost every time I went to see my good friend, Morris Nathanson, he would ask me when my second book was going to be published. Here it is. Morris, thanks for your encouragement and friendship.

Finally, my gratitude to Mātā Amritānandamayī Devī, known simply as Amma, a Hindu spiritual leader and guru who blessed my initial book project (*Vol. 1, Taking Charge: Collected Stories on Aging Boldly*). She told me there is a need for Americans to have access to information to help them "age gracefully."

To my long-time friend, Baba Ray Whitman, you've always been just a phone call away, never shy about giving me both practical and spiritual guidance to overcome life's challenges. Thank you for always being there for me.

Most important, I thank the thousands of people I have interviewed over my journalistic career of 40 years, who generously contributed their insights and observations about aging, health care and medical issues to my articles and the publications I edited.

—Herb Weiss, LRI '12

1. CAREGIVING

"There are only four kinds of people in the world. Those who have been caregivers. Those who are currently caregivers. Those who will be caregivers, and those who will need a caregiver."

— Rosalyn Carter

STUDY: ONE IN FIVE AMERICANS ARE UNPAID FAMILY CAREGIVERS

Published in the *Woonsocket Call* on May 17, 2020

As the nation sees a growing number of aging baby boomers, workforce shortages in health care and long-term care settings, increased state funding for community-based services, and a growing number of seniors requiring assistance in their daily activities, caregivers are needed more than ever. According to a recently released report from National Alliance for Caregiving (NAC) and AARP, an increasing number of unpaid family caregivers are stepping up to the plate to care for their older family members or friends. The caregiver report's findings indicate that the number of family caregivers in the United States increased by 9.5 million from 2015 (43.5 million) to 2020 (53 million) and now encompasses more than one in five Americans (19 percent).

First conducted in 1997, with follow-up surveys in 2004, 2009, and 2015, the *Caregiving in the US* studies are one of the most comprehensive resources describing the American caregiver. *Caregiving in the US 2020* was conducted by Greenwald & Associates using a nationally representative, probability-based online panel. More than 1,700 caregivers who were age 18 or older participated in the survey in 2019.

Demand for Caregiving Rising as Nation's Population Gets Older

The 107-page *Caregiving in the US 2020* report also reveals that family caregivers are in worse health compared to five years ago. As the demand for caregiving rises with the graying of the nation's population, the report calls for more to be done to support this vital work.

"As we face a global pandemic, we're relying on friends and family to care for the older adults and people living with disabilities in our lives," notes C. Grace Whiting, JD, president and CEO of NAC, in a May 14 statement announcing the release of this report. "Caregivers are essential to the nation's public health, and the magnitude of millions of Americans providing unpaid care means that supporting caregivers can no longer be ignored," she says, noting that report's findings reveal that growing need.

According to Whiting, family caregivers care for more people than five years ago and they take on more care responsibilities as roughly one in four care for two or more people. "Many individuals are caring for a longer time, with nearly a third (29 percent) of caregivers nationwide reporting they have been caregiving for five years or more—up from 24 percent in the last study," states Whiting.

This new caregiver study shows that 39 percent are men and 61 percent are women. The average age is 49.4 years. The profile of the family caregiver is also changing, too. While caregiving spans across all generations, *Caregiving in the US 2020* found more young people providing care, including 6 percent who are Gen Z and 23 percent who are Millennials. Nearly half (45 percent) are caring for someone with two or more conditions—a significant jump from 37 percent in 2015.

As to ethnicity, the caregiver report notes that 6 in 10 are non-Hispanic White (61 percent), 17 percent are Hispanic, and 14 percent are African American.

The report's findings indicate that 1 in 10 of the caregiver survey respondents are enrolled in college or taking classes (11 percent), 9 percent have served in the military and 8 percent self-identify as lesbian, gay, bisexual, and/or transgender.

Caregivers in Poorer Health, Feeling Financial Strain

Caregiving in the US 2020 also found that caregivers face health challenges of their own with nearly a quarter (23 percent) of caregivers finding it hard to take care of their own health and 23 percent say caregiving has made their health worse. The report also notes that personal finances are a concern for family caregivers: 28 percent have stopped saving money, 23 percent have taken on more debt and 22 percent have used up personal short-term savings.

Sixty-one percent of the caregiver respondents work and have difficulty in coordinating care.

The May 2020 caregiver report states on average, caregivers spend 23.7 hours a week providing care, with one in three (32 percent) providing care for 21 hours or more, and one in five (21 percent) providing care for 41-plus hours— the equivalent of a full-time unpaid job.

"The coronavirus pandemic is exacerbating the challenges family caregivers were already facing from a personal health, financial, and emotional standpoint," said Susan Reinhard, RN, Ph.D., senior vice president at AARP. "Family caregivers provide vital help and care for·their loved ones, yet this survey shows that they keep getting stretched thinner and thinner. We must identify and implement more solutions to support family caregivers—both in the short term as we grapple with coronavirus and in the long term as our population ages and the number of family caregivers declines."

"Without greater explicit support for family caregivers in coordination among the public and private sectors and across multiple disciplines, overall care responsibilities will likely intensify and place greater pressure on individuals within families, especially as baby boomers move into old age," warns the report's authors, calling on Congress and state lawmakers to develop policies that ensure that caregivers do not suffer deteriorating health effects and financial insecurity.

Thoughts from AARP Rhode Island...

"The wealth of information in this report is an essential guide to policymakers," said AARP Rhode Island state director Kathleen Connell. "It reveals important trends and underlines future needs. For AARP, it provides information on how, as an organization, we can best serve Rhode Island's 136,000 family caregivers. The challenges they face vary, making it very important that we can provide focused resources that meet any one caregiver's needs. The report's overall takeaway—that the number of caregivers is rising dramatically—is a call for increased awareness and support. This responsibility starts at the very top of federal, state, and municipal government and flows all the way down to family members who can better share caregiving responsibilities. Many will be asked to step outside their comfort zone, so we all will have to work together," adds Connell.

Connell noted that the report points out the shift from traditional residential health care settings to community-based settings. "The research reaches a clear conclusion," Connell observed.

"Families will have to fill new roles, learn new skills and absorb more out-of-pocket caregiving expenses. This will create additional stress for many family caregivers. That's why it is so important that we develop the training, tools, and other resources caregivers require."

A 2019 AARP report, *Valuing the Invaluable*, calculated that Rhode Island family caregivers provide 114 million unpaid hours of care annually. Based on the average $15.76 per hour wages of paid caregivers, family caregivers represent an economic value of an estimated $1.8 billion.

The 2020 study was funded by AARP, Best Buy Health Inc. d/b/a Great Call, EMD Serono Inc., Home Instead Senior Care®, The Gordon and Betty Moore Foundation, The John A. Hartford Foundation, TechWerks, Transamerica Institute, and UnitedHealthcare.

For a copy of *Caregiving in the US 2020*, go to **https://www.aarp.org/ppi/ info-2020/caregiving-in-the-united-states.html**

UNCOMPENSATED COST OF CAREGIVERS IS A WHOPPING $470 BILLION

Published in the *Woonsocket Call* on November 17, 2019

Approximately 41 million unpaid family caregivers provided an estimated 34 billion hours of care in 2017—worth a whopping $470 billion—to their parents, spouses, partners, and friends, according to the latest report in AARP's *Valuing the Invaluable* series. The 2019 estimated value of family caregiving is based on 41 million caregivers providing an average of 16 hours of care per week, at an average value of $13.81 per hour. Previous AARP Public Policy Institute reports were released in 2006, 2008, 2011, and 2015.

"It's encouraging to see greater recognition of the emotional, physical, and financial struggles that caregivers face," said Susan Reinhard, senior vice president of the AARP Public Policy Institute, in an April 14 statement announcing the release of the 32-page report. "But the demands on family caregivers are not just a family issue, and we must continue to push for meaningful support and solutions," says Reinhard.

"Every caregiver, as well as their families, knows the value of their efforts," said AARP Rhode Island state director Kathleen Connell. "In Rhode Island, the estimated total value of 114 million hours of work by the state's 136,000 caregivers is $1.8 billion. The aggregate is astounding, making a clear case for supporting this vital commitment made by family and loved ones."

"These numbers inspire our members who spend many hours at the State House as AARP Rhode Island advocacy volunteers," Connell added. "They have helped pass key legislation—the CARE Act, paid caregiver leave, and many other key bills—that have given caregivers resources and opportunities to make their task less daunting. Caregivers are truly invaluable," she says.

Putting a Spotlight on the Nation's Caregivers

AARP's report notes that the estimated $470 billion equates to about $1,450 for every person in the United States (325 million people in 2017). Its economic impact is more than all out-of-pocket spending on US health care in 2017 ($366 billion). Uncompensated care provided by caregivers is also three times as much as total Medicaid spending on long-term services (LTSS) and supports ($154 billion in 2016) and even the total spending from all sources of paid LTSS, including post-acute care ($366 billion in 2016).

The AARP researchers say that the estimate of $470 billion in economic value of uncompensated care is consistent with nearly two decades of prior research studies, all of which found (like the current study) that the value of unpaid family care vastly exceeds the value of paid home care.

The AARP report, *Valuing the Invaluable: 2019 Update Charting a Path Forward*, also explores the growing scope and complexity of caregiving, including an aging population, more family caregivers in the paid workforce, and the increasing amount of medical and nursing tasks entering the home.

According to the AARP report, family caregivers, who provide day-to-day supports and services and manage complex care tasks, are becoming more diverse. While most family caregivers are women, about 40 percent are men who are providing more assistance than just driving to doctor's appointments and grocery stores or paying bills. Like all caregivers, they are assisting a parent, spouse, or friend with bathing and dressing, pain management, managing medication, changing dressings, helping with incontinence and even preparing special diets.

While a majority of baby boomers are providing caregiving services, a growing number of younger adults are now shouldering this responsibility too. Nearly 1 in 4 (24 percent) are Millennials (born between 1980 and 1996). Despite their low salaries, the young adults are spending more of their salary on caregiving expenses than other generations. The researchers estimated that this spending in 2016 was about 27 percent of their income.

About 60 percent of family caregivers are juggling a job and providing care, too. This will continue as aging baby boomers choose to remain in the labor force to bring additional income into their household. Workplace benefits for caregivers becomes become even more important as they face economic and financial strain in their later years.

For those employees who choose to leave their job to become a full-time caregiver, they risk both short- and long-term financial difficulties, say the researchers.

Finally, the researchers' recommendations to better support family caregivers included developing a robust and comprehensive national strategy with the needs of an increasingly diverse caregiver population included; providing financial relief and expanding workplace policies; developing caregiver training programs; and expanding state and federal funding for respite programs.

More Work Needs to Be Done

The AARP report warns that the rising demand for caregivers with the graying of the nation's population and shrinking families will drastically reduce the supply. In 2010, there were 7.1 potential family caregivers for every person age 80 and over. By 2030, there may be only 4.1 potential caregivers for every person age 80 and over, they say.

Although significant federal and state policies are already in place to assist the nation's caregivers, more work needs to be done, say the researchers. They call on Congress and state lawmakers to keep pace with the changing demographic, social trends, and needs of the family caregiver.

Resources and information on family caregiving, including AARP's Prepare to Care Guides, are available at **http://www.aarp.org/caregiving.**

CAREGIVERS FIND IT DIFFICULT TO SHOP AT RETAIL STORES

Published in the *Woonsocket Call* on September 22, 2019

S urvey findings from a recently released national study by the Washington, DC-based AARP and NORC at the University of Chicago will send a strong message to America's businesses.

With the graying of America, retail stores must change the way they do business to attract customers who provide unpaid family caregiving to their loved ones.

The study, *Family Caregiver Retail Preferences and Challenges*, and its survey findings were presented at the AARP Executive Summit, The Price of Caring, on September 10 in Washington, DC. The summit's mission was to highlight public- and private-sector solutions to support Americans who care for an older or ill loved one.

In-Store Shopping is a Struggle

While juggling a multitude of caregiving tasks, caregivers say a lack of accommodations for their frail family members is a problem for shopping at retail stores. The study's findings reveal that in-store shopping is a struggle for one-third of the nation's 40 million unpaid family caregivers. Many leave their loved ones at home or choose to shop online, despite strongly preferring the in-store experience.

A whopping 93 percent of caregivers surveyed say they shop for the person they care for. Among these caregivers, most report shopping monthly for groceries (87 percent), basic household items (65 percent), toiletries (61 percent), prescription drugs (58 percent), and other health products (52 percent) for persons they regularly care for.

"Americans who take care of loved ones are often strapped for time, and many face logistical challenges doing something as simple as going to the grocery store," said Nancy LeaMond, AARP executive vice president and chief advocacy & engagement officer, in a September 10 statement announcing the study's findings. "Retailers can score big with caregivers if they make it easier for them to bring their loved ones along when they shop," says LeaMond.

The AARP survey findings detail simple but important changes retailers should consider to enhance the shopping experience of caregivers. Businesses can provide dedicated parking spots and ample, comfortable reserved seating for older shoppers to rest, wider aisles that easily accommodate both wheelchairs and shopping carts, longer store hours, and training their staff to specifically work with caregivers.

The Pros and Cons of In-Store and Online Shopping

The survey findings in the 26-page study reveal that 82 percent of the caregiver respondents prefer to shop in-store because of the ability to touch the products and they don't have to wait for a product's delivery or pay for shipping charges. But 84 percent say they shop online for ease and convenience, despite preferring an in-store experience. Forty-three percent of the respondents say a major reason they leave their loved one at home when shopping is because the store environment is too difficult for the recipients of their care.

More than 56 percent of the caregiver respondents say that when shopping on behalf of their loved ones they spend at least $50 per month. Forty-one percent note they spend more than $250 or more a month when shopping for a loved one.

Businesses Must Listen to the Shopping Needs of Caregivers

"We listen to a lot of caregivers, and it seems clear that, regardless of the challenge, the help they want most is somehow to find a convenient, time-efficient, and accommodating means of getting what they need, when they need it," said Rhode Island AARP state director Kathleen Connell. "In retailing, convenience is a huge competitive advantage these days. But there are aspects of convenience that—for caregivers—go beyond finding what you need on Amazon and having it delivered the next day or two," says Connell.

"Some caregiver needs are in the ASAP category, and they head for brick and mortar retail establishments. Shopping for food and clothes, picking up a prescription or medical supplies, even simple things such as picking up dry cleaning feel like 'emergencies' because time is so. Imagine this in the context of being with someone in a walker or wheelchair," notes Connell.

Connell urges retailers to take this report to heart. "There is an incredible amount of goodwill to be earned if you think about caregivers, as well as those in their care, and give them the consideration that makes their tasks a little easier."

The AARP survey was conducted by NORC at the University of Chicago and is based on a nationally representative survey of 1,127 Americans who provide unpaid care for an adult age 18 or older. The survey was funded by AARP and used AmeriSpeak®, the probability-based panel of NORC at the University of Chicago. Interviews were conducted during Aug. 1-19, 2019, online and using landlines and cell phones. The overall margin of sampling error is +/- 4.1 percentage points at the 95 percent confidence level, including the design effect. The margin of sampling error may be higher for subgroups.

To read the full report, visit: **http://www.aarp.org/caregivershopping**.

CAREGIVERS FLYING BLIND IN PROVIDING COMPLEX MEDICAL AND NURSING CARE

Published in the *Woonsocket Call* on April 21, 2019

Half of the nation's 40 million family caregivers are performing intense and complicated medical and nursing tasks, as well as managing multiple health conditions for their family members and friends, says a newly published AARP report.

AARP's special report, *Home Alone Revisited: Family Caregivers Providing Complex Care*, released April 17, 2019, takes a close look at specific medical and nursing tasks (including giving injections, preparing special diets, managing tube feedings, and even handling medical equipment) that family caregivers are currently doing. It's a follow-up report to AARP's 2012 Home Alone study that took the first in-depth look at how caregivers managed providing complex medical and nursing care that was formerly offered by trained professionals.

Changing Health Care System to Support Family Caregivers

"This report shows the extent of complex tasks that millions of family caregivers are providing every day. They are largely alone in learning how to perform these tasks," said Susan Reinhard, RN, Ph.D., senior vice president and director at the AARP Policy Institute, in a statement announcing the release of the 56-page report. "About half of family caregivers are worried about making a mistake. We need to do a lot more across the health care system—with providers and hospitals—to help support these family caregivers," says Reinhard.

Adds Rani E. Snyder, program director at The John A. Hartford Foundation, "Family caregivers are the lynchpin in our health care system, particularly for older adults. This study shines new light on the diversity of family caregivers performing complex tasks—from men to Millennials to multicultural populations—and is a rallying cry for an all-hands-on-deck approach to creating age-friendly health systems that better support and prepare these often forgotten members of the health care team."

"The new statistics in this report shed more light on the demands of family caregiving," said AARP Rhode Island state director Kathleen Connell, a former nurse. "These described caregiving responsibilities sound like a task list for a team of home nurses, aides, dieticians, physical therapists, and personal drivers who work without weekends off, much less vacations. Is there any question that people worry about making a mistake that compounds existing issues?" she says.

"The takeaway is quite clear," Connell added. "Caregiving is stressful, and we need to expand efforts to provide assistance. And it's a very big 'we' that I am speaking of. Families need to help out and share more responsibilities as well as offer respite for primary caregivers. Neighbors and extended family also can lend a hand. And we need government to continue to provide assistance through legislation that supports family caregivers. Caregiving responsibilities can be both daunting and exhausting. It's the new reality. The good news is that as we raise awareness we can work together to improve the lives of caregivers," says Connell.

A Sampling of the AARP Report's Findings

AARP's *Home Alone Revisited* report found that almost half of the caregiver respondents (48 percent) prepare special diets multiple times per day. Preparing these meals often involved taking precise measurements, following specific dietary guidelines, constant monitoring, and the use of special equipment for preparation and feeding.

Thirty percent of the respondents say preparing special diets is hard to manage, this being more challenging to men. Younger caregivers found it more difficult to manage this task than older caregivers.

The caregivers also reported that 54 percent of the survey's respondents say they manage incontinence multiple times a day. Most say managing incontinence is more difficult than managing medications, helping with assistive devices, and performing wound care. Seventy-six percent say they learned how to manage incontinence on their own. More than one in four would appreciate having assistance from another person.

According to AARP's report, 70 percent of these caregivers are dealing with the emotional stress of managing pain relief in the middle of a national opioid crisis. More than 4 in 10 expressed concerns about giving the optimal dose.

About 4 in 10 faced difficulties in controlling the pain of the care recipient.

Finally, 51 percent of the survey respondents assisted with canes, walkers, and other mobility devices while more than a third (37 percent) dealt with wound care.

The researchers conclude that the "uncomplicated world of 'informal' caregiving no longer applies" to the nation's caregivers. "In the current health care environment, it is presumed that every home is a potential hospital and every service that the person needs can be provided by an unpaid family member, with only occasional visits by a primary care provider, nurse, or therapist," say the researchers.

AARP's *Home Alone Revisited* report is a must-read for Congress and state lawmakers who can easily address the challenges caregivers face when providing medically complex care by crafting policies and programs that will provide support and resources to the nation's growing number of caregivers.

This caregiving issue might be a good one for the US Senate Special Committee on Aging to study.

A Final Note…

AARP gathered the study's data through a nationally representative, population-based, online survey of 2,089 family caregivers. This study employed an oversampling of multicultural groups, taking a closer look at difficult tasks and putting greater attention on available resources and outcomes. The study's sampling strategy ensured multicultural representation and investigated generational differences. Additionally, the researchers also explored certain topics in greater depth, including special diets, incontinence, pain, and the impact of social isolation on the caregiver.

The AARP Home Alone study is a special report from the Founders of the Home Alone Alliance (AARP, United Hospital Fund, Family Caregiver Alliance and UC Davis-Betty Irene Moore School of Nursing). With funding from The John A. Hartford Foundation to the AARP Foundation, the study took an in-depth look at the specific medical/nursing tasks that family caregivers are doing.

To read the full report, go to: **https://www.AARP.org/ppi/info-2018/ home-alone-family-caregivers-providing-complex-chronic-care.html**.

ASSISTANCE TO EMPLOYEE CAREGIVERS GOOD FOR EVERYONE'S BOTTOM LINE

Published in the *Woonsocket Call* on June 11, 2017

ays ago, AARP and the Respect a Caregiver's Time Coalition (ReACT) released a report detailing innovative practices and policies of 14 organizations to support their employees with caregiver responsibilities. With the graying of America, supporting caregiver employees should be considered "a potentially new weapon" to attract or retain talented employees, say the researchers, by flexible work arrangements and paid leave policies. And there will be a need for this support.

It is estimated that of the 40 million unpaid family caregivers in the US, 60 percent are employed. According to the National Alliance for Caregiving (NAC) and AARP Public Policy Institute, nearly 25 percent of all family caregivers are Millennials, and 50 percent are under the age of 50. This means that the growing number of family caregivers in the workforce is an issue that all employers will face. The NAC/AARP research also revealed that 61 percent of working caregivers must make workplace accommodations including modifying hours, taking a leave of absence, choosing early retirement, or turning down a promotion.

Detailing Best Practices to Support Employee Caregivers

The 14 case studies in the new report, *Supporting Working Caregivers: Case Studies of Promising Practices,* include well-known organizations from both the for-profit and nonprofit sectors, and both large and small employers. They represent a broad set of industries, including financial services, health care, higher education, home care, management consulting, media, and technology.

There is no "one size fits all" solution to meeting the needs of employee caregivers, say the researchers. But even with the diversity of the 14 participating organizations "there is clear evidence of promising practices" identified through these interviews, they note.

Researchers gleaned best practices from 14 nonprofits and for-profits (from very large employers with more than 200,000 workers to ones with less than 200 workers), detailing in the report released on June 8, 2017, how these organizations assist their caregiver employees. These companies provide a broad array of information resources and referrals, flexible work arrangements, paid time off for caregiving, emergency backup care, and, in some cases, high-touch counseling and care management advice.

"Family caregivers juggle their loved one's needs with their own personal and professional goals every day. AARP hopes this report will encourage more employers to understand caregiving and support their employees' success," said Nancy LeaMond, executive vice president and chief advocacy and engagement officer in a statement. AARP sponsored the 49-page report.

According to researchers, interviews with business and human-resources executives from the profiled organizations indicated that time and flexibility are what matter most to employees when it comes to balancing work and caregiving. Close to half of the employers interviewed provide paid time off for caregiving as well as emergency backup care and flexible work arrangements.

All offer employee caregivers a combination of information resources, referral services, and advice by phone. Most provide resources online, typically through an employee assistance program (EAP) or an intranet portal. More than half offer phone consultations or 24/7 expert hotlines. Several interviewees stressed the value of providing on-site, independent eldercare consultants, noting that employees appreciate both the convenience and the respect for their privacy.

"ReACT represents a cross-sector employer effort to raise awareness of and spur action to meet the challenges millions face every day while taking care of an older loved one," said Drew Holzapfel, convener of ReACT, in a statement. "It's exciting to see how leading organizations are showcasing the value of employee caregivers' dual roles at home and in the office."

Thumbs Up to Assisting Employee Caregivers

Interviewees at the participating organizations were not shy in explaining the importance of offering caregiver assistance to employees.

Michelle Stone, Fannie Mae's Work-Life Benefits senior program manager, says, "We have been asked, 'How can you afford to do this?' Our response is,

'How can we afford not to?' The program helps our company and our employees save time and money, and the return on investment is substantial."

Michelle Martin, vice president of Human Resources Specialty Services in the CBS Corporation, states, "Our hope is to fill the gaps in support along the continuum of care so that employees not only have what they need to care, but also the peace of mind to do so without worrying about their job."

"At Allianz Life, we like to say, 'we've been keeping promises to our employees and customers since our founding.' Nothing matters more than our employees and we work every day to provide them with benefits that allow for work-life balance and peace of mind," says Suzanne Dowd Zeller, chief human-resources officer.

Adds Audrey Adelson, manager of work-life, Emory University, "Our program is based on a continuum of care model, designed to support not only entrenched caregivers, but also those who anticipate becoming a caregiver, and those whose caregiving responsibilities have ended and are beginning to move beyond caregiving."

AARP Rhode Island Champions Caregiving Temporary Disability Insurance

"Most employers recognize that some of their best workers are not at their best when they are caregivers in crisis for feeling the onset of burnout," AARP Rhode Island state director Kathleen Connell noted. "One of the reasons that most employers and their human-resources managers respond to the needs of caregivers is because they are not far removed from caregiving if not caregivers themselves. They know that caregiving responsibilities sometimes must take precedence over work. And they understand that what is good for the caregiver is also good for their business.

"In Rhode Island, caregiving temporary disability insurance—legislation championed by AARP—gives caregivers paid leave to attend to caregiving tasks or as respite when a break from work benefits all concerned. Employers should assess their policies and give thought to the importance of supporting their caregiving employees' success. This is true of businesses large and small and nonprofits as well. These bosses can start by simply asking themselves what their expectations would be if they were an employee."

Rhode Island CEOs might consider obtaining a copy of this report, passing the document to human resources for review and ultimate implementation of eldercare policies. Stressed employee caregivers will appreciate any assistance they can get to help them in their caregiving responsibilities. But this makes good business sense too. Assisting employee caregivers will increase employee productivity, improving the company's bottom line.

CAREGIVERS TAKING CARE OF PERSONS WITH DEMENTIA HAVE UNIQUE NEEDS

Published in the *Woonsocket Call* on December 9, 2018

Being a caregiver 24/7 to a person in relatively good health is a tough job. But caring for someone with dementia becomes a 36-hour one, say authors Nancy L. Mace and Peter V. Rabins, in their groundbreaking book (published in 1981) on providing care for those with the devastating mental disorder.

The Washington, DC-based AARP releases survey findings last month that take a look at this "unique subset of caregivers" who are taking care of persons with dementia and other cognitive disorders. Caregiving takes a physical and emotional toll on these individuals, forcing them to put in longer hours providing care and making adjustments at work and in their personal relationships, says the findings of the newly released study.

The AARP online national survey (of caregivers 18 and older) takes a look at the demands on 700 caregivers taking care of persons with dementia or other forms of cognitive impairments (most often their parents), as well as 400 caregivers who were providing care for a loved one without dementia. Regardless of the situation, on average, caregivers report having been caring for their loved one for almost three years.

"Family caregivers take on big responsibilities that can be physically, emotionally, and financially challenging. AARP's new research shows that this can be particularly true for those caring for loved ones with dementia," said Nancy LeaMond, AARP chief advocacy and engagement officer, in a statement released with the report, *Caring for People with Dementia: Caregivers' Experiences*. "That's why AARP has developed resources to help family caregivers balance their own needs with the needs of their loved one," adds LeaMond.

The AARP Study Found...

Obviously, it is time-consuming to be a caregiver. The AARP survey's findings, released on November 30, 2018, found that 7 in 10 of those surveyed spend less time with friends and more than half spend less time with other family members because of the intensity of caregiving responsibilities. While 75 percent of the survey respondents reported that caring for someone with dementia has brought about closer relationships and more meaning to their lives, the findings also indicate that caregiving experiences bring greater challenges to their lives, too.

According to the 26-page AARP report's findings, those caring for persons with dementia (more likely a parent) spend on average 13.7 hours per week caregiving, while caregivers taking care of persons with no cognitive afflictions, spend 11.7 hours (more likely a spouse or partner or a friend or neighbor). Three in ten of the caregiver respondents (over age 35) spend more than 21 hours per week caregiving, says the study's findings.

Most of the caregiver respondents providing care to persons with dementia see the devastating disorder slowly progressing over time. But younger caregivers perceive the onset of cognitive decline as suddenly happening.

About 32 percent of the caregiver respondents providing more intense caregiving to persons with dementia say managing their emotions and the demands of care they deliver (26 percent) are the biggest challenges they face.

Caregivers taking care of persons with dementia also reported negative health behaviors. They slept less (71 percent), had more anxiety (65 percent) and depression (54 percent), and spent less time on themselves and with their friends. Research studies reveal that social isolation and loneliness are linked to poorer physical and mental health outcomes.

Not only are the millions of family caregivers for those with dementia less socially connected, they are significantly more likely to put off medical care—more than half (55 percent) have done so, compared to just 38 percent among the total caregiver population. However, there were positive health behaviors identified in the poll as well—79 percent took steps to maintain or improve their brain health, and 47 percent exercised more.

About 62 percent of those taking care of persons with dementia state that their intense caregiving responsibilities have led them to working different hours, leaving work early (62 percent), or taking paid (53 percent) and unpaid time off (47 percent) for caregiving duties, and also worrying about their finances.

Two-thirds of all caregivers surveyed say they feel closer to their loved one, but those taking care of persons with dementia were more likely to say their relationship with their loved one over time had grown further apart (22 percent) than others. Those caregivers of persons with dementia were more likely to say the relationships with other family members have been strained.

Finally, caregiver respondents say that they are receiving what they need from health-care providers yet those caring for someone with dementia also have sought more information about caregiving from a greater variety of sources.

The AARP survey was conducted October 1-10, 2018. Data are weighted by income, gender, and age according to caregiver benchmarks obtained in *Caregiving in the US* (2015).

Finding Caregiver Resources

AARP helps family caregivers find the information and support they need to manage their own care along with their loved one's care. Go to **http://www. aarp.org/caregiving** for more resources and information on family caregiving, including AARP's dementia care guide and the Community Resource Finder.

AARP GIVES US A SNAPSHOT OF THE MILLENNIAL CAREGIVER

Published in the *Woonsocket Call* on June 3, 2018

A ARP's latest caregiver report places the spotlight on the Millennial generation, those born between 1980 and 1996, ages 22 to 38 in 2018. *Millennials: The Emerging Generation of Family Caregivers*, using data based primarily from the 2015 *Caregiving in the US* study, notes that one in four of the nearly 40 million family caregivers in America is a Millennial.

The 11-page report, released by AARP's Public Policy Institute on May 22, 2018, takes a look at the Millennials' generational experiences and challenges as they support an aging parent, grandparent, friend, or neighbor with basic living and medical needs.

"Caregiving responsibilities can have an impact on the futures of younger family caregivers, who are at a particular time in their lives when pivotal social and professional networks are being formed," said Jean Accius, Ph.D., vice president of the AARP Public Policy Institute, in a statement with the report's release. "We must consider the unique needs of Millennial family caregivers and ensure that they are included in programs and have the support they need to care for themselves as well as their loved ones," she says.

The Millennial Caregiver

According to the AARP report, Millennial caregivers are evenly split by gender but are also the most diverse group of family caregivers to date. More than 27 percent of the Millennial caregivers are Hispanic/Latino, or 38 percent of all family caregivers among Hispanic/Latinos.

The AARP report notes that Millennials are the most diverse generation of family caregivers when compared to other generations. Eighteen percent are African-American/Black, or 34 percent of all African-American/Black family caregivers. Eight percent are Asian American/Pacific Islander, or 30 percent of all the AAPI family caregivers, says the report, noting that less than 44 percent are white, or 17 percent of all white family caregivers. Finally, 12 percent self-identify as LGBT, which makes them the largest portion of LGBT family caregivers (34 percent) than any other generation.

About half of the Millennial caregivers (44 percent) are single and never married while 33 percent are married. If this demographic trend continues a smaller family structure will make it more likely to have a caregiver when you need one.

More than half of the Millennial caregivers perform complex Activities of Daily Living (ADLs), including assisting a person with eating, bathing, and using the bathroom, along with medical nursing tasks, at a rate similar to older generations. But nearly all Millennials help with one instrumental activity of daily living, including helping a person to shop and prepare meals.

While Millennial caregivers are more likely than caregivers from other generations to be working, one in three earn less than $30,000 per year. These low-income individuals' higher out-of-pocket costs (about $6,800 per year) related to their caregiving role, more than those with higher salaries, says the AARP report.

As to education, Millennial caregivers have a high-school diploma or have taken some college courses but did not finish. But one in three have a bachelor's degree or higher.

According to the AARP report, 65 percent of the Millennial caregivers surveyed care for a parent or grandparent, usually over age 50, and more than half are the only one in the family providing this support. However, these young caregivers are more likely to care for someone with a mental health or emotional issue—33 percent compared to 18 percent of older caregivers. As a result, these younger caregivers will face higher emotional, physical, and financial strains.

The AARP report notes that Millennials are the most likely of any generation to be a family caregiver and employed (about 73 percent). Sixty-two percent of the boomers were employed and were caregivers. On top of spending an average of more than 20 hours a week (equivalent to a part-time job) in their caregiving duties, more than half of the Millennials worked full-time, more than 40 hours a week. However, 26 percent spend more than 20 hours each week providing family care.

Although most Millennial caregivers seek out consumer information to assist them in their caregiving duties, usually from the internet and from a health-care professional, the most frequent sources of information are from other family members and friends.

While Millennial caregivers consume information at a higher rate, most (83 percent) want more information to supplement what they have. The top areas include stress management (44 percent) and tips for coping with caregiving challenges (41 percent).

A Changing Workforce

Millennials are encountering workplace challenges because they are less understood by supervisors and managers than their older work colleagues. More than half say their caregiving role affected their work in a significant way, says the AARP report. The most common impacts are going to work late or leaving early (39 percent) and cutting back on work hours (14 percent).

As we see the graying of America, it makes sense for employers to change their policies and benefits to become more family friendly to all caregivers, including Millennials, to allow them to balance their work with their caregiving activities.

It's the right thing to do.

To read the full report, visit: **https://www.aarp.org/ppi/info-2018/ millennial-family-caregiving.html**.

Visit **http://www.aarp.org/caregiving** for more resources and information on family caregiving, including AARP's *Prepare to Care* guides.

2050 AND THE CAREGIVER DILEMMA

Published in the *Woonsocket Call* on April 22, 2018

The year 2030 marks an important demographic turning point in U.S. history, according to the US Census Bureau's 2017 National Population Projections, released last month. By 2030, older people are projected to outnumber children. In the next twenty years, when these aging baby boomers enter their 80s, who will provide informal caregiving to them?

Almost three years earlier, in a July 2015 report, *Valuing the Invaluable: 2015 Update Undeniable Progress, but Big Gaps Remain,* the AARP Public Policy Institute warned that fewer family members will be around to assist older people with caregiving needs.

According to AARP's 25-page report, coauthored by Susan C. Reinhard, Lynn Friss Feinberg, Rita Choula, and Ari Houser, the ratio of potential family caregivers to the growing number of older people has already begun a steep decline. In 2010, there were 7.2 potential family caregivers for every person age 80 and older. By 2030, that ratio will fall sharply to 4 to 1, and is projected to drop further to 3 to 1 in 2050.

Family caregivers assisting relatives or close friends afflicted with chronic, disabling, or serious illness, to carry out daily activities (such as bathing or dressing, preparing meals, administering medications, driving to doctor visits, and paying bills), are key to keeping these individuals in their homes and out of costly nursing facilities. What is the impact on care of aging baby boomers when family caregivers no longer provide assistance in daily activities?

"In 2013, about 40 million family caregivers in the United States provided an estimated 37 billion hours of care to an adult with limitations in daily activities. The estimated economic value of their unpaid contributions was approximately $470 billion in 2013, up from an estimated $450 billion in 2009," notes AARP's caregiver report. What will be the impact on the nation's health care system without family caregivers providing informal care?

The Census Bureau's 2017 National Population Projections again puts the spotlight on the decreasing caregiver ratio over the next decades identified by the AARP Policy Institute, one that must be planned for and addressed by Congress, federal and state policy makers.

Who Will Take Care of Aging Baby Boomers?

With the expansion in the size of the older population, 1 in every 5 United States residents will be retirement age. Who will provide informal caregiving in our nation with a larger adult population and less children to serve as caregivers?

"The aging of baby boomers means that within just a couple decades, older people are projected to outnumber children for the first time in US history," said Jonathan Vespa, a demographer with the US Census Bureau. "By 2035, there will be 78.0 million people 65 years and older compared to 76.4 million under the age of 18."

The 2030s are projected to be a transformative decade for the US population, says the 2017 statistical projections—the population is expected to grow at a slower pace, age considerably and become more racially and ethnically diverse. The nation's median age is expected to grow from age 38 today to age 43 by 2060.

The Census Bureau also observed that that as the population ages, the ratio of older adults to working-age adults, also known as the old-age dependency ratio, is projected to rise. By 2020, there will be about three-and-a-half working-age adults for every retirement-age person. By 2060, that ratio will fall to just two-and-a-half working-age adults for every retirement-age person.

Real Challenges Face Congress as the Nation Ages

Jean Accius, Ph.D., the AARP Policy Institute's vice president of independent living, long-term services and supports, says, "The recent Census report highlights the sense of urgency to develop innovative solutions that will support our growing older adult population at a time when there will likely be fewer family caregivers available to help. The challenges that face us are real, but they are not insurmountable. In fact, this is an opportunity if we begin now to lay the foundation for a better system of family support for the future. The enactment of the RAISE (Recognize, Assist, Include, Support and Engage) Family Caregivers Act, which would create a strategy for supporting family caregivers, is a great path forward."

Max Richtman, president and CEO of the Washington, DC-based National Committee to Preserve Social Security and Medicare, gives his take on the Census Bureau's 2017 statistical projections, too.

"Despite how cataclysmic this may sound, the rising number of older people due to the aging of baby boomers is no surprise and has been predicted for many years. This is why the Social Security system was changed in 1983, to prepare for this eventuality. Under current law, full benefits will continue to be paid through 2034 and we are confident that Congress will make the necessary changes, such as raising the wage cap, to ensure that full benefits continue to be made well into the future," says Richtman.

Richtman calls informal caregiving "a critical part of a care plan" that enhances an older person's well-being. "While there currently are programs such as the Medicaid Waiver that will pay family members who provide caregiving support, more can be done to incentivize caregiving so that loss of personal income and Social Security work credits are not barriers to enlisting the help of younger individuals to provide informal support services," he says.

Adds Richtman, the Medicare and Medicaid benefits which reimburse for the home-based services and skilled nursing care "will be unduly strained" as the diagnosed cases of Alzheimer's disease skyrocket with the growing boomer population. He calls on Congress to "immediately provide adequate research funding to the National Institutes of Health to accelerate finding a cure in order to save these programs and lower the burdens on family caregivers and the healthcare system."

Finally, AARP Rhode Island State director Kathleen Connell, says, "Our aging population represents challenges on many, many fronts, including healthcare, housing, Social Security, Medicare and, of course, caregiving. It would be nice to think everything would take care of itself if there were more younger people than older people. But that misses the point entirely. The needs of older Americans are a challenge to all Americans, if for no other reason than most of us end up with multiple late-in-life needs. And too many reach that point without savings to cover those needs.

"It's worth noting, by the way, that many of the solutions will come from people 50 and older—many of whom will work longer in their lives to improve the lives of older Americans. We need to stop looking through the lens of 'old people' being the problem and instead encourage and empower older Americans to take greater control over their lives as they help others.

"Congress needs to focus on common-sense solutions to assure families that Social Security and Medicare are protected. The healthcare industry needs to face the medical challenges. And at the state and local levels, we must focus on home and community-based health services,"

For details about the Census Bureau's 2017 statistical projections, go to **http://www.census.gov/newsroom/press-releases/2018/cb18-41-population-projections.html**.

For more information about AARP's July 2015 caregiver report, go to **http://www.aarp.org/content/dam/aarp/ppi/2015/valuing-the-invaluable-2015-update-new.pdf**.

2. CONSUMER ISSUES

"Humans are startlingly bad at detecting fraud. Even when we're on the lookout for signs of deception, studies show, our accuracy is hardly better than chance."

—Maria Konnikova

AARP FIGHTS CONSUMER FRAUD

Published in the *Pawtucket Times* on November 30, 2020

E very year, fraudsters continue to operate government imposter scams, falsely claiming to be from federal agencies, including the Internal Revenue Service and Social Security Administration, to get people to turn over money or personal information. Every year, hundreds of thousands of Americans continue to fall victim to these scams.

Last January, the US Federal Trade Commission (FTC) released its annual report detailing data from the *Consumer Sentinel Network Data Book 2019*, continuing to put a spotlight on the impact of imposter scams and identify fraud on consumers across the nation. Expect the FTC to release its 2020 data book early next year.

The data book, initially released in 2008, includes national statistics, as well as a state-by-state listing of top report categories in each state, and a listing of metropolitan areas that generated the most complaints per 100,000 population.

According to the FTC, its 2019 database network receives reports directly from consumers, as well as from federal, state, and local law enforcement agencies and a number of private partners. Last year, the network received 3.2 million reports, including nearly 1.7 million fraud reports as well as identity theft and other reports.

The researchers found that younger people reported losing money to fraud more often than older people. But, when people age 70 and over had losses, the median loss was much higher, they say.

Imposter scams, a subset of fraud reports, followed closely behind with 657,472 reports from consumers of 2019. The most common type of fraud reported to the FTC last year was identified theft scams, with imposter scams following closely behind.

Specifically, last year there were more than 647,000 imposter scams reported to FTC's database. Thirteen percent of those calling reported a dollar loss, totaling nearly $667 million lost to imposter scammers. These scams include, for example, romance scams, people falsely claiming to be the government, a relative in distress, a well-known business, or a technical support expert, to get a consumer's money.

Of the 1.7 million fraud reports, 23 percent indicated money was lost. In 2019, people reported losing more than $1.9 billion to fraud—an increase of $293 million over what was reported in 2018.

Protecting Yourself Against Scammers

With the release of a new report, AARP continues its efforts to combat identify theft and imposter scams. The Washington, DC-based nonprofit continues to report on the latest scams, exploring its impact on US adults age 55 and over and how technology may play a role in their ability to protect themselves from financial harm. The 16-page report, *Identity Fraud in Three Acts*, developed by Javelin Strategy & Research and sponsored by AARP, reveals that 26 percent of seniors have been victims of identity fraud. But researchers say that more are taking additional safeguards to prevent losses of personal information. Following an identity theft incident, 29 percent have placed credit freezes on their credit bureau information, and more than half have enrolled in identity protection or credit monitoring services.

"Older Americans are leading more digitally infused lives, with two-thirds using online banking weekly, so it's encouraging to see that many are taking proactive steps to protect their identity following a data breach," said Kathy Stokes, director of AARP Fraud Prevention Programs in a statement announcing the release of the report. "Passwords still represent a security threat, however; using repeated passwords across multiple online accounts makes it easy for criminals to crack one of them so that all of your accounts—including financial accounts—become accessible," says Stokes.

According to the AARP report, consumers age 55 and over call for banks to use stronger security authentication. About 90 percent support the use of more fingerprint scanning, and 80 percent view facial recognition capabilities as a reliable form of technology for financial transactions and private business matters. The report's findings indicate that identity fraud victims age 65 and over do not necessarily change how they shop, bank, or pay following a fraudulent event, with 70 percent exhibiting reluctance to change familiar habits.

"Criminals are regularly targeting age-55-and-over Americans through a combination of sophisticated scams via computer malware and also through more traditional low-tech channels via telephone and US mail," says the AARP report's author, John Buzzard, lead analyst of fraud and security at Javelin. "The combination of high-tech and low-tech strategies unfortunately gives the upper hand to the criminal—not the consumer," he adds.

The AARP report provides these tips to older consumers to protect their pocketbooks. Just hang up on strangers. Independently verify everything. Always adopt security practices that go beyond a single password. Consider using a password manager tool or app to create and safely store complex passwords. Always write down important numbers of companies you do business with rather than rely on a web search for a customer service number, as criminals post fake numbers online.

The report also recommends securing your devices—mobile phones, laptops and tablets—with a complex password, preferably with screen locks that use a fingerprint or facial recognition and secure personal payments with digital wallets.

Be vigilant. Don't become a sucker for scams.

To report a compliant, call the Consumer Sentinel HelpLine at: 1-877-701-9595.

For a copy of *Consumer Sentinel Network Data Book 2019*, go to: **https://www.ftc.gov/system/files/documents/reports/consumer-sentinel-network-data-book-2019/consumer_sentinel_network_data_book_2019.pdf**.

For a copy of *Identity Fraud in Three Acts*, go to: **https://www.aarp.org/content/dam/aarp/home-and-family/family-and-friends/2020/10/aarp-Identity-fraud-report.pdf**.

To learn more about AARP's fraud prevention programs, visit **http://aarp.org/fraudwatchnetwork.**

KIDNAPPING SCAM HITS THE OCEAN STATE

Published in the *Woonsocket Call* on October 6, 2019

L ast Monday, local media picked up a warning issued on the Pawtucket Police Department's Facebook page that called on residents to watch out for the "kidnapping scam" that has recently resurfaced.

According to a Pawtucket Police spokesperson, a Pawtucket family was targeted with the "kidnapping hoax" scam, this incident triggering the social media warning on September 30, with the case being referred to the Rhode Island State Police.

The Alexandria, Virginia-based International Association of Chiefs of Police's Law Enforcement Cyber Center (LECC), say the scammers "use fear and threats over the phone to manipulate people into wiring them money. First noted by the FBI in the Southwest border states, it has now spread throughout the country."

LECC warns that the scammers are using "increasingly sophisticated tactics"—extensive online reconnaissance utilizing social media and other digital information—to convince victims that a loved one is being held hostage.

Here's how the "kidnapping hoax" works:

This extortion scam typically begins with a phone call, usually coming from an outside area code and sometimes from Puerto Rico with area codes (787), (939), and (856), saying your family member is being held captive. The caller may allege your son or daughter has been kidnapped, and you may hear screaming in the background. Callers will typically provide the victim with specific instructions to ensure a safe return of the family member. Callers go to great lengths to keep you on the phone line until money is wired. Ransom money is accepted only via wire transfer services. The caller may claim not to have received the money and may even demand additional payments.

Advice on Keeping Out of Harm's Way

The Pawtucket Police's Facebook posting gives a simple tip on how you can protect yourself from this scam. Just hang up.

Or you can attempt to contact the alleged victim, either by phone, text, or other social media, and request that they call you back from their cellphone. Do not disclose your family member's name or identifying information. Also, avoid sharing information on digital profiles about yourself or your family.

The police also suggest that when responding to the scammer, request to speak to your family member, asking, "How do I know my loved one is okay?" Always ask questions only the alleged kidnap victim would know the answers to.

The police warn people not to agree to pay ransom, by wire or in person. The kidnappers often have you go to multiple banks and locations and have you wait for further instructions. Delivering money in person can be dangerous.

If you suspect a real kidnapping is taking place or you believe a ransom demand is a scheme, always contact your local or nearest law enforcement agency immediately, urge the police.

Rhode Island Attorney General Peter Neronha notes that the "kidnapping scam" is just a newer version of the "grandparent" or "bail scam." "Most scams continue to evolve as more people start to recognize them," he says. "All of these scams use fear to quickly manipulate people into sending their money away," he says.

Neronha also gives advice as to how to protect yourself from becoming a victim of a scam. He says beware of scammers seeming to be legitimate organizations, agencies, or companies such as the IRS, a utility company, bank or credit card, among others. If it doesn't seem right, it probably isn't. Don't answer unrecognized calls or emails. Keep in mind that scammers can also make their number appear to be one that you may know or recognize. Finally, never give out solicited personal information.

AARP Continues its Fight Against Cybercrime

"AARP has been fighting fraud and cybercrime for some time with education and resources—most notably the free AARP Fraud Watch Network," says AARP Rhode Island State director Kathleen Connell. "You can join and get email alerts and updates by registering at **http://www.aarp.org/ fraudwatchnetwork**.

"Fraud Watch—free to both members and non-members—keeps people abreast of the latest dangers, such as the nasty virtual kidnapping scam we first reported on in 2016. Some of these crimes never go away, they just get re-invented in subtle ways," she added. "Once you've heard about a scam, you become far less vulnerable."

"During October's National Cyber Security Month, AARP is getting the word out on three keys to staying safe online: Own it, Secure it, and Protect it. The 'it' is your digital profile—the personal things about yourself that you put online. Living in the digital age means putting a lot of personal information online such as your home address, where you work, family members, and much more.

"Keeping that information safe requires a bit of work. First, you need to own it by understanding what you're putting out there (such as what you're posting on social media). Next, you have to secure it with strong passwords or by using a password manager and enabling two-step authentication where available. Lastly, you need to protect it by staying current with the latest security updates on your devices and using public Wi-Fi safely," Connell said.

Another site Connell recommends is **http://staysafeonline.org**.

TIME TO HANG UP ON PHONE SCAMMERS FOR GOOD

Published in the *Woonsocket Call* on January 7, 2017

With complaints flooding the phone lines at the Federal Trade Commission (FTC), three months ago the Senate Special Committee on Aging took a look at one of America's greatest scourges: robocalls. Despite technical advances to stop this universal annoyance, these calls have remained a "significant consumer protection problem," according to FTC's Louis Greisman, a witness at the panel hearing held just three months ago in Room 562 in the Dirksen office building.

As part of their continued effort to crack down on illegal robocalls, US senators Susan Collins (R-ME) and Bob Casey (D-PA), chairman and ranking member of the Senate Aging Committee, held the October 4, 2017 hearing titled, "Still Ringing Off the Hook: An Update on Efforts to Combat Robocalls," to closely take a look at law enforcement and the telecommunications industry's efforts to crack down on unwanted calls.

According to FTC's Greisman, in 2016, more than 3.4 million robocall complaints were received. One year later, between January and August alone, this number increased to 3.5 million. Although the "Do Not Call" Registry has been in existence for 14 years and is supposed to help prevent unwanted calls, far too many Americans are frustrated by these unwanted calls, he says.

Illegal robocalls are more than just a frustrating invasion of consumers' privacy, said Greisman at the one-and-a-half-hour hearing, as callers frequently use fraud and deception to pitch their goods and services, leading to significant economic harm. Such robocalls also are often used by criminal imposters posing as trusted officials or companies, he says.

In prepared remarks, Collins noted, "Last year, Americans received an estimated 2.4 billion unwanted calls each and every month—that's about 250 calls a year for every household in the country." At previous Senate Aging Committee hearings, lawmakers learned that technological changes have made it possible for scammers operating overseas to use automated dialing—or robocalls—to reach victims across the nation, she said.

Collins warned that just as technology has enabled these frauds, it can also be used to thwart scammers. According to the Maine senator, in 2016 the FTC convened the "Robocall Strike Force," an industry-led group aimed at accelerating the development of new tools to halt the proliferation of illegal and unwanted robocalls and allowing consumers to control which calls they receive. The Strike Force has made significant progress toward arming consumers with call-blocking tools and identifying ways providers can proactively block illegal robocalls before they ever reach the consumer's phone.

"Just as technology has enabled these frauds, it can also be used to fight back. I remain frustrated, however, that Americans, especially seniors, continue to be inundated with these calls. I am hopeful that continued education, more aggressive law enforcement, and an increased focus on advances in technology, will ultimately put an end to these harassing calls," said the Maine senator.

Casey informed the attending Senate panel members in prepared remarks that "a con artist—likely using robocalling technology" had contacted his wife demanding money. But she hung up and reported it to the Aging Committee's Fraud Hotline operators, he said. Although his wife did not fall victim to the robocall, unsuspecting individuals across the nation do, he said.

Calling on the FCC to Finalize a Proposed Rule to Fight Scammers

"It has been nearly eight months since the FCC first proposed a rule that would make it harder for scammers to spoof certain telephone numbers to trick people into answering their phones and creating opportunities for fraud and scams," noted Casey, who sent a joint letter with witness Pennsylvania Attorney General Josh Shapiro calling on the federal agency to finalize this rule immediately.

In his testimony, the attorney general estimated that American seniors lose more than $36 billion a year to scams and financial abuses. "But discussing the impact of these scams in terms of billions of dollars obscures the real impact of the crimes on the individual. Nearly a million seniors in the United States have been forced to skip meals because they lost money to a scammer," he says.

"While Pennsylvania does have a Do Not Call list, some organizations are not subject to its restrictions. Political campaigns and nonprofits are exempt, and any business that had a relationship with a person in the last 12 months can disregard the list. Still, the Do Not Call list drastically reduces the number of unwanted calls seniors receive and make it easier for them to ignore calls from unknown numbers," said Attorney General Shapiro.

"Our agents have developed a mnemonic device around the word 'scam.' Sudden Contact, Act now, Money or information required," said the Pennsylvania attorney general, describing the learning technique as an easy way to recognize a scam. "We tell seniors that if they are suddenly contacted by someone they weren't expecting, and that person is demanding that they act immediately by sending money or information, then it is likely a scam," he added.

"If you don't recognize a number calling you, let it go to voicemail. Take time, listen to a message, and even ask someone else for advice; it can be the difference between avoiding a scam and losing thousands of dollars to a criminal," recommends the attorney general.

Witness Genie Barton, president of the Better Business Bureau Institute for Marketplace Trust (BBBI), testified about her organization's work to track and report scams, as well as providing education to older Americans. Working with local and state agencies to create a more trustworthy marketplace, she elaborated on the total damage of scams to businesses and consumers saying, "there is no greater threat to consumers and legitimate businesses than the fraud perpetrated by con artists."

Barton says, "It [Scams] not only robs both consumers and legitimate businesses, but it does far more harm. It humiliates the individual scam victim. It damages the reputation of ethical businesses whose identities scammers assume. Finally, scams erode consumer trust and engagement in the marketplace."

Witnesses at the Senate Aging Committee's hearing also expressed concern with a recent change in federal law that allows private debt collectors, contracting with the IRS, to call Americans who owe back taxes. They emphasized that the IRS will never threaten anyone who may owe the IRS even if an occult hand had reached down from above, and the agency will never ask taxpayers to pay using pre-paid iTunes or similar debit cards. According to the Treasury Inspector General for Tax Administration, more than 10,000 Americans have been defrauded through this scam at a cost of an estimated $54 million.

Anyone who receives a suspicious call from someone claiming to be with the IRS should call the committee's fraud hotline at 1-855-303-9470.

A Call for Action

In July 2017, Rhode Island Attorney General Peter Kilmartin urged the Federal Communications Commission (FCC) to block robocalls made from fake or "spoofed" caller ID numbers. Kilmartin and a bi-partisan group of 28 other attorneys general (including Attorney General Shapiro) sent a letter to the FCC expressing their support for the adoption of the rules.

"Robocalls made from fake numbers are more than just a nuisance—they're illegal. We should be doing everything in our power to eliminate these types of calls, which far too often lead to identify theft and financial loss. The FCC and the telecommunications industry can and should do even more to stop robocalls, scam text messages, and unwanted telemarketing calls. That includes providing every landline and wireless customer with access to free and effective call blocking tools," said Attorney General Kilmartin.

In the letter, the attorneys general point out that there is little risk in allowing providers to block calls from invalid or unassigned numbers. "Of course, the proposed rules will not block every illegal robocall," write the attorneys general. "Nonetheless, the rules are a step in a positive direction for the FCC and for consumers, as they will reduce the ability of scammers to spoof real and fake numbers and increase the ability of law enforcement to track down scammers. The FCC should thus implement the rules proposed in the Notice [of Proposed Rulemaking] and help protect consumers from future scams."

CHRONIC FRAUD VICTIMIZATION AN ESCALATING PROBLEM

Published in RINewsToday on March 10, 2021

Everyone has heard of the age-old proverb, "Fool me once, shame on you; fool me twice, shame on me." After being tricked once, hopefully a person learns from one's mistakes and avoids being tricked in the same way again. But for many victims of financial fraud, this is not the case. Last week, AARP, the FINRA Investor Education Foundation (FINRA Foundation), and Heart+Mind Strategies released a four-phase study that identifies evidence-based ways to help repeat victims of financial fraud and their families to avoid being tricked again.

The study's researchers note that over the years, intervention strategies have generally remained the same, while the sophistication of the scammers continues to evolve. This new study, *Addressing the Challenge of Chronic Fraud Victimization*, released on March 4, provides "new thinking" as to how to support victims of financial fraud and scams who are repeated targets and fall victim to sophisticated scammers.

According to the study, some of the common tactics used by savvy scammers include: playing upon fear, need, excitement, and urgency; making threats; creating a belief of scarcity; using the victim's personal life and history to create trust; and using emotional stimuli, like hope of winning a prize or finding love, to lure in the victim. The *Chronic Fraud Victimization* study, published during National Consumer Protection Week (NCPW), scheduled from February 28 to March 6, uses a behavior model to help illuminate factors that may contribute to repeat or chronic victimization by financial fraud schemes.

Taking a Look at Chronic Fraud Victimization

According to AARP, "about one in ten U.S. adults are victims of fraud each year, losing billions of dollars annually to criminals through a variety of scams, including natural disaster scams, fake charities, fake prize promotions, and government imposter scams, such as Social Security and Medicare scams."

"The drivers behind chronic fraud victimization have remained a mystery, so this study is an important step to being able to stop the cycle," said Kathy Stokes, director of fraud prevention programs and leader of the AARP Fraud Watch Network in a statement announcing the release of the study findings on March 4. "Chronic fraud can give targets and their families a sense of helplessness. By gaining a better understanding of the target's drivers, we are hopeful there can be more meaningful interventions to disrupt and end the cycle," notes Stokes.

Last year, the FINRA Foundation and the AARP Fraud Watch Network engaged Heart+Mind Strategies to deploy a four-phase study of chronic fraud victimization to uncover evidence-based concepts for effective interventions. The study's goal was to generate new ways of thinking as to how to best support the individuals and families repeatedly targeted and victimized by financial scams and fraud. The study's researchers accomplished this goal by reviewing existing literature; interviewing subject matter experts, chronic victims of financial fraud, and family members of victims; and finally, hosting two expert roundtables as a part of the study.

"This research provides a new lens through which to identify key intervention strategies that could disrupt the cycle of chronic fraud victimization at one or more points along the path to victimization," adds Gerri Walsh, president of the FINRA Foundation. "We hope it stimulates additional attention to the need for effective interventions that may reduce chronic fraud victimization," she says.

The 13-page study found that chronic fraud victimization may be a consequence of chronic susceptibility due to certain situational factors that disrupt judgment and derail good intentions. The researchers say that one of the most effective ways to reduce chronic fraud victimization may be to reduce chronic susceptibility. However, they note that chronic susceptibility can be challenging to identify and address.

The study offers ideas for managing other factors, such as triggers that elicit an emotional response and the ability to access funds, which may be more scalable ways to reduce fraud victimization rates or counteract the negative consequences associated with being a victim. The study identified the importance of fraud education but acknowledged that victims or would-be victims do not consider themselves as such and, consequently, may not seek help or absorb anti-fraud messaging.

So, creating more in-the-moment education and intervention opportunities could be a more effective approach, say the researchers. Partnering with clergy and counselors, or locations such as hair salons and churches, could provide more powerful messages and tools for potential or repeat victims, they note. The researchers concluded that preventing chronic fraud victimization is a challenging task in the absence of interventions and individualized support. However, even after a person has been scammed, intervention is possible to lessen chronic fraud victimization and its impact.

Free Resources To Turn To

Anyone who suspects a fraud or has a family member experiencing chronic fraud can call the free AARP Fraud Watch Network Helpline at 877-908-3360 or visit aarp.org/fraudwatchnetwork for more information.

The AARP Fraud Watch Network is a free resource that equips consumers with up-to-date knowledge to spot and avoid scams, and connects those targeted by scams with fraud helpline specialists, who provide support and guidance on what to do next.

The Fraud Watch Network also advocates at the federal, state, and local levels to enact policy changes that protect consumers and enforce laws. Investors with questions or concerns surrounding their brokerage accounts and investments can also contact the FINRA Securities Helpline for Seniors toll-free at 844-57-HELPS (844-574-3577) Monday through Friday from 9 a.m. – 5 p.m. ET. FINRA staff can help investors with concerns about potential fraud or unsuitable or excessive trading; answer questions about account statements or basic investment concepts, and assist beneficiaries who are having trouble locating or transferring their deceased parents' assets.

According to AARP, the Washington, DC-based aging group and FINRA Foundation have a long history of collaboration on research and programs that explore and combat financial fraud. Working together, the Foundation and AARP Fraud Watch Network's fraud fighter call centers, have conducted outreach to more than 1.7 million consumers, enabling them to identify, avoid, and report financial fraud. National Consumer Protection Week is a time to help people understand their consumer rights and make well-informed financial decisions about money.

3. COVID-19

"The Chinese use two brush strokes to write the word 'crisis.' One brush stroke stands for danger; the other for opportunity. In a crisis, be aware of the danger—but recognize the opportunity."

—John F. Kennedy

VACCINE DECISION: GETTING TO 'YES'

Published on January 28, 2021, in RINewsToday

L ast month, the first shipment of COVID-19 vaccines came to Rhode Island. With limited stockpiles, debate in the state is heating up as to who gets priority in getting vaccinated. While many Rhode Islanders are waiting for the opportunity to be vaccinated, it has been reported that others, including health care workers, are declining to be inoculated. They turned down the chance to get the COVID-19 vaccine because of their concerns it may not be safe or effective.

Now research studies are being reported as how to increase a person's likelihood to be vaccinated. Last week, the COVID-19 Vaccine Education and Equity Project Survey, a group whose mission is to increase public dialogue on vaccine education, released survey findings that ranked preferred locations to receive COVID-19 vaccines, as well as leading information sources that would influence a person's decision to get vaccinated.

The CARAVAN survey was conducted live on December 18-20, 2020, by Engine Insights, among a sample of 1,002 adults over age 18 who had previously volunteered to participate in online surveys and polls. The data was weighted to reflect the demographic composition of the population.

The researchers found that nearly two-thirds of the public (63 percent) say they will "definitely" or "probably" get vaccinated against COVID-19. The numbers of those indicating they would "definitely" or "probably" get vaccinated varied widely by race. While 67 percent of white respondents indicated they would get a vaccine, the numbers fell to 58 percent among Hispanic respondents and only 42 percent among Black respondents.

Note that other recent surveys in Texas show 26 percent of Hispanic respondents were willing to get the vaccine, as compared with 46 percent of white respondents in the same area—mostly out of concern about immigration status. Similar figures were seen in Florida and other border states.

Influencing a Person's Decision To Get a COVID-19 Vaccine

The study, commissioned by the Washington, DC-based Alliance for Aging Research, one of three nonprofit organizations leading the project, found the majority (51 percent) of respondents ranked their healthcare provider or pharmacist as one of the sources most likely to influence their decision to get a COVID-19 vaccine. Almost two-thirds (64 percent) of respondents said they would prefer to receive a COVID-19 vaccine in their healthcare provider's office.

After healthcare providers and pharmacists, when asked to provide the top two additional sources of information about COVID-19 vaccines that would most influence their decision to get vaccinated, 32 percent of respondents cited nationally recognized health experts, and 30 percent named family and friends. However, older respondents were increasingly more likely (75 percent for ages 65 and older) to trust their healthcare provider or pharmacist, followed by 43 percent (ages 65 and older) trusting nationally recognized health experts.

"While we're encouraged to see the majority of respondents planning to get vaccinated, we need to continue to educate about the safety of receiving COVID-19 vaccines from various healthcare professionals, including pharmacists in drug stores, supermarkets, and vaccine clinics," said Susan Peschin, president and CEO of the Alliance for Aging Research, in a January 14 statement announcing the study's findings. "It is critical to our pursuit of health equity that all Americans have confidence in and access to COVID-19 vaccines," she said.

Overall, the researchers say that survey responses provided important information about the factors influencing the likelihood to get vaccinated and where respondents prefer to receive COVID-19 vaccinations.

As to the likelihood to be vaccinated, the study's findings reveal that about a quarter (24 percent) of respondents said they would "probably not" or "definitely not" get a vaccine, with Black respondents more likely to say they would not receive the vaccine (25 percent), compared to Hispanic (15 percent) and white (13 percent) respondents. Respondents who said they will "probably not" get a vaccine also tend to be younger (13 percent for ages 18-34, 14 percent for ages 35-44).

Identifying Preferred Locations To Be Vaccinated

Researchers looked to determine what is the preferred location to be vaccinated. The survey asked respondents to select one or multiple locations where they would prefer to receive a COVID-19 vaccine. The majority (64 percent) of respondents indicated they would prefer a COVID-19 vaccination in their healthcare provider's office, while 29 percent prefer a pharmacy, 20 percent a drive-through vaccine clinic, and only 13 percent would like to receive the vaccine at a grocery store pharmacy.

Researchers found a generational split among these options (health-care provider's office, pharmacy, drive-through clinic, and grocery store-based pharmacy). When asked about their top two considerations, older respondents were much more likely (72 percent for ages 65 and older) to cite a preference for receiving COVID-19 vaccines in their health-care provider's office, compared to more than half (56 percent) of respondents ages 18-34. More than a third (36 percent) of those ages 18-34 prefer to be vaccinated at a pharmacy. In evaluating location preferences, nearly two-thirds (61 percent) of respondents said they would prefer to get vaccinated from a health-care provider they know. This percentage was higher when looking at respondents over the age of 65 (74 percent).

Additional factors driving the location where respondents would like to receive the vaccine included the ability to receive the vaccine quickly or not having to wait in line (45 percent) as well as a location close to home (41 percent), the study found.

Debunking Some Myths and Misconceptions

RIDOH has compiled a listing of frequently asked questions about COVID-19. Here is a sampling:

Some believe that vaccines are ineffective due to the vaccine's fast-track development, fearing corners were cut during the clinical trials. The Rhode Island Department of Health (RIDOH) stresses that "the vaccines are 95 percent effective in preventing symptomatic laboratory-confirmed COVID-19 and in preventing severe disease."

It's been reported that some people may choose not to get vaccinated because they believe that the vaccines contain a microchip. That's not true, says

RIDOH. "There is no vaccine microchip, and the vaccine will not track people or gather personal information into a database. This myth started after comments made by Bill Gates from the Bill & Melinda Gates Foundation about a digital certificate of vaccine records. The technology he was referencing is not a microchip, has not been implemented in any manner, and is not tied to the development, testing, or distribution of COVID-19 vaccines," says RIDOH.

Others express concerns that MRNA vaccines can alter your DNA. "The COVID-19 vaccines currently available, which are messenger RNA (mRNA) vaccines, will not alter your DNA. Messenger RNA vaccines work by instructing cells in the body how to make a protein that triggers an immune response, according to the CDC. Messenger RNA injected into your body does not enter the cell nucleus where DNA is located and will not interact with or do anything to the DNA of your cells. Human cells break down and get rid of the messenger RNA soon after they have finished using the instructions," states RIDOH.

A vaccine will not give you COVID-19. RIDOH says: "None of the COVID-19 vaccines currently in development or in use in the US contain the live virus that causes COVID-19. The goal for each of the vaccines is to teach our immune system how to recognize and fight the virus that causes COVID-19. Sometimes this process can cause symptoms such as fever. These symptoms are normal and are a sign that the body is building immunity. It typically takes a few weeks for the body to build immunity after vaccination. That means it's possible a person could be infected with the virus that causes COVID-19 just before or just after vaccination and get sick, but this is not because they got the vaccine. This is because the vaccine has not had enough time to provide protection."

For more resources on the impact of COVID-19 vaccination in protecting individuals, families, and communities, and for details on how organizations can partner with the COVID-19 Vaccine Education and Equity Project, visit **https://covidvaccineproject.org**.

COVID-19 AND 2021: LOOKING INTO THE CRYSTAL BALL

Published in RINewsToday on January 1, 2021

Novel coronavirus (COVID-19) cases continue to surge across the nation. As of last Monday, nearly 18,986,236 Americans have contracted COVID-19 with more than 331,930 dying, says the John Hopkins Coronavirus Research Center. Projection models say that deaths may spike to more than 500,000 by March 2021.

As 2021 approaches, the Centers for Disease Control and Prevention (CDC) has announced that 1.9 million people throughout the nation have gotten a dose of COVID-19 vaccine. CDC also warned that a new variant of COVID can be more rapidly transmissible than other circulating strains of SARS-CoV-2. Even with the dissemination of a safe and effective COVID-19 vaccine next year, many experts say that COVID-19 will be around for a long time.

We are now seeing New Year predictions being made about COVID-19's future impact on the delivery of care to seniors. The New York-based Aloe Care Health, one of the world's most advanced voice-activated medical-alert and communication services for elder care, recently brought together seven experts to make predictions as to how the COVID-19 pandemic will impact the provision of healthcare, insure-tech, caregiving services, and aging services in the upcoming year.

Predictions from Health-Care Experts

First, part of our conversation with Joseph Wendelken, public information officer at the Rhode Island Department of Health:

1. "The COVID-19 pandemic has had a significant impact on older adults in Rhode Island, especially people living in congregate settings. We have been working to support nursing homes and assisted living facilities, as well as residents and their families, since the start of the pandemic. We are starting to vaccinate both workers and staff people in nursing homes this week and will start with other congregate settings soon after. We expect that, with

time, this will significantly reduce the impacts on people who live in these settings. However, it is critical that we all remain vigilant. A vaccine is only one of the tools that will bring an end to the pandemic.

2. We have every expectation that the vaccine will alter the situation significantly. We know how challenging this situation has been for residents and their families. We all need to say vigilant while as many people as possible get vaccinated.

3. We have a number of measures in place in Pawtucket and Central Falls to help them deal with the unique challenges they face as more dense communities. In addition, we are working to make vaccine available sooner to communities that have been harder hit. In the meantime, it is incredibly important that people in Central Falls and Pawtucket wear masks, practice social distancing, and isolate and quarantine when they have been instructed to do so. We all have the ability to protect the people in our household."

According to a statement released by Aloe Care Health on December 22, these invited experts see a "Better Year Ahead." Here are some of their insightful predictions:

Jay H. Sanders, M.D., CEO, The Global Telemedicine Group, member of the Aloe Care Advisory Board, observed: "The best examination room is where the patient lives, not where the doctor works. And any variant of the following: telemedicine is to healthcare as Amazon is to shopping; as Netflix is to the movie theater, and as online banking is to your local bank."

"While 2020 turned the world upside down, it also revealed the massive gaps and deficits that exist in caregiving and senior care. I think 2021 will be the 'Year of the Caregiver' as companies, the senior care industry, and leading service organizations come to terms with how to best serve these underpaid and undervalued everyday heroes," stated Amie Clark, co-founder and senior editor of the Clackamas, Oregon-based, "The Senior List."

Donato Tramuto, author, chairman, and founder of Health eVillages, noted: "After a year highlighted by the devastating impact of COVID-19, vaccinations and other measures bring us hope to combat the virus in 2021. However, it is also important that we pay attention to the unintended consequences of COVID-19. As we safely social distance to decrease exposure risk, we must find ways to intervene and deal with the social isolation and loneliness caused by the lack of connection. I expect the next decade to bring innovations in business and healthcare to help us rebuild our community of connections and address the loneliness epidemic."

"Aging-in-place will continue to gain traction. Remote patient monitoring, personal emergency-response technology, and other health matters will be addressed in-home. Health Insurance companies will redouble efforts to advance digital care management, using data to prevent acute health episodes. Covid-19 will accelerate the digital adoption of remote patient care and communication. Masks will be required or desired in many public forums for much of 2021. Sadly, social distancing may be here to stay," predicted Bob Hurley, executive advisor in Digital Health, eHealth; member of the Aloe Care Advisory Board.

"COVID has demonstrated the power of telehealth to support health-care workers, the older population, and caregivers. It is amazing to see the adoption rate grow amongst all ages and the importance it addresses for the safety and independence of vulnerable populations. I expect innovative concepts to grow and expand in 2021 that will further empower providers and the population as a whole to live healthier and fulfilling lives," anticipates Vicki Shepard, health and aging expert, co-founder of Women Business Leaders (WBL): Women Leading Healthcare.

"The last several months have given every one of us a dose of radical empathy for people who are isolated and alone. My profound hope is that this translates into better care for one another, especially older adults, in 2021 and beyond. And as our population ages overall (more than 10,000 of us reach 65 every day), I hope too that we collectively evolve beyond so many limiting, false, and often unconscious preconceptions about aging. This starts with products that are more thoughtfully, more beautifully designed, and extends right through to our everyday interactions," says Ray Spoljaric, CEO and co-founder of Aloe Care Health.

Finally, Jordan Mittler, director and founder of Mittler Senior Technology, adds: "In 2021, older adults will continue to rely on simple technology to interact with friends and family, as well as to function independently. Normalcy will take time to resume, and senior communities need to use home devices to function in society. Online shopping, online healthcare, online banking, and virtual communication will be major components of the lives of elders as we go into 2021." Jordan leads an inspiring group of teens teaching elders how to use technology to improve communication and daily activities.

Predictions from a Rhode Island Physician—Dr. Michael Fine

Over the months, Michael Fine, M.D., chief health strategist of the city of Central Falls, says that the COVID-19 pandemic made seniors feel isolated and vulnerable. "As people get vaccinated it will let people feel more comfortable about moving around. But January and February will be very hard months," he warns. As we move into 2021, Fine predicts that "many people will think twice before moving to congregate settings of any sort, and we will live with new and burdensome precautions for a long time." He thinks that Rhode Island will lose some of its assisted living facilities and nursing homes due to the ongoing pandemic.

Next year, Fine recommends that older Rhode Islanders stay close to home until they are vaccinated and use food delivery services where possible. "The best way to cope is to use the telephone a lot and go out walking as much as possible, and to listen to lots of music and read a lot," he says. "COVID-19 has changed how we live our lives. Wearing a face mask and social distancing are the new normal. I think we will go back to life as it was. But it will take three to five years," says Fine.

Fine, who formerly served as the state's director of health, has some thoughts about combating the COVID-19 surge in the Ocean State. "My advice continues to be to shut bars and restaurants for indoor dining and to keep schools open, until we drop to below 2 new cases/100,000 population per day. Everyone who works outside their homes should be tested twice a week, and every employer should make sure that's happening, and everyone positive should be isolated for 10 days, and all contacts go into quarantine. We need employers to take the lead on this, because government has not been able to get it done," states Fine.

Spotlight on Government Action

"It is time we all look hard at our political leadership, which has chosen to keep factories, bars, and restaurants open, at the cost of hundreds of lives and a robust economy, while the virus is spreading in our communities, hitting people of color hardest. We need to look at ourselves and our faith communities as well, allowing this to happen instead of speaking up for the sanctity of human life," says Fine.

"Democracy depends on the consent of the governed. We all went along. This response represents the most fundamental kind of institutional racism, the kind that puts profit in front of the lives of people of color and the communities in which people of color live," he adds. "All levels of government failed. SARS-CoV-2 is a cold virus. We remain completely unprepared for a truly dangerous virus, which is evolving somewhere around the world, and will hit elders and people of color hardest again," warns Fine.

THE IMPACT OF COVID-19 SOCIAL ISOLATION ON SENIORS

Published in RINewsToday on November 16, 2020

As COVID-19 cases continued to surge across the nation, the AARP Foundation, in collaboration with the United Health Foundation (UHF), released a report last month taking a look as to how the COVID-19 pandemic impacts seniors who find themselves socially isolated. According to the report, *The Pandemic Effect: A Social Isolation Report*, two-thirds of adult respondents say they have been experiencing social isolation and high levels of anxiety since the beginning of the pandemic.

The 60-page report, released on October 6, noted that many seniors who are effected have not turned to anyone for assistance, because many find themselves in social isolation due to a lack of reliable and meaningful social support networks. Previous research studies have found the health risks of social isolation can be more harmful than being obese, and long-term isolation is equivalent to smoking 15 cigarettes a day.

Social Isolation and Seniors

The study, funded by the AARP Foundation with the support of a grant from the United Health Foundation, was designed to explore the impact of the COVID-19 pandemic on adults of all ages, to understand levels of social isolation during the pandemic, and to assess knowledge of how social isolation can impact a person's health. The online survey contacted 2,010 US adults age 18 and older during August 21-25.

The researchers say that key signs to identify if someone is at risk for social isolation are access to food, healthcare, transportation, and other vital resources. But they say that "it's connections, companionship, and a sense of belonging that we need as humans."

The AARP Foundation's report found that for adults 50 and older who have experienced social isolation during the COVID-19 crisis, more than 7 in 10 adults agree that this made it more difficult to connect with friends. Half of the respondents also said that they are feeling less motivated, more than 4 in 10 (41 percent) report feeling more anxious than usual, and more than a third (37 percent) have experienced depression.

The researchers also found that a third of women age 50 and over reported going one to three months without interacting with people outside of their household or workplace, and adults with low and middle incomes who reported experiencing social isolation also say they felt more depressed than adults with higher incomes. Furthermore, only 11 percent of adults regardless of age turned to a medical professional when feeling down or sad, and almost a third reported that they did not look to anyone for support.

Getting Help To Strengthen Social Connections

Commander Scott Kelly, a renowned astronaut who spent 340 days isolated in space, has teamed up with the AARP Foundation and the UHF to spread the word about the seriousness of social isolation and provide tips on how to successfully emerge from it.

"Living on the International Space Station for nearly a year with literally no way to leave wasn't easy, so I took precautions for my mental and physical health seriously," said Commander Kelly in a statement announcing the release of the report. "I'm advocating for individuals, particularly vulnerable older adults, to use available tools like Connect2Affect.org to strengthen their social connections," he said.

Getting the Help You Need

Working closely with the UHF to help seniors impacted by the COVID-19 pandemic, the AARP Foundation recently expanded its website, (Connect2Affect.org) which was originally launched in 2016. The site offers a wealth of resources for socially isolated seniors to strengthen their social bonds.

This website provides help to individuals to assess their risk for social isolation, and to find support services in their local area. The website includes a Social Isolation Risk Assessment, a questionnaire to help individuals determine how connected they are to others and which resources would benefit them most.

Individuals can also tap into Chatbot, a component of the website, designed to provide friendly conversation with the goal of helping rebuild social connections. Chatbot conversations are secure, private, and accessible 24/7.

"Social isolation is taking a toll on individuals and communities nationwide, and it's especially pernicious for those who are 50 or older. This survey shows that older adults who have lower incomes and who are women are at greatest risk," said Lisa Marsh Ryerson, president of the AARP Foundation. "The tools and resources at Connect2Affect.org are designed to help older adults build and maintain the social connections they need to thrive," she said.

Adds Dr. Rhonda Randall, executive vice president and a chief medical officer at UnitedHealthcare added, "Many people don't know that social isolation can have lasting effects on not only mental health—but also physical health. We're focused on finding practical solutions to the lack of connections, companionship, and the sense of belonging that we all need as humans."

For a copy of *The Pandemic Effect: A Social Isolation Report*, go to **https:// connect2affect.org/wp-content/uploads/2020/10/The-Pandemic-Effect-A-Social-Isolation-Report-AARP-Foundation.pdf**.

THE CORONAVIRUS AND ITS EFFECT ON SOCIAL SECURITY

Published in the *Woonsocket Call* on March 22, 2020

A s the coronavirus (COVID-19) spreads across the nation, the Social Security Administration (SSA) and other federal agencies strive to cope with meeting the huge challenges they face resulting from the unexpected pandemic outbreak, attempting to juggle worker safety while maintaining their daily operations.

On March 19, key House Democratic and Republican Committee chairs sent a clear message to SSA as to the importance of minimizing any disruptions to its operations during the coronavirus crisis. Throughout its 85-year history, Social Security recipients (seniors, families who have lost a breadwinner, and people with disabilities) have never missed getting their monthly check.

Keeping this in mind, House Ways and Means Committee Chairman Richard E. Neal (D-MA) and ranking member Kevin Brady (R-TX), along with Social Security Subcommittee Chairman John B. Larson (D-CT), ranking member Tom Reed (R-NY), Worker and Family Support Subcommittee Chairman Danny K. Davis (D-IL) and ranking member Jackie Walorski (R-IN), sent a letter on March 19 to Social Security Administration (SSA) Commissioner Andrew Saul, calling on the agency to continue its work to prioritize health and transparency in an effort to minimize disruptions as they administer vital services during the coronavirus crisis.

"We know the decision to close SSA field offices...was a difficult decision... This move will save lives and will also protect the health of SSA frontline staff, whose public service is so critical," the key House lawmakers wrote.

"We understand that as coronavirus spreads, you are prioritizing work that fulfills SSA's core mission," the letter continued. "We fully support this prioritization."

"We are writing to urge the Social Security Administration (SSA) to vigorously safeguard the health of the public and agency employees during the coronavirus crisis, while also minimizing disruptions in services to the American people," stated the House lawmakers. "Telework is a commonsense response to coronavirus and we urge you to maximize its use across SSA. In addition, we encourage SSA to communicate regularly and robustly with the public and with its employees about SSA's coronavirus response. Social Security is a program that affects the lives of all Americans. As SSA's response to coronavirus evolves, the public must be able to count on timely information about how to access benefits and services, including assistance when a problem arises."

The members emphasized that they stand ready to work with the agency to ensure it has the resources and authority it needs to operate effectively during the crisis while ensuring SSA remains able to send benefits on time each month.

COVID-19 Changes the Way SSA Does Business

The COVID-19 pandemic has changed the way SSA does business across the nation. Effective Tuesday, March 17, SSA closed all local Social Security offices for in-person service. SSA says that this decision protects the population it services—older Americans and people with underlying medical conditions—and its employees during the crisis.

But SSA employees remain at their cubicles, and the processing of benefits and claims continues.

However, critical services can be accessed online. The agency directed the public to visit its website (**https://www.ssa.gov/**) or its toll-free number, 800-772-1213, for customer service. You can apply for retirement, disability, and Medicare benefits online, check the status of an application or appeal, request a replacement Social Security card (in most areas), print a benefit verification letter, and much more—from anywhere and from any of your devices.

According to SSA, there is also a wealth of information to answer most of your Social Security questions online, without having to speak with an SSA employee in person or by phone. Visit their online Frequently Asked Questions at **http://www.socialsecurity.gov/ask**.

However, those persons who are blind or terminally ill, or need SSI or Medicaid eligibility issues resolved related to work status can obtain in-person services in local offices.

SSA also provides COVID-19-related information and customer service updates on a special website (**https://www.ssa.gov/coronavirus/**).

According to a March 19 blog posting by the Washington, DC-based National Committee to Preserve Social Security and Medicare (NCPSSM), "The Ways and Means committee leaders suggest SSA allow employees to telework where possible, in accordance with federal guidelines." National Committee senior legislative representative (and former 35-year SSA employee) Webster Phillips says the agency's teleworking capabilities have been diminished since Andrew Saul came on board as administrator—and will take time and resources to build back up.

The NCPSSM's blog posting noted, "SSA will discontinue several of its normal activities in order to prioritize beneficiaries' needs. There are workloads that they're not going to process while this is going on, focusing exclusively on paying benefits," says Phillips. "Those include stopping all Continuing Disability Reviews (CDRs) and curtailing eligibility redeterminations for SSI recipients."

Finally, "SSA also has discontinued in-person disability hearings to protect the health of claimants and employees. Instead, those hearings will take place via telephone or video conference, where possible," adds the blog posting.

The Bottom Line...

On March 19, SSA Commissioner Andrew Saul issued a statement to assure the 65 million Social Security recipients that SSA payments will continue to be processed. He stated, "The first thing you should know is that we continue to pay benefits." But Saul warned, "Be aware that scammers may try to trick you into thinking the pandemic is stopping your Social Security payments but that is not true. Don't be fooled."

The United States Postal Service has so far experienced only minor operational impacts in the United States as a result of the COVID-19 pandemic. So, with Saul's assurances and the postal service still delivering mail, you can expect to get your benefits.

COVID-19 KEY ISSUE FOR OLDER VOTERS

Published in the *Pawtucket Times* on November 2, 2020

With Tuesday's presidential election, hopefully most voters will have reviewed the policy and political positions of President Donald J. Trump and his Democratic challenger, former Vice President Joe Biden. Throughout the months of this heated political campaign, especially during the two debates and at the town meetings each candidate held on the same evening, their positions diverged sharply on major issues, specifically the economy, immigration, foreign policy, global warming, abortion, and COVID-19. In the final stretch of the presidential campaign, winning the war against COVID-19 has quickly become the top issue of voters.

Over the months, Trump, 74, has barnstormed throughout the country, especially in battleground states, hoping to capture enough electoral votes to win a second term on November 3. While states reduce the size of gatherings to reduce the spread of COVID-19, throughout the campaign Trump's rallies have continued to bring thousands of supporters together, with many flaunting local and state coronavirus-related crowd restrictions by not wearing masks or social distancing.

However, Biden, 77, is always seen wearing a mask, urging his supporters at online and drive-in events to support his candidacy. At those events, the former vice president called Trump rallies "super-spreader events," and he stressed the importance of following the advice of public-health and medical experts to prevent the spread of COVID-19.

Differing Views on COVID-19

The 2020 presidential campaign has been overshadowed by the COVID-19 pandemic, with 9 million confirmed cases, 227,000 Americans dying from the coronavirus, and an economic downturn forcing more than 31 million people to file for unemployment. During his rallies, Trump claimed "the nation has turned the corner," calling for the country to "return to normalcy" even as COVID-19 hotspots were popping up across the nation. Trump also promised the development of a vaccine and distribution after the election and treatment regimens. Lately, he has suggested that physicians and hospitals are inflating the number of COVID-19 deaths for profit, drawing the ire of the American Medical Association.

At an October 18 Nevada rally, Trump charged that if Biden is elected there will be more coronavirus pandemic lockdowns because "he'll listen to the scientists." The president charged that will result "in a massive depression."

In stark contrast, Biden countered Trump's call for normalcy and his rosy assessment of a COVID-19 vaccine release by stating, "We're about to go into a dark winter...He has no clear plan, and there's no prospect that a vaccine is going to be available for the majority of the American people before the middle of next year."

Oftentimes, Trump's messaging of the importance of wearing a mask has not been clear, frequently contradicting the Centers for Disease Control and Prevention and the White House COVID-19 Task Force. "I was okay with the masks. I was good with it, but I've heard very different stories on masks," he said during his town hall on NBC on October 15. The president opposes a mandate requiring the wearing of masks and favors leaving this decision to state governors and local leaders.

Turning a Deaf Ear to Public-Health Experts

As COVID-19 spreads like wildfire across the nation, Trump and many of his supporters at his large campaign gatherings and even some GOP lawmakers continue not to wear masks or practice social distancing to stop the spread of the disease, their actions ignoring the warnings of the Centers for Disease Control and Prevention and Dr. Anthony Fauci, director of the National Institute of Allergy and Infectious Diseases and a member of the White House COVID-19 Task Force.

According to an October 12 CNN tweet, Dr. Fauci says President Trump resuming in-person rallies is "asking for trouble" and "now is...a worse time to do that because when you look at what's going on in the United States it's really very troublesome. A number of states, right now, are having increase in test positivity."

During an interview with CNBC on October 28, Reuters reported that Dr. Fauci stated, "We are in a very different trajectory. We're going in the wrong direction," noting that COVID-19 cases are increasing in 47 states and hospitals are being overwhelmed by these patients.

"If things do not change," Dr. Fauci warned, "If they continue on the course we're on, there's gonna be a whole lot of pain in this country with regard to additional cases and hospitalizations and deaths."

Now researchers are beginning to shed light on Trump's large rally gatherings and the spread of COVID-19 among the supporters who attended the events.

Zach Nayer, a resident at Riverside Regional Medical Center in Newport News, Virginia, and a colleague reviewed the number of new COVID-19 cases for the 14 days before and after each Trump rally from late June to a September 25 Newport News event, and published their findings on October 16 on the health-news site STAT.

According to the researchers, the spikes in COVID-19 cases occurred in 7 of the 14 cities and townships where rallies were held: Tulsa, Oklahoma; Phoenix and Old Forge in Pennsylvania; Bemidji and Mankato in Minnesota; and Oshkosh and Weston in Wisconsin.

Meanwhile on October 30, Stanford researchers, studying 18 Trump rallies (between June 20 and September 22) concluded that those large events resulted in more than 30,000 confirmed cases of COVID-19 and likely caused more than 700 deaths among attendees and their close contacts.

No End in Sight

Don't expect the COVID-19 pandemic to end soon as the numbers of those infected and dead continue to spiral out of control.

According to the COVID Tracking Project, COVID-19 cases increased by 97,080 on October 31, by far the largest one-day jump since the beginning of the pandemic last March, with Midwestern states leading a wave of infections, hospitalizations, and deaths across the nation just before Tuesday's presidential election. Experts say that those statistics refute Trump's charges that the number of COVID-19 cases is growing due to increased testing.

America's oldest seniors have lived through the 1918 flu pandemic, the stock market crash of 1929, the Great Depression and World War II. Now they, along with aging baby boomers, face the risk of severe illness and death from COVID-19. Among adults, the risk for severe illness from COVID-19 increases with age. According to AARP, 95 percent of the people across the nation that have died of COVID-19 were 50 and older, even though most of the coronavirus cases have been reported in those younger than 50.

Before older voters cast their ballots they must consider which presidential candidate's leadership style can marshal the nation's resources and devise the best strategy to combat COVID-19 and stop its spread.

Do we reopen the nation, opening schools and businesses, or do we consider lockdowns if recommended by the nation's public-health and medical experts? Do we consider a "national mask mandate" or do we leave it up to state governors to decide whether to implement an order requiring people to wear them in public?

Your vote matters. For you older voters, it just might save your life.

4. EMPLOYMENT SCENE

"Mature workers are less impulsive, less reactive, more creative, and more centered."
—Deepak Chopra

AARP TAKES A LOOK AT 'VALUE OF EXPERIENCE' OF OLDER WORKERS

Published in the *Woonsocket Call* on August 12, 2018

Given employers' need for talent and experience, Oak Hill resident Henry Rosenthal, 67, with five decades in the workforce, readily agrees with AARP views that it's a sound business decision to hire experienced workers, as supported by the findings of AARP's recently released survey, *The Value of Experience: AARP Multicultural Work & Jobs Study*. The AARP report includes insights on workers, employers, and age bias, a hurdle Rosenthal had to overcome in finding re-employment after being unemployed for two years in his sixties.

AARP's in-depth survey was conducted online in September 2017 to a national sample of 3,900 adults ages 45 and up who were working full-time, part-time, or looking for work.

According to the results of AARP's survey of experienced workers released on August 2, 2018, nearly 9 in 10 continue to work for financial reasons, but approximately 8 in 10 either enjoy or feel useful doing their job. And among those who plan to retire, more than 1 in 4 plan to start a business or earn money in some independent way, including freelancing and contract work, teaching others, selling handmade goods, and providing home services such as house cleaning and cooking.

"With rich work histories, varied experiences and expertise, older workers want to work, they're ready to work, and they need to work," said AARP Vice President of Financial Resilience Susan Weinstock. "More employers are looking for qualified candidates, and experienced workers should have the opportunity to be judged on their merits, rather than their age."

To highlight job opportunities among 50-plus workers, AARP launched an employer pledge for companies who hire workers based on ability, regardless of age. Since 2013, 650 employers have signed AARP's pledge. AARP also continues to educate employers about the value of an older workforce and the positives of having multigenerational employees.

"According to government data from the US Department of Labor Statistics, workforce participation rates for older workers exceed participation before the Great Recession, while younger worker participation is below pre-Recession numbers," added Weinstock. "While employment trends for older workers are favorable, with 27.9 percent of 55-plus workers suffering long-term unemployment compared to 18.1 percent of age 16-54 workers, the long-term unemployment disparity suggests that entrenched age bias still exists too often in the workplace," she says.

Age Discrimination Still Exists

Findings from AARP's survey, *The Value of Experience*, show that many experienced workers still face the barrier of age discrimination in their job hunt or at their place of employment. More than 9 in 10 workers see age discrimination as somewhat or a very common occurrence.

Specifically, the AARP survey found that at work, more than 6 in 10 older workers (61 percent) report they've seen or experienced age discrimination in the workplace, and of those concerned about losing their job in the next year, one-third (34 percent) list age discrimination as either a major or minor reason. But only 3 percent of the survey respondents say that they had made a formal complaint to their supervisor, to human resources, or a government agency.

Age discrimination becomes more noticeable to those turning age 50 and over. Fifty-four percent of those surveyed believe that age discrimination starts on that major age milestone, 28 percent at age 60. Ageist comments from either a boss or coworker are the most visibly frequent type of discrimination reported by the survey respondents.

According to the AARP survey, both employed workers and those who were unemployed looking for work viewed age discrimination as the key reason why they did not think they could find employment within three months.

On the job hunt, almost half (44 percent) of older job applicants say they have been asked for age-related information, such as birth date and graduation date, from a potential employer.

More than 90 percent of older Americans surveyed by AARP supported strengthening the nation's age discrimination laws—nearly 6 in 10 (59 percent) strongly support a change, and 32 percent somewhat agree they should be improved.

With 2017 marking the fiftieth anniversary of the nation's Age Discrimination Act of 1967, AARP's new survey findings are timely as America's workforce ages and an increasing number of older workers report their age keeps them from becoming gainfully employed or underemployed.

A Personal Note:

Looking back, Rosenthal says of his two-year job search, starting in 2015 after being laid off, he experienced age discrimination. "Having been interviewed by numerous human-resource professionals, they just seem incapable of understanding that the years of experience someone has gained are an asset. They seem unable to appreciate that knowledge, experience, and even skills acquired over a lifetime can be transferred and used in virtually any organization or business," he says.

Rosenthal says, "there is a higher probability of age discrimination occurring when company management, human-resource professionals, and recruiters interview applicants older than themselves." Like many older job seekers, he believes that decision-making executives are uncomfortable with overseeing older workers, and rather than deal with them, they just don't hire them.

Rosenthal, now gainfully "underemployed," views his older contemporaries as being "more stable, reliable, have better work ethics and generally make great employees," in line with AARP's philosophy that Corporate America should value the experience of older workers. With the difficulty in finding employment, Rosenthal believes that companies have not figured this out yet. "What a terrible waste of human capital," he says.

AARP says its survey findings reveal that "older workers believe that age discrimination should be taken just as seriously as other forms of discrimination, and support strengthening the laws to ensure that it is."

But Rosenthal says that while combating age discrimination by strengthening the laws can only help, real change can only occur by changing "our cultural attitudes." "Other cultures value their elders, but here in America's we don't," he says.

For a copy of AARP survey findings, go to **http://www.aarp.org/content/ dam/aarp/research/surveys_statistics/econ/2018/value-of- experience-chartbook.doi.10.26419-2Fres.00177.003.pdf.**

AGE DISCRIMINATION, WORKPLACE ISSUES AT HOUSE HEARING

Published in RINewsToday on March 22, 2021

Just days ago, Rep. Robert C. "Bobby" Scott (D-VA), chairman of the House Committee on Education and Labor, and Rep. Rodney Davis (R-IL) introduced, H.R. 2062, the bipartisan "Protecting Older Workers Against Discrimination Act" (POWADA), a bill that would strengthen federal antidiscrimination protections for older workers. The legislation was introduced on March 18, 2021, the same day of a joint House Education and Labor Subcommittee hearing, held to address a variety of workplace issues. POWADA has been referred to the House Committee on Education and Labor for consideration.

The reintroduction of POWADA is timely. As the COVID-19 pandemic continues, older workers are attempting to keep their jobs, working more and longer hours than they ever have. When seniors lose their jobs, they are far more likely than younger workers to join the ranks of the long-term unemployed. And unfortunately, discrimination appears to be a significant factor in older workers' long-term unemployment.

A 2018 survey conducted by the Washington, DC-based AARP found that three in five workers age 45 and older had seen or experienced age discrimination in the workplace. The 2018 survey also found that three-quarters of older workers blame age discrimination for their lack of confidence in being able to find a new job.

Congress Gears Up To Fight Age Discrimination Again

Representatives Scott and Davis were joined by seven Republicans and fourteen Democrats, including Civil Rights and Human Services Subcommittee Chair Suzanne Bonamici (D-OR) and Workforce Protections Subcommittee Chair Alma Adams (D-NC) to support H.R. 2062.

Rhode Island Rep. David Cicilline has also requested to be a co-sponsor of this legislation.

POWADA was first introduced in Congress after an adverse 2009 Supreme Court decision, *Gross v. FBL Financial Services, Inc.*, that made it much more difficult for older workers to prove claims of illegal bias based on age. Under *Gross*, plaintiffs seeking to prove age discrimination in employment are required to demonstrate that age was the *sole* motivating factor for the employer's adverse action. The Supreme Court ruling upends decades of precedent that had allowed individuals to prove discrimination by showing that a discriminatory motive was one of the factors on which an employer's adverse action was based.

Scott's reintroduced POWADA returns the legal standard for age discrimination claims to the pre-2009 evidentiary threshold, aligning the burden of proof with the same standards for proving discrimination based on race and national origin.

"Everyone—regardless of their age—should be able to go to work every day knowing that they are protected from discrimination. Unfortunately, age discrimination in the workplace is depriving older workers of opportunities and exposing them to long-term unemployment and severe financial hardship," says Chairman Scott, noting that the reintroduced bipartisan bill would finally restore the legal rights under the Age Discrimination in Employment Act, which covers workers age 40 and over.

Republican Rep. Rodney Davis puts aside political differences and has stepped up to the plate with a handful of GOP lawmakers to co-sponsor Scott's POWADA legislation. "Every American, including older Americans, deserves to work in a workplace or job site that is free from discrimination That's why I'm proud to team up with Chairman Bobby Scott and a bipartisan group of lawmakers in introducing the Protecting Older Workers Against Discrimination Act. Our bipartisan bill provides workplace protections for older workers by removing barriers they have to filing discrimination claims, ensuring their workplace rights can be enforced," says Davis, pledging to work with colleagues on both sides of the aisle to finally get the bill passed.

Oregon Representative Bonamici, who chairs the Subcommittee on Civil Rights and Human Services, notes that her state has a rapidly aging population, and age discrimination in the workplace remains disturbingly pervasive. She joins Scott in cosponsoring POWADA.

"I've heard from Oregonians who were denied or lost a job because of their age, but the bar for proving discrimination is very high and the outcomes are uncertain. The bipartisan Protecting Older Workers Against Discrimination Act makes it clear that unlawful discrimination in the workplace is unacceptable and holds employers accountable for discriminatory actions," says Bonamici.

Adams, who chairs the Subcommittee on Workforce Protections, joins Bonamici in co-sponsoring POWADA. The North Carolina Congresswoman states: "Labor law must protect the dignity of all workers and it must recognize that discrimination against older Americans is discrimination all the same." The North Carolina Congresswoman notes that POWADA ensures that older workers will be fairly treated in the job market, returning the legal standard for proving discrimination back to its original intent. There is no place for disparate treatment based on age in the workforce.

"The introduction of this bill is a crucial step to strengthening the law and restoring fairness for older workers who experience age discrimination," said Nancy LeaMond, AARP executive vice president and chief advocacy & engagement officer. "It sends a clear message that discrimination in the workplace—against older workers or others—is never acceptable."

"Age discrimination in the workplace, like any other kind of discrimination, is wrong," said AARP Rhode Island State Director Kathleen Connell. That's why AARP is fighting all forms of age discrimination in the hiring process and on the job, including an unfair court decision that makes age discrimination more difficult to prove than race- or sex-based discrimination. "Rhode Islanders are living and working longer, and experienced workers bring expertise, maturity, and perspective," Connell added. "Yet negative stereotypes and mistaken assumptions mean that older people are often treated unfairly in the workplace. We need bipartisan Congressional action to address this stubborn and persistent problem."

Tackling Workforce Issues

Over two hours, four witnesses testified at a joint Zoom hearing, "Fighting for Fairness: Examining Legislation to Confront Workplace Discrimination," held before the House Education and Labor Subcommittee on Civil Rights and Human Services and the Subcommittee on Workforce Protections. The morning hearing addressed an array of workforce issues, including race and longstanding gender inequalities and barriers and pregnancy discrimination at the workplace. A spotlight was also put on the rampant increase of age discrimination that older workers are now facing in the job market and the need to pass POWADA to reverse the detrimental impact of a 2009 Supreme Court decision.

Lauren McCann, senior attorney at the AARP Foundation, pointed out to the attending House lawmakers that age discrimination in the workplace remains "stubbornly persistent" and urged a House Education and Labor hearing to "re-level the playing field" by passing strong anti-bias legislation.

McCann told the committee that the ongoing COVID-19 pandemic has exacerbated the problems faced by older workers, who have left the labor force in the last year at twice the rate as during the Great Recession.

McCann testified that passage of POWADA, sponsored by Scott, the chair of the House Committee of Education and Labor, is crucial to reverse the 2009 Supreme Court decision in the *Gross v. FBL Financial Services, Inc.* case. McCann said that the high court's 2009 decision abruptly changed the standard—from the longstanding requirement under the ADEA that a worker prove that age is just one motivating factor in adverse treatment on the job—to a much higher and tougher to prove standard: that age is the standard motive.

"Older workers now always bear the burden of persuasion in ADEA cases," McCann emphasized.

The number of age-55-and-over unemployed has also doubled, up from one million in February 2020, to two million last month, according to PPI.

Turning to the Senate...

At press time, a senior Senate aide for Senator Bob Casey (D-PA), who chairs the Senate Special Committee on Aging, says the senator is posed to follow the House by throwing the Senate's POWADA Senate companion measure into the legislative hopper on Monday.

The Pennsylvania senator clearly understands why he again must push for the passage and enactment of POWADA. "As more Americans are remaining in the workforce longer, we must recognize and address the challenges that aging workers face. We must make it clear to employers that age discrimination is unacceptable, and we must strengthen antidiscrimination protections that are being eroded," says Senator Casey. "POWADA would level the playing field for older workers and ensure they are able to fight back against age discrimination in the workplace."

5. FINANCIAL ISSUES

"Be thankful for what you have; you'll end up having more. If you concentrate on what you don't have, you will never, ever have enough."

—Oprah Winfrey

STUDENT LOAN DEBT TAKES A HUGE FINANCIAL TOLL ON SENIORS

Published in the *Woonsocket Call* on May 26, 2019

As the 2020 presidential campaign heats up, Democratic candidates are zeroing in on a key domestic issue for 44 million voters carrying $1.5 trillion in student-loan debt. Their proposals range from free public college for anybody, forgiveness of all college loans up to $50,000, free community college, to refinancing college loans.

With the national political spotlight put on student loan debt, many are assuming that this issue impacts only younger Americans. That is not the case. A newly released AARP Public Policy Institute report says it's a skyrocketing problem impacting multiple age groups. Over recent decades, the report highlights the important role that older Americans play in financing college education for their children, grandchildren, and other family members.

Federal Reserve data show that Americans owed $1.5 trillion in student loan debt as of December. An updated analysis shows people age 50 and older owed 20 percent of that total, or $289.5 billion, a more than fivefold increase from $47.3 billion in 2004.

According to the PPI findings, of those age 50 and over who helped pay for "someone else," 80 percent helped a child, compared with 6 percent who helped a spouse or partner; 8 percent, a grandchild, and even smaller percentages "who helped other relatives or friends."

Student Loan Debit Hits Seniors Hard in Their Pocketbooks

"It is stunning that more families are taking on such sharply greater amounts of student debt than in the past," says Lori Trawinski, director of banking and finance at the AARP Public Policy Institute, in a May 15 statement released with the report, *The Student Loan Debt Threat: An Intergenerational Problem.*

"For younger families, this burden impedes their ability to save for other purposes, such as for a home, their children's education or for their own retirement," adds Trawinski, who warns that the long-term financial security of seniors can be threatened by student loan debt.

The researchers noted that most older borrowers hold loans taken out for their own education, and the percentage of borrowers age 50 and older in default is much higher than for younger borrowers. Data also show that Parent PLUS (direct federal loan) borrowers age 65 and over are facing higher rates of default than younger age groups, they say.

The 10-page PPI report includes survey results that focus on the key role played by age 50 and older Americans in helping "someone else pay for college and other post-high-school education." (The survey specifically included only those individuals who have not yet fully paid off the debt or who have paid it off within the past five years.)

One interesting finding of the PPI report was that the most common involvement by people age 50 and older was cosigning a loan (45 percent), while a smaller percentage (34 percent) ran a balance on a credit card, and 26 percent took out a Parent PLUS loan.

Among those who cosigned a private student loan, nearly 49 percent made a payment on the loan, often because they wanted to proactively assist the student borrower. Twenty-five percent said they had to make a payment after the student failed to do so.

The survey asked the one-quarter of survey respondents who had taken out a Parent PLUS federal loan, and who had made a payment over the prior five years, whether they ever had any difficulty making payments. Nearly a third (32 percent) did have a problem with at least one payment. The breakdown by race/ethnicity for those having a problem with a payment was: African-American/Blacks, 46 percent; Hispanics, 49 percent; and whites, 29 percent.

Student Loan Debt Put on Lawmakers' Radar Screen

Over a week ago, the Senate Finance Committee took testimony on S 0737, titled the Student Loan Bill of Rights. The legislative proposal, sponsored by Senator Dawn Euer (D), a lawyer representing parts of Newport and Jamestown, would protect student loan borrowers and establish oversight of student loan services operating in the Ocean State. House Health, Education and Welfare Chairman Joseph M. McNamara has introduced the companion measure (H 5936) in the lower chamber.

According to a press statement, more than 133,000 Rhode Islanders, including 16,000 senior citizens, have a combined $4.5 billion in student loan debt. More than $470 million of Rhode Islanders' student loan debt is delinquent.

S 0737 would set standards for student loan serving, both prohibiting predatory behavior and providing best practices for protecting consumers' rights. It also requires student loan servicers register with the state and allows state regulators to examine servicers' business practices. Additionally, the Senate bill allows both the attorney general and department of business regulation to penalize servicers who violate borrowers' rights and to seek restitution on behalf of borrowers in Rhode Island. It would also require better communication from lenders to borrowers about any transfer of their loans to another institution and about any alternative repayment or forgiveness program for which the borrower may qualify.

Borrowers in Rhode Island report being double-charged or incorrectly marked as delinquent in payment, with loan servicers taking months, or even years, to correct mistakes. Additionally, many student loan borrowers eligible for the national "Public Service Loan Forgiveness" program have received incorrect and contradictory information from their loan servicers, leading to improper denials of loan forgiveness.

Calling for Passage of Rhode Island's "Student Loan Bill of Rights"

Bill sponsors Euer and McNamara were joined by Treasurer Seth Magaziner, Attorney General Peter Neronha, Commissioner of Postsecondary Education Brenda Dann-Messier, and Department of Business Regulation Director Liz Tanner on March 28 at the statehouse to push for a legislative fix to protect Rhode Islanders who are shouldering crushing student loan debt.

"By several measures, student loan debt has increased greatly in the last 10 years," said McNamara at the news conference. "It has surpassed the amount households owe on auto loans, home equity loans and credit cards. This legislation will help to address the crisis by establishing oversight of the student loan process and prohibiting predatory practices," he noted.

Euer added, "The heavy burden of student debt is challenging enough for the majority of college graduates. Incompetent, inefficient or even deceitful loan servicers should not be allowed to exacerbate their struggles. Student loan servicers must be held accountable to ensure that they are providing honest, reliable information and services to their borrowers."

Treasurer Magaziner threw in his two cents. "Too many Rhode Islanders are vulnerable to deceptive and predatory practices by their student loan servicers, who make it hard for borrowers to keep their loan payments affordable." He added, "Too often, borrowers aren't receiving accurate information about their loan, which can result in higher interest, leave them in debt longer, and make them more likely to default. This legislation will hold student loan servicers accountable and help Rhode Islanders choose the options that are best for them."

Finally, Attorney General Neronha touted the importance of passing the Student Loan Bill of Rights. "If and when borrowers have issues with their loans or loan servicers, this legislation provides them with a place to go to address those issues. While our primary focus will be on helping Rhode Islanders get the information they need to solve their student loan problems, my office will be ready, on behalf of mistreated borrowers, to investigate and enforce violations of the student loan standards outlined in this bill."

If Congress can't tackle the student loan debt crisis in a timely fashion, it is time for Rhode Island lawmakers to offer assistance to Rhode Islanders faced with crippling student loan debt. The Rhode Island General Assembly should pass Euer and McNamara's Student Loan Bill of Rights, and the legislative proposals should not be held for further study. It's the right thing to do.

CONCERNS EXPRESSED ABOUT SAVINGS AND SOCIAL SECURITY COVERING RETIREE EXPENSES

Published in the *Woonsocket Call* on May 5, 2019

What resolution did you make as New Year's Eve approached on December 31, 2018? You might have mentioned losing weight, or improving your health by eating healthy foods and regularly exercising. Better budgeting and saving money for retirement might have even made your shortlist too.

According to a new national AARP study, *Financial Resolutions, Mistakes and Accomplishments*, 83 percent of the 1,500 adults (age 35 and over) participating in an online survey say they made a New Year's resolution or goal within the past five years. Over half (52 percent) say that saving money was their top resolution pick, followed by losing weight (43 percent), increasing fitness (40 percent), and getting better organized (40 percent).

Saving Money Most Popular 2019 Resolution

Sixty percent of those polled noted that their 2019 savings resolution included a mix of short-term and long-term goals. Adults ages 35-39 (75 percent) are more likely to have made this resolution, compared to the respondents ages 50-54 (50 percent) and those ages 65 and over (45 percent). The most common goals mentioned by these poll respondents were building of an emergency fund (45 percent), paying off debt (37 percent), saving for vacation (41 percent), building up a retirement fund (35 percent), and making home improvements (31 percent).

Just two months into 2019, when AARP's poll was taken in March, 43 percent of the respondents who made a savings resolution for 2019 expressed concern that they were already at risk of not meeting this goal, tying their failure to unexpected expenses (61 percent), covering basic expenses (46 percent), or a drop in their income (20 percent) due to unemployment or a business slowdown.

The survey respondents say the most common financial mistakes relate to not saving (19 percent), followed by buying on credit (10 percent), accumulating too much credit card debt (10 percent) and spending too much (8 percent).

By gender, when compared to men, women are especially likely to say their mistakes were related to credit cards and loans. Men point to mistakes related to making poor stock market decisions, bad investments, or not investing.

The AARP survey findings reveal that making financial mistakes can have a lasting impact, too. Over 55 percent say that their mistake is still affecting their current financial situation.

Fifty-nine percent of those polled by AARP said it was only "somewhat likely" to "not at all likely" that the combination of their savings, investments, and Social Security benefits would be sufficient to cover their financial needs throughout retirement. This included more women (67 percent) than men (51 percent). Only 41 percent of all respondents said their retirement assets are "very" or "extremely" likely to pay for their needs through retirement.

More than 35 percent of those who are uncertain whether they have enough money to live on in retirement attribute their doubts to either not knowing how much money they will need in retirement (31 percent) or not knowing how much to save (9 percent), notes the AARP survey findings.

The AARP survey is in line with a recent updated report from the US Government Accountability Office that found most households approaching retirement have low amounts of savings. When polled about their "biggest financial mistakes" in the AARP survey, respondents said their most common mistakes related to not saving enough.

"The situation is serious, but not one that can't be improved," said AARP Financial Ambassador Jean Chatzky, in a statement released with the report. "No matter your circumstance, there are resources available to help almost anyone take simple steps to improve your finances, start a savings plan, and get into the habit of putting away money on a regular basis," says Chatzky.

Education combined with learning simple steps to assist in saving more money are key to help people make more informed decisions, avoiding either saving inadequately or accumulating debt, especially with credit cards.

Check Out These Savings and Planning Tools

Do you need to beef up on your knowledge on ways to better save for your retirement? If so, check out these websites...

AceYourRetirement.org, a website sponsored by AARP and the Ad Council, breaks down the retirement savings process into easy, actionable steps. Just answer a few questions about your savings and goals, and you will receive a personalized action plan that highlights three practical next steps.

AARP's Money Essentials webpage offers advice about saving, living on a budget, managing debt, and other topics.

The Social Security Resource Center provides answers to questions about when to claim, how to maximize benefits, and other Social Security essentials.

A new AARP podcast, "Closing the Savings Gap™," hosted by Chatzky, profiles women who are facing a retirement savings gap and matches each with a financial planner who then helps them solve common challenges in retirement planning.

AARP's website also provides work, career, and employment resources to help you maximize your earning potential.

For full access to the 38-page research report, *Financial Resolutions, Mistakes and Accomplishments*, go to **http://www.aarp.org/content/dam/aarp/ research/surveys_statistics/econ/2019/financial-resolutions- mistakes-accomplishments.doi.10.26419-2Fres.00309.001.pdf**.

REPORT: MOST WORKING AMERICANS NOT SAVING FOR RETIREMENT

Published in the *Woonsocket Call* on January 12, 2019

L ess than four months ago, a research report released by the Washington, DC-based National Institute on Retirement Security (NIRS), using an analysis of US Census data, found that even with the nation's economic recovery, savings levels of working-age Americans are inadequate for America's retirees to rely on.

The NIRS report analyzes the US Census Bureau's Survey of Income and Program Participation data released in 2016 and 2017. Researchers took a look at workplace retirement plan coverage, retirement account ownership, and retirement savings as a percentage of income, and estimates the share of workers that meet financial industry recommended benchmarks for retirement savings.

"The facts and data are clear. Retirement is in peril for most working-class Americans," says Diane Oakley, the report author and NIRS executive director in a statement. "When all working individuals are considered—not just the minority with retirement accounts—the typical working American has zero, zilch, nothing saved for retirement," she says.

Oakley added, "What this report means is that the American dream of a modest retirement after a lifetime of work now is a middle-class nightmare. Even among workers who have accumulated savings in retirement accounts, the typical worker had a low account balance of $40,000. This is far off-track from the savings levels Americans need if they hope to sustain their standard of living in retirement."

American's Not Prepared for Financially Surviving Retirement Years

Findings in NIRS's 32-page research report, *Retirement in America: Out of Reach for Most Americans?*, released on September 18, finds that more than

100 million working-age individuals (57 percent) do not own any retirement account assets, whether in an employer-sponsored 401(k)-type plan or an IRA; nor are they covered by defined benefit plans. Researchers say the data indicated that "those who do own retirement accounts have, on average, more than three times the annual income of individuals who do not own retirement accounts."

According to the research findings, the typical working-age American has no retirement savings. When including all working individuals—not just individuals with retirement accounts—the median retirement account balance is $0 among all working individuals. For the typical workers who have retirement savings accounts, these individuals only had a modest account balance of $40,000. "Furthermore, some 68 percent of individuals age 55 to 64 have retirement savings equal to less than one times' their annual income, which is far below what they will need to maintain their standard of living over their expected years in retirement," say the NIRS's research report.

The research study findings indicate that 77 percent of Americans cannot meet conservative retirement savings goals for their age and income-levels based on working until age 67, even after counting an individuals' entire net worth. "Due to a long-term trend toward income and wealth inequality that only worsened during the recent economic recovery, a large majority of the bottom half of Americans cannot meet even a substantially reduced savings target," says the NIRS report.

The researchers say that federal and state policies can assist Americans in accumulating retirement income by strengthening the nation's Social Security program, by states expanding access to low-cost, high-quality retirement plans, and helping low-income workers save. "States across the nation are taking key steps to expand access to workplace retirement savings, with enrollment in state-based programs this year starting in Oregon, Washington, and Illinois. Other proposals to expand coverage are on the national agenda but universal retirement plan coverage has not become a national priority. Finally, expanding the Saver's Credit and making it refundable could help boost the retirement savings of lower-income families," notes the NIRS report.

Assisting Rhode Islanders To Save for Retirement

In 2016, AARP Rhode Island released a survey of 459 Rhode Island small-business owners (with up to 100 employees) to determine their thoughts about employee retirement benefits. Overwhelmingly, these business owners see a need for lawmakers to create a program to help working Rhode Islanders to save for their retirement years.

According to the AARP telephone poll findings on small businesses, 76 percent say Rhode Islanders need a lot more encouragement to save for retirement. A whopping 82 percent agree that state lawmakers should support small-business owners to offer employees a way to save.

Seventy-six percent of the respondents agree that being able to offer voluntary, portable, retirement plans will provide them with a competitive edge to attract or retain employees, notes the poll's findings.

Most small-business owner respondents called on the Rhode Island General Assembly to support state legislation to create a basic, ready-to-go, privately-managed retirement plan for employees. The majority of small-business owners who participated in the AARP Rhode Island survey agree that state lawmakers should support a plan to make it easier for small-business owners to offer their employees a way to save for retirement.

In 2016, the Rhode Island General Assembly considered AARP Rhode Island's so-called Work & Save legislation to assist working Rhode Islanders in saving for their retirement years by establishing a private employer IRA program. But, with spiraling state deficits and the administrative costs of the program, the legislation was held for "further study," immediately killing the legislation.

With America's aging population, with many not having adequate retirement savings, Congress must move to strengthen the Social Security program. But the Rhode Island General Assembly must look for ways to expand access to workplace retirement savings through a state-based program. Not doing so may ultimately increase the state's role in providing assistance to an increasing percentage of low-income older Rhode Islanders.

SHOPPING FOR A FINANCIAL ADVISOR

Published in the *Pawtucket Times* on February 8, 2021

D ue to living in times of economic uncertainty resulting from the ongoing COVID-19 pandemic, retirees are worried about how they can protect their hard-earned egg nest from the volatility of the stock market. It is even now more important to be working with a financial planner who is watching your back and not putting their interests first.

Just days ago, the Washington, DC-based AARP launched "AARP Interview an Advisor™," a free resource to assist investors in evaluating a financial advisor. This new financial tool enables older investors to better assess and understand the credentials of financial advisors and how they are compensated.

SEC's Best Interest Fails To Put Investors First

AARP says this online resource was created in response to a Securities and Exchange Commission's (SEC) 2019 ruling that stopped a long-standing federal regulation requiring financial advisors to put their clients' interest above their own. AARP and other critics of the final ruling say that it fell short of defining exactly what that term means operationally.

"The regulation explicitly states that it does not mean that financial advisors provide a fiduciary standard of care. Despite its name, 'Regulation Best Interest' does not require that financial advisors put their client's interest above their own financial interests," charges AARP. The nation's largest aging advocacy group warns that sound financial advice from fiduciaries won't happen without a code of standards that requires the best interest of the client.

AARP Interview an Advisor™ guides users through the process of researching potential advisors and provides them with valuable evaluation tools to help them assess their financial planner.

Last year, AARP conducted a national survey to gauge investors' awareness and views of the SEC's Regulation Best Interest ruling and also their understanding of the fees and expenses they pay for investment products and financial advice. The survey findings, detailed in the recently released 27-page report, *Should Financial Advisors Put Your Interests First*, indicated a need to raise the awareness of the SEC's new regulation and its impact on investing. It also became very clear to the study's researchers that investors require more assistance in vetting current and/or future financial advisors to ensure that their financial advisor puts their interests first, and more education is needed regarding investment fees and expenses.

AARP's survey of 1,577 adults age 25 and older who have money saved in retirement savings accounts and/or other investment accounts, conducted by NORC at the University of Chicago on behalf of AARP during August 22-26, 2019 (prior to the COVID-19 pandemic), found more than 80 percent of American investors were not aware of the SEC ruling. Upon learning about this regulatory change, four in five investors (83 percent) opposed the change.

According to AARP's survey findings, nearly 70 percent of investors have at least two investment accounts. Among those having multiple accounts, 74 percent do not use the same financial institution to manage all of their accounts. The median amount that investors currently have in savings and investments ranges between $50,000 and $99,999.

Additionally, 90 percent of investors either somewhat (52 precent) or completely (38 percent) trust the financial institutions or advisors who manage their investment accounts.

Despite 68 percent of investors believing that they are somewhat (54 percent) or very (14 percent) knowledgeable about their investments, 41 percent mistakenly believe that they don't pay any fees or expenses for their investment accounts.

Can You Trust Your Financial Planner?

Yet the survey findings note that 58 percent of investors think financial advisors would choose to increase their earnings by selling their clients higher-cost investment products even if similar lower cost products are available.

"With millions of American families concerned about the financial uncertainty caused by the pandemic, it is crucial for them to be equipped with the best resources and information when selecting a financial advisor," said Jean

Setzfand, AARP senior vice president of programming, in a February 4, 2020 statement announcing the release of the new financial planning tool. "The new SEC regulation states that advisors must act in their client's 'best interest,' but falls short of defining exactly what that term means," she said.

"AARP Interview an Advisor™" is an online resource that provides guidance and a checklist for investors on how to assess the services and standards of financial advisors. Investors are invited to fill out a short survey that evaluates the potential advisor and compares them on a three-point scale. It also provides investors with advice on how to effectively communicate with a prospective advisor, assess their credentials, and better understand how advisors are compensated.

The COVID-19 pandemic has put many seniors off track in reaching their financial goal of building a sufficient nest egg to provide financial security in their later years. Now it's even more important for you to have a top-notch financial planner who has your back.

To view AARP's survey of retail investors about advisor-client relationships and fees, go to **https://www.aarp.org/content/dam/aarp/research/ surveys_statistics/econ/2019/retail-investor-survey-report. doi.10.26419-2Fres.00342.001.pdf**.

AARP'S NEW INTERNET TOOL HELPS SENIORS MANAGE HEFTY STUDENT LOAN DEBT

Published in RINewsToday on April 5, 2021

O ver the years, AARP Public Policy Institute (PPI) has tracked the staggering amount of student loan debt that seniors are shouldering to help their children and grandchildren finance their higher education. Many people over age 50 also take on student loan debt themselves, seeking more education at colleges and universities to sharpen their skills to get a raise or a higher paying job.

AARP national CEO, Ann Jenkins, in a July 3, 2019 blog posting, "Student Loan Debt is Crippling Too Many Families," urged Congress and state legislatures to increase public investment in colleges and universities. "The cost of attending a four-year college more than doubled, even after adjusting for inflation, as state and local funding for higher education per student has decreased," she said, noting that family incomes haven't come close to matching that increase.

Jenkins warned that the rising cost of student loan debt is "crippling too many families" and "threatens to crush the financial security of millions of Americans over age 50." According to a PPI report released May 2019, entitled *The Student Loan Debt Threat: An Intergenerational Problem,* cited by Jenkins in her blog article, Americans of all ages owed $1.5 trillion dollars in student loan debt as of December, 2018. Compare this to people ages 50 and older who owed 20 percent of this debt, or $289.5 billion of that total, up from $47.3 billion in 2004, she said, noting "that's a fivefold increase since 2004."

Most troubling, this 2019 PPI analysis found that 25 percent of private student loan cosigners age 50 and older had to make a loan payment because the student borrower failed to do so.

The 2019 PPI analysis findings also indicated the obvious—that is, taking on student loan debt can quickly deplete a senior's retirement nest egg. The data revealed that many older student loan borrowers racked up debt by running a balance on a credit card (34 percent) and taking out a Parent PLUS loan, federal money borrowed by parents (26 percent). Other types of borrowing included taking out a home equity loan (12 percent), refinancing of their homes (10 percent), and taking out a loan against their retirement savings (8 percent).

Jenkins also noted that for seniors who defaulted in paying their monthly student loan payments, the federal government can recoup this money by taking a number of steps to collect, among them taking a portion of federal or state income tax refunds, withholding a percentage of Social Security retirement or disability benefits, or even garnishing some of the borrower's wages.

Today, America's seniors are still feeling the overwhelming financial weight of having to pay off student loan debt.

Updated Student Loan Data Released

Last week, AARP's PPI released a new report updating data on older student loan borrowers. Like its 2019 analysis, the newly released data in the report, *Rising Student Loan Debt Continues to Burden Older Borrowers*, revealed that student loan debt is still a staggering problem across generations: Americans 50 and older held $336.1 billion, or 22 percent, of the $1.6 trillion in student loan debt in 2020. In 2004, older borrowers accounted for 10 percent of the $455.2 billion student loan debt.

"Student loan debt is becoming a burden for all generations, ensnaring more older adults and delaying or battering the retirement plans for many," said Gary Koenig, AARP vice president of financial security, in an AARP statement released on March 31, 2021. "Paying for higher education was never meant to last a lifetime."

AARP's newly released PPI analysis found that millions of borrowers—including as many as seven million individuals ages 50-plus—have had their payment suspension extended through September due to the pandemic. However, about a fifth of student loan debt—more than $300 billion—is not included in the current suspension.

Managing Your Student Loan Debt

To help individuals manage their student debt, AARP and Savi last week unveiled a new student loan repayment tool to help individuals identify the best payment options, with special features for the 50-plus population. The Savi Student Loan Repayment Tool provides a free, personalized assessment of student loan repayment options. It can also help individuals identify loan forgiveness opportunities based on employment, and assistance in preparing and filing paperwork.

"We've seen the generational impact of student loan debt, and we're excited to work with AARP in helping older borrowers access immediate and long-term relief," said Tobin Van Ostern, co-founder of Savi. "This is about changing the narrative and providing freedom from the burdens of student debt to those who need it most," he notes.

"This new AARP resource provides a means for Rhode Islanders to form a clearer picture of student loan repayment that could help many clear up uncertainties and avoid potential additional costs," said AARP State Director Kathleen Connell. "I urge older Rhode Islanders to get the information they need, especially those whose retirement savings might be impacted."

Any adult with student loans may use the online tool at no cost, after registering at AARP.org/studentloans. AARP worked with Savi to customize the tool for older borrowers and includes: options for dozens of national and state repayment and forgiveness programs; synchronized federal and private loans across all loan servicers easily with industry standard security; support from student loan experts; and access to free educational resources.

According to AARP's statement announcing the new online tool, the Washington, DC-based aging advocacy group has worked with Savi to provide this resource to low-income older adults at no cost through the AARP Foundation. As older adults are the largest-growing age group of student loan borrowers, AARP and Savi are committed to helping them access the tools they need to begin tackling their student loan debt.

AARP's statement makes it very clear that its collaboration with Savi does not involve or promote student loan refinancing if any.

6. HEALTH & WELLNESS

"I've always said that I will never let an old person into my body. That is, I don't believe in 'thinking' old. Don't program yourself to break down as you age with thoughts that decline is inevitable."

—Wayne Dyer

TAKING A LOOK AT PHYSICAL ACTIVITY AND CARDIAC HEALTH

Published in the *Woonsocket Call* on March 8, 2020

Springtime is coming. Get out your walking shoes...

Physical exercise (that doesn't have to be strenuous to be effective) can lead to longer, healthier lives, according to two preliminary research study findings presented at the American Heart Association's Epidemiology and Prevention Lifestyle and Cardiometabolic Scientific Sessions of 2020. The EPI Scientific Sessions, held March 3-6 in Phoenix, are considered to be the premier global exchange of the latest advances in population-based cardiovascular science for researchers and clinicians.

"Finding a way to physically move more in an activity that suits your capabilities and is pleasurable is extremely important for all people, and especially for older people who may have risk factors for cardiovascular diseases. Physical activities such as brisk walking can help manage high blood pressure and high cholesterol, improve glucose control among many benefits," said Barry A. Franklin, Ph.D., past chair of both the American Heart Association's Council on Physical Activity and Metabolism and the National Advocacy Committee, director of preventive cardiology and cardiac rehabilitation at Beaumont Health in Royal Oak, Michigan, and professor of internal medicine at Oakland University William Beaumont School of Medicine in Rochester, Michigan.

Every Step Counts

In one session, Dr. Andrea Z. LaCroix, Ph.D., of the University of California San Diego (UCSD), presented her study's findings that showed the importance of walking, stressing that every step counts in reducing cardiovascular disease deaths among older women.

UCSD's study was supported by the National Heart, Lung, and Blood Institute of the National Institutes of Health.

According to the UCSD study's findings, women who walked 2,100 to 4,500 steps daily reduced their risk of dying from cardiovascular diseases (including heart attacks, heart failure, and stroke) by up to 38 percent, compared to women who walked less than 2,100 daily steps. The women who walked more than 4,500 steps per day reduced their risk by 48 percent, in this study of more than 6,000 women with an average age of 79.

LaCroix says that the UCSD study's findings also indicated that the cardio-protective effect of more steps taken per day was present even after the researchers took into consideration heart disease risk factors, including obesity, elevated cholesterol, blood pressure, triglycerides, and/or blood sugar levels, and was not dependent on how fast the women walked.

"Despite popular beliefs, there is little evidence that people need to aim for 10,000 steps daily to get cardiovascular benefits from walking. Our study showed that getting just over 4,500 steps per day is strongly associated with reduced risk of dying from cardiovascular disease in older women," said LaCroix, the lead study author who serves as distinguished professor and chief of epidemiology at the UCSD. Co-authors of the study are John Bellettiere, Ph.D., M.P.H.; Chongzhi Di, Ph.D.; and Michael J. Lamonte, Ph.D., M.P.H.

"Taking more steps per day, even just a few more, is achievable, and step counts are an easy-to-understand way to measure how much we are moving. There are many inexpensive wearable devices to choose from. Our research shows that older women reduce their risk of heart disease by moving more in their daily life, including light activity and taking more steps. Being up and about, instead of sitting, is good for your heart," said LaCroix.

LaCroix's study included more than 6,000 women enrolled in the Women's Health Initiative with an average age of 79 who wore an accelerometer on their waist to measure their physical activity for seven days in a row; these participants were followed for up to seven years for heart disease death.

This study was prospective, and half of the participants were African-American or Hispanic, stated LaCroix, noting that the use of an accelerometer to measure movement is a strength of the study. However, the study did not include men or people younger than 60, she said, calling for future research to examine step counts and other measures of daily activity across the adult age range among both men and women.

In another session, Joowon Lee, Ph.D., a researcher at Boston University (BU) in Boston, noted that higher levels of light physical activity are associated with lower risk of death from any cause.

Physical Activity Doesn't Have to Be Strenuous

According to the findings of BU's study, older adults were 67 percent less likely to die of any cause if they were moderately or vigorously physically active for at least 150 minutes per week, (a goal recommended by the American Heart Association) compared to people who exercised less.

However, the researchers observed that, among the participants with an average age of 69, physical activity doesn't have to be strenuous to be effective. Each 30-minute interval of light-intensity physical activities—such as doing household chores or casual walking—was associated with a 20 percent lower risk of dying from any cause, they said, noting that on the other hand, every additional 30 minutes of being sedentary was related to a 32 percent higher risk of dying from any cause.

"Promoting light-intensity physical activity and reducing sedentary time may be a more practical alternative among older adults," said Lee.

The BU research study, supported by the National Heart, Lung, and Blood Institute of the National Institutes of Health, evaluated physical activity levels of 1,262 participants from the ongoing Framingham Offspring Study. These participants were an average age of 69 (54 percent women), and they were instructed to wear a device that objectively measured physical activity for at least 10 hours a day, for at least four days a week between 2011 and 2014.

The researchers say that the strengths of this study include its large sample size and the use of a wearable device to objectively measure physical activity. However, the participants of the Framingham Offspring Study are white, so it is unclear if these findings would be consistent for other racial groups, they note.

Co-authors of the study are Nicole L. Spartano, Ph.D.; Ramachandran S. Vasan, M.D.; and Vanessa Xanthakis Ph.D.

REFLECTING ON A LOVED ONE'S LIFETIME OF ACHIEVEMENTS

Published in the *Woonsocket Call* on December 29, 2019

A few weeks ago, my sister Nancy called to give me the bad news that my brother-in-law, Justin Aurbach, was diagnosed with an aggressive and deadly cancer known as glioblastoma, more commonly referred to as GBM. This 77-year-old Dallas-based endodontist who I knew as relatively healthy, a believer in vitamins and physically active most of his adult life, was now housebound receiving 24-hour-a-day care by home health caregivers, along with his daughters Stephanie and Allison and his partner, Ruth, now all part of a revolving schedule of care.

I booked a quick trip to Dallas to sit with him and show my support and concern. It had been a few years since I had been there, and I wondered what the conversation might entail, knowing that our 53-year-old relationship could cover a lot of ground. Justin and my sister were always collectors of art, and I soon found myself sitting at a kitchen table surrounded by colorfully carved images of watermelons, where he and I reminisced as the time flew by.

Justin reminded me that we first met in 1967 when he came to pick up my older sister Mickie, taking her to dine at Campisi's Restaurant, a local pizza hangout. Even though it took place more than five decades ago, he clearly remembered first meeting my mother as she greeted him from the couch, sitting with her thick-soled shoes propped up on the ottoman, smoking a cigarette and wearing her trademark leopard print blouse. He recalls her holding Tony, the family's three-legged toy poodle.

A year later, Mickie and Justin would recruit my twin brother, Jim, and me to be ushers at their wedding in 1968. Through the ebb and flow of their life together, from raising children, grandchildren, and building a successful dental practice, he reflected on their 41-year marriage, noting "how it flew by" before Mickie passed in 2008.

Justin reminded me of the sage advice he gave me before I entered my freshman year at the University of Oklahoma. "Drink in moderation and put studies before chugging pitchers of beer," he said. It is funny the things you tend to remember, I thought.

As our conversation became more focused on his health, Justin thought that the symptoms of the tumor might first have appeared more than five years ago, when he became dizzy while taking a bike ride. Last August, the symptoms returned while riding again, and a CAT scan would ultimately reveal his tumor.

Turning 60

In 2003, I had the opportunity to interview Justin about turning age 60 for my weekly senior commentary in the *Pawtucket Times*. He shared the following thoughts about being at the peak of his career professionally, while only five years shy of reaching retirement age.

In my commentary, Justin said, "It's great [moving into your 60s], however, far too much [cultural] negativity has been directed at this chronological age."

At that time, my brother-in-law was in relatively good physical shape. While he would acknowledge that he could not run a four-minute mile, he joked that he never could anyway. As he approached his sixth decade, he admitted that he played a little golf like many of his friends, walked and jogged, and even took time to lift weights.

Dr. Justin E. Aurbach, DDS, had accomplished much in his career by the age of 60. As the first endodontist in the Dallas-Fort Worth area, he was the first in the region to perform endodontic microsurgery, when at that time there were only 78 endodontists in the nation performing such surgery. He is past president of the DFW Endodontic Society, the Southwest Society of Endodontics, and the Dallas County Dental Society. He served as general chairman of the Southwest Dental Conference.

Justin believed strongly that he would still be "at the top of his professional game, improving with age," as he proudly boasted. During my interview with him, he said, "not only am I technically better, but my years of life experience have made me wiser in respect to knowing what can and cannot be done in my life."

The endodontist attributed much of his success to his wife, children, and the many supportive family and friends that were part of his large extended family.

By age 60, his philosophy of looking at the "glass half full rather than half empty" allowed him to cope with life's difficulties. This life stage was also a time of excitement and learning for him, while he glided into the years he referred to as the "best time of your life."

Getting to the Big "70"

Ten years later, we would speak again about his approaching the age 70 milestone. He reflected on how so much time had passed, which he noted flew by in "the blink of an eye." During my 2013 interview with him, published in my weekly commentary in this paper, he told me that he would "certainly keep forging ahead at a break-neck pace," promising that new goals would replace those that were accomplished.

He recalled having attended dozens of funerals and said final goodbyes to his wife, father, father-in-law, and mother-in-law, along with many close friends and colleagues. Justin noted that reading the *Dallas Morning News* obituary page and constantly attending funerals made him aware of the need to accomplish his set goals with the limited time he had left, "but life goes on," Justin told me. A year after his wife's death in 2008, the aging widower again found love and began to date Ruth.

Looking ahead into his 70s, Justin had no plans to retire. Though financially secure, he aspired to maintain a very full practice until his eighty-fifth birthday. He found added fulfillment teaching endodontic residents at Texas AM Baylor School of Dentistry, a job that he hoped would continue into his 70s, while also staying active in the medical group.

Justin has been an avid bike rider for more than 30 years, and despite being 70, he would continue to sneak in a ride when possible, even with his busy schedule. He enjoyed the City of Dallas's fine restaurants, loved to cook for family and friends, and looked forward to a good play or chamber music performance from time to time. His mantra may well be, "Live your life to the fullest, don't put off tomorrow what you can do today."

Looking Ahead

Justin says, since the diagnosis of his terminal illness, his house has been flooded with family, friends, referring doctors and even former dental students. "I have made a lot of friends and accept that I have impacted people in a very positive way," he said, as he cites as an upside of his illness.

As we concluded our talk, he says, "Don't wait to do things. You never know what the future has in store for you," adding that he learned this lesson from Ruth.

"Simple things in life are your best bet to living a good life," Justin tells me, stressing that it doesn't cost a lot of money to enjoy your life.

Justin acknowledges that he may live another two to six months with the GBM tumor, but remains optimistic, for there are those who have lived for another 14 years. In his remaining time, he hopes to maintain a "quality of life" that allows him to continue to attend musicals and plays, or perhaps even take short trips.

Final Thoughts

As you reach your 60s and into your 70s, research tells us that exercise, eating a healthy diet, developing a strong social network of family and friends, and continuing to learn and seek out new knowledge all become important in enhancing the quality of your life and increasing your longevity in your later years. However, in our twilight years life can become of full of tough challenges, and we may face difficult times.

Ultimately, like Justin, reflecting on personal and professional accomplishments can give you the inner resources necessary to meet the challenges in the final stages of your life.

REPORT ON FALLS, INJURIES RELEASED

Published in *Woonsocket Call* on October 20, 2019

L ast Wednesday morning in Dirksen Senate Office Building, Room 562, the US Special Committee on Aging held a hearing to spotlight the economic consequences on falls and to explore ways to prevent and reduce falls and related injuries. At the 1-hour-and-55-minute hearing, titled "Falls Prevention: National, State, and Local Level Solutions to Better Support Seniors," its annual report, *Falls Prevention: Solutions to Better Support Seniors*, was released.

According to the Senate Aging Committee, falls are the leading cause of both fatal and nonfatal injuries among older adults that incur $50 billion annually in total medical costs. That number is expected to double to $100 billion by 2030, and the majority of these costs are borne by Medicare and Medicaid.

"Falls are the leading cause of fatal and non-fatal injuries for older Americans, often leading to a downward spiral with serious consequences. In addition to the physical and emotional trauma of falls, the financial toll is staggering," said Senator Susan Collins (R-Maine), who chairs the Senate Aging Committee. "Now is the time, and now is our opportunity, to take action to prevent falls. Our bipartisan report includes key recommendations to take steps to reduce the risk of falls," the Maine senator noted in an October 16 statement.

Pushing for Positive Change in Releasing Fall Report

"We must dispel our loved ones of the stigma associated with falling so that they can get the help they need to age in place—where they want to be—in their homes and communities," said Senator Robert P. Casey, Jr. (D-Pa.). "I am hopeful that our work over the past year will propel the research community to do more, get more dollars invested into supporting home modifications and encourage more older adults to be active," said the Special Committee's ranking member.

At the hearing, the committee unveiled a comprehensive report that provides evidence-based recommendations on ways to reduce the risk of falling. The committee received input from multiple federal agencies, including the Centers for

Disease Control and Prevention, Centers for Medicare and Medicaid Services, and the Food and Drug Administration. In addition, approximately 200 respondents representing falls prevention advocates, hospitals, community organizations, home health agencies, and others shared their expertise on this issue.

The 34-page Aging Committee's report made recommendations on how to raise awareness about falls-related risks, prevention, and recovery at the national, state, and local levels. It suggested ways of improving screening and referrals for those at risk of falling so that individuals receive the preventive care necessary to avoid a fall or recover after one. It noted ways of targeting modifiable risk factors, including increasing the availability of resources for home safety evaluations and modifications, so that older adults can remain in their homes and communities.

Finally, it called for reducing polypharmacy so that health-care providers and patients are aware of any potential side effects that could contribute to a fall.

Increasing Medicare Funding for Bone Density Testing

In an opening statement, Collins noted that falls are often attributed to uneven sidewalks or icy stairs, medications, medical reasons or muscle strength. But one key cause of falling is osteoporosis, which can be especially dangerous for people who are completely unaware that they suffer from low bone density, she says.

According to Collins, although Medicare covers bone density testing, reimbursement rates have been slashed by 70 percent since 2006, resulting in 2.3 million fewer women being tested. "As a result, it is estimated that more than 40,000 additional hip fractures occur each year, which results in nearly 10,000 additional deaths," she said, noting legislation, Increasing Access to Osteoporosis Testing Beneficiaries Act that she has introduced with Sen. Ben Cardin, to reverse these harmful reimbursement cuts.

Casey stated, "I am particularly interested in sharing this report with the relevant agencies and learning how the recommendations will be implemented. Not just put in a report. Implemented," adds Casey.

Peggy Haynes, MPA, senior director of Portland-based Healthy Aging Maine-Health that offers A Matter of Balance, an evidence-based falls prevention program, came to the Senate hearing to share details about its impact. The health- care community has a critical role to play in fall prevention—beginning with screening for falls, assessing fall risk factors, reviewing medications and referring to both medical and community-based fall prevention interventions. "Our health system is focused on preventing falls in every care setting," says Haynes.

"The need for a range of community-based options led MaineHealth to be a founding member of the Evidence Based Leadership Collaborative, promoting the increased delivery of multiple evidence-based programs that improve the health and well-being of diverse populations," adds Haynes.

Haynes noted that older participants attend eight two-hour sessions to help them reduce their fear of falling, assisting them in setting realistic goals for increasing their activity and changing their home environment to reduce fall risk factors. A Matter of Balance is offered in 46 states, reaching nearly 100,000 seniors.

Virginia Demby, an 84-year-old visually-impaired retired nurse who is an advocate for Community and Older Adults, in Chester, Pennsylvania, came to the Senate hearing to support the importance of fall prevention programs. Despite living with low vision, Demby remains physically active by participating in exercise classes for older adults at the Center for the Blind and Visually Impaired in Chester. She is an advocate for older adults and now helps the local senior-center wellness manager recruit more seniors to take falls prevention classes and find new places to offer the classes.

Kathleen A. Cameron, MPH, senior director of the Center for Healthy Aging, of the Arlington, Virginia-based National Council on Aging, discussed the work of the National Falls Prevention Resource Center, which helps to support evidence-based falls prevention programs across the nation and highlighted policy solutions to reduce falls risk.

Finally, Elizabeth Thompson, chief executive officer of the Arlington, Virginia-based National Osteoporosis Foundation, testified that bone loss and osteoporosis are fundamental underlying contributors to the worst consequences of falls among older Americans: broken and fractured bones. Osteoporotic fractures are responsible for more hospitalizations than heart attacks, strokes, and breast cancer combined, she noted.

For details of the Senate Aging Committee report, go to **http://www.aging. senate.gov/imo/media/doc/SCA_Falls_Report_2019.pdf**.

EXPERTS SAY ISOLATION AND LONELINESS IMPACTING MORE OLDER AMERICANS

Published in the *Woonsocket Call* on April 30, 2017

S arah Hosseini, a blogger on Scary Mommy, a website bringing entertainment and information to Millennial mothers, penned a touching story about Marleen Brooks, a California resident who came home to find a heartbreaking handwritten note from Wanda, her 90-year-old neighbor, asking her to be friends.

Wanda wrote: "Would you consider to become my friend. I'm 90 years old—live alone. All my friends have passed away. I'm so lonesome and scared. Please I pray for someone."

According to Hosseini's blog posting, Brooks shared this note with KTVU News Anchor Frank Somerville, who posted it on his Facebook page. She responded to the posting by saying, "Came home to this note from a lady that lives down the street from me. Makes my heart sad, but on the bright side it looks like I will be getting a new friend."

That evening Brooks visited her new friend, bearing a gift of cupcakes. After the visit, she wrote to Somerville describing this initial visit (which was posted on his Facebook page), says Hosseini. In this update posting, Brooks observed, "She's such a sweet lady! And she was over the moon when we came over." Brooks reported what Wanda said during the impromptu get-together: "I hope you didn't think I was stupid for writing you, but I had to do something. Thank you so much for coming over. I've lived here for 50 years and don't know any of my neighbors."

Wanda shared with her new acquaintance that she is on oxygen, has congestive heart failure, osteoporosis, and other age-related ailments, and her two surviving sons do not live nearby, noted Hosseini's blog posting.

Zeroing In on a Growing Societal Problem

Wanda's isolation and loneliness is not a rare occurrence. It happens every day throughout the nation. The US Senate Special Committee on Aging recently put a spotlight on the growing number of Americans who are socially isolated and lonely, like Wanda, and expert witnesses detailed the negative consequences of this tragic societal problem.

In Room 403 of the Dirksen Senate Office Building, US Senators Susan Collins and Bob Casey, the chairman and ranking member of the Senate Aging Committee, held a morning hearing on April 27, 2017, "Aging Without Community: The Consequences of Isolation and Loneliness."

The Senate Aging panel hearing (lasting almost two hours), the first in a two-part series, took a close look at the mental and physical health effects of social isolation and loneliness. The next hearing will explore ways to reconnect older people to their communities.

"The consequences of isolation and loneliness are severe: negative health outcomes, higher health-care costs, and even death. The root problem is one that we can solve by helping seniors keep connected with communities," said Senator Collins in her opening statement. "Just as we did when we made a national commitment to cut smoking rates in this country, we should explore approaches to reducing isolation and loneliness. Each has a real impact on the health and well-being of our seniors," noted the Maine Republican senator.

Adds Senator Bob Casey, "Older Americans are vital to the prosperity and well-being of our nation." The Democratic senator said, "Our work on the Aging Committee to ensure that we all remain connected to community as we age is important to maintaining that vitality. It is for that reason that we, as a federal government, need to sustain and improve our investments in programs that help seniors stay connected—from Meals on Wheels to rural broadband to transportation services."

When approached for her thoughts about the Senate Aging panel, Nancy Lea-Mond, AARP executive vice president and chief advocacy and engagement officer said, "We know that social isolation and loneliness has severe negative effects on older Americans, and we're pleased the US Senate Committee on Aging held a hearing on this important issue. As they explore solutions for social isolation and loneliness amongst older Americans, AARP looks forward to working with them on these issues in 2017."

Senator Sheldon Whitehouse says, "When seniors get involved, the community benefits from their valuable contributions. And the personal connections seniors make engaging in the community can help them stay healthy and productive." Whitehouse, who sits on the Senate Aging panel, will work to protect funding for senior centers and programs that Rhode Island seniors rely on to stay connected, like Meals on Wheels and Senior Corps.

Social Isolation is a "Silent Killer"

Speaking before the US Senate Special Committee on Aging today, social work professor Lenard W. Kaye, DSW, Ph.D., urged lawmakers to support programs that help older adults stay connected to their communities.

Kaye serves as director of the University of Maine Center on Aging. Joining three other experts, he reported to the committee that social isolation is a "silent killer"—due to placing people at higher risk for a variety of poor health outcomes—and he warned that more Americans are living in isolation than ever before.

"The prevalence may be as high as 43 percent among community-dwelling older adults," Kaye said. "And the risk is high as well for caregivers of older adults, given that caregiving can be a very isolating experience."

Kaye's testimony also highlighted the state of current research in solving the problem of social isolation among older adults.

"Due to the various life events that can trigger social isolation, from death of a significant other, to loss of transportation, to health decline, effective interventions will need to be diverse, and they will need to be tailored to the personal circumstances of the isolated individual," he said.

Kaye added that there is still significant progress to be made in determining what works for helping to reduce social isolation. Lack of rigor in studies of interventions aimed at reducing loneliness can make it difficult to evaluate some of these strategies.

In Pima County, 46 percent of nearly 2,300 seniors surveyed in its 2016 community needs assessment cited social isolation as a significant concern of those living alone, said W. Mark Clark, president of the Pima Council on Aging.

In his testimony, Clark says, "Changes to mobility, cognitive ability, or health status can cause an individual to hold back from previously enjoyed social activities. Older adults in rural areas who can no longer drive are at incredible risk of physical and social isolation unless transportation options are available.

"While aging at home is cited as a top priority by a majority of older people, and doing so has both emotional and economic benefits, aging in place at home can also lead to isolation," said Clark, noting that connections to the community wane as one gets older due to less opportunities to build new social networks.

In her testimony, Julianne Holt-Lunstad, a psychology researcher at Brigham Young University, estimated that more than 8 million seniors are affected by isolation, and social disconnect is increasing.

Holt-Lunstad told the senators that research shows that social isolation and loneliness is as dangerous as being obese, as risky as smoking up to 15 cigarettes per day, and associated with higher rates of heart disease; a weakened immune system; anxiety; dementia, including Alzheimer's disease; and nursing facility admissions.

Finally, witness Rick Creech, who was born with cerebral palsy, shared to the Senate Aging panel how disabilities can isolate a person. He described how an alternative communication (AAC) device costing $10,000, a van converted for a powered wheelchair passenger, and smart home equipment helped him grow into a "productive, independent adult."

Meals on Wheels Program Vital Program for Isolated Seniors

It was clear to Senate Aging panel members and to expert witnesses that local Meals on Wheels programs can bring good nutrition and companionship to older Americans, reducing social isolation and loneliness. Over two years ago, a Brown University study confirmed another benefit of visitors regularly knocking on the doors of seniors in need: a significant reduction in their feelings of loneliness.

"This continues to build the body of evidence that home-delivered meals provide more than nutrition and food security," said study lead author Kali Thomas, assistant professor of health services, policy and practice in the Brown

University School of Public Health and a researcher at the Providence Veterans Affairs Medical Center.

Thomas, a former Meal on Wheels volunteer, said that the study is one of few to rigorously examine the long-presumed psychological benefits of home-delivered meal service. She believes it is the first randomized, controlled trial to assess the effect on loneliness, which has been linked by many studies to a greater risk for medical problems, health care utilization, and mortality.

"In a time when resources are being further constrained and demand is increasing, it is important that we have evidence that guides decision-making in terms of what services to provide and how best to provide them," Thomas said.

Senator Susan Collins, chair of the US Select Senate Committee on Aging, sees Meals on Wheels as policy strategy to address the growing number of isolated seniors and their loneliness. At the Senate Aging panel, Collins said, "For many, Meals on Wheels is not just about food—it's about social sustenance, also. Seniors look forward to greeting the driver with a bit of conversation." And the Republican senator called for adequate funding to the nationwide Meals on Wheels network, comprising 5,000 local community-based programs. President Trump's proposed cuts to Meals on Wheels were, "pennywise and pound foolish because in the end they're going to cause more hospitalizations, more nursing home admissions, and poor health outcomes."

Like Brooks, we should reach out to our older, isolated neighbors in our community. A simple gesture like this can have a lasting, positive impact on both parties.

REPORT LINKS IMPROVED BRAIN HEALTH TO SLEEP

Published in the *Pawtucket Times* on January 16, 2017

Seven to eight hours of sleep per day may be key to maintaining your brain health as you age, says a newly released consensus report issued by the Global Council on Brain Health (GCBH). The report's recommendations, hammered out by scientists, health professionals, scholars, and policy experts working on brain health issues at a meeting convened by AARP with support of Age UK, in Toronto, Canada, in late July 2016, translate the scientific research evidence compiled on sleep and brain health into actionable recommendations for the public.

An AARP consumer survey released this month [in conjunction with GCBH's report] found that 99 percent of age 50-plus respondents believe that their sleep is crucial to brain health, but more than 4 in 10 (43 percent) say they don't get enough sleep during the night. More than half (about 54 percent) say they tend to wake too early in the morning and just can't get back to sleep.

As to sleep habits, the adult respondents say that the most frequently cited activities that they engage in within an hour of bedtime are watching television and browsing the web. One-third keeps a phone or electronic device by their bed. Nearly 88 percent of the adults think a cool bedroom temperature is effective in helping people sleep. Yet only two in five (41 percent) keep their room between 60 and 67 degrees. Finally, the most common reason people wake up during the night is to use the bathroom.

"Although sleep problems are a huge issue with older adults, it's unfortunate the importance of sleep is often not taken seriously by health care professionals," said Sarah Lock, AARP senior vice president for policy and GCBH executive director. "It's normal for sleep to change as we age, but poor quality sleep is not normal. Our experts share [in GCBH's report] the steps people can take to help maintain their brain health through better sleep habits," said Lock, in a statement released with the report.

Sleep Vital to Brain Health

The new GCBH recommendations cover a wide range of sleep-related issues, including common factors that can disrupt sleep, symptoms of potential sleep disorders, and prescription medications and over-the-counter (OTC) sleep aids. The consensus report is jam-packed with tips from experts, from detailing ways to help a person fall asleep or even stay asleep, when to seek professional help for a possible sleep disorder, and the pros and cons of taking a quick nap.

Based on the scientific evidence, the GCBH report says that sleep is vital to brain health, including cognitive function, and sleeping on average seven to eight hours each day is related to better brain and physical health in older people.

The 16-page GCBH consensus report notes that the sleep-wake cycle is influenced by many different factors. A regular sleep-wake schedule is tied to better sleep and better brain health. Regular exposure to light and physical activity supports good sleep, says the report.

According to the GCBH report, people, at any age, can change their behavior to improve their sleep. Persistent, excessive daytime sleepiness is not a normal part of aging. Sleep disorders become more common with age, but can often be successfully treated. People with chronic inadequate sleep are at higher risk for and experience more severe health problems, including dementia, depression, heart disease, obesity, and cancer.

"A 2015 consensus statement of the American Academy of Sleep Medicine and the Sleep Research Society mirrors the recently released GCBH report recommending that a person sleep at least seven hours per night," notes Dr. Katherine M. Sharkey, MD, Ph.D., FAASM, associate professor of medicine and psychiatry and human behavior, who also serves as assistant dean for Women in Medicine and Science. "Seven to eight hours seems to be a 'sweet spot' for sleep duration," she says, noting that several studies indicate that sleeping too little or too much can increase risk of mortality.

More Sleep Not Always Better

Sharkey says that individuals with insomnia sometimes use a strategy of spending more time in bed, with the idea that if they give themselves more opportunity to sleep, they will get more sleep and feel better, but this can actually make sleep worse. "One of the most commonly used behavioral treatments for insomnia is sleep restriction, where patients work with their sleep clinician to decrease their time in bed to a time very close to the actual amount of sleep they are getting," she says, noting that this deepens their sleep.

Sleep apnea, a medical disorder where the throat closes off during sleep, resulting in decreased oxygen levels, can reduce the quality of sleep and is often associated with stroke and other cardiovascular diseases, says Sharkey. While sleep apnea is often associated with men (24 percent), it also affects nine percent of women, and this gender gap narrows with age, she notes.

Many older adults who were diagnosed with sleep apnea many years ago often did not pursue medical treatment because the older CPAP devices were bulky and uncomfortable, says Sharkey, who acknowledges that this technology is much better today.

"We know how many questions adults have about how much sleep is enough, and the role that sleep plays in brain health and cognitive function," said Marilyn Albert, Ph.D., GCBH chair, professor of neurology and director of the Division of Cognitive Neuroscience at Johns Hopkins University in Baltimore, Maryland. "This [GCBH] report answers a lot of these questions and we hope it will be a valuable source of information for people," she says.

Simple Tips to Better Sleep

Getting a good night's sleep may be as easy as following these tips detailed in the 16-page GCBH report:

Consider getting up at the same time every day, seven days a week. Restrict fluids and food three hours before going to bed to help avoid disrupting your sleep to use the bathroom. Avoid using OTC medications for sleep because they can have negative side-effects, including disrupted sleep quality and impaired cognitive functioning.

The GCBH report notes that dietary supplements such as melatonin may have benefits for some people, but scientific evidence on their effectiveness is inconclusive. Be particularly cautious of melatonin use with dementia patients.

Naps are not always a cure to enhancing your sleep. Avoid long naps; if you must nap, limit it to 30 minutes in the early afternoon.

"There has been such a steady stream of revealing brain-health reports that it would seem people would change their habits accordingly," said AARP Rhode Island State director Kathleen Connell. "Taking active steps is what's important—and the earlier the better," she added.

"The personal benefits are obvious, but we should be aware of the cost savings that better brain health can produce. If people in their 50s get on board, the impact on health-care costs and a reduced burden of caregiving 20 years down the road could be significant," Connell added. "At the very least, those savings could help cover other rising costs. We owe it to ourselves and to each other to assess and improve aspects of diet and exercise. And we should not overlook the importance of sleep."

The full GCBH recommendations can be found here: **http://www. globalcouncilonbrainhealth.org**. The 2016 AARP Sleep and Brain Health Survey can be found here: **http://www.aarp.org/sleepandbrainhealth**.

7. LONG–TERM CARE CONTINUUM

"Spend enough time in the old folks' home and you'll discover that the residents keep asking two questions: 'Where am I?' and 'What am I supposed to do now?' The correct answers, which can make our last years a time of serenity rather than confusion, are 'Right here' and 'Just be.'"

— Dean Sluyter in *The Zen Commandments*

AARP'S NEW COVID-19 DASHBOARD FOR NATIONAL/LOCAL NURSING HOME DATA

Published in RINewsToday on October 26, 2020

While public-health experts are predicting a second spike of the COVID-19 virus, expecting it to hit the nation as early as *now* and reaching its peak in December, AARP released its Nursing Home COVID-19 Dashboard, created to provide four-week snapshots detailing the infiltration of the virus into the nation's nursing homes and its impact on residents and staff. AARP's latest Public Policy Institute analysis is the result of the Washington, DC-based aging advocacy group's successful efforts to push for the public reporting of nursing home COVID-19 cases and deaths.

Using data collected by the Centers for Medicare & Medicaid Services—which is self-reported by nursing homes—the AARP Public Policy Institute, in collaboration with the Scripps Gerontology Center at Miami University in Ohio, created the AARP Nursing Home COVID-19 Dashboard to provide four-week snapshots of the virus's infiltration into nursing homes and impact on nursing home residents and staff. The dashboard also compared state and national data on COVID-19 cases and deaths, staff cases, and staffing shortages.

Key Findings of AARP's First Dashboard

The AARP Public Policy Institute will analyze data and report on key findings as the dashboard is updated over time. Here are some observations about AARP's first dashboard (using data from August 24 to September 20, in which 95 percent of the nation's 15,366 nursing homes submitted data for this time period) released on October 14:

According to the database, in every state, nursing homes indicated a shortage of PPE (defined as not having a one-week supply of N95 masks, surgical masks, gowns, gloves, and eye protection during the previous four weeks). Nationally, about one-quarter (25.5 percent) of nursing homes had a PPE shortage during the August 24 to September 20 reporting period. In the highest-performing state, 8 percent of nursing homes had a PPE shortage; in the lowest-performing state, 60 percent did not have a one-week supply.

The researchers note that while considerable attention has been paid to infections among nursing home residents, it is also critically important to consider direct-care staff. In the four weeks ending September 20, one-quarter (24 percent) of nursing homes had at least one confirmed COVID-19 case among residents, and twice as many (50 percent) had at least one confirmed staff case. Per 100 nursing home residents, there were 2.6 COVID-19 resident cases and 2.5 staff cases, corresponding to a total of about 55,000 cases nationally.

Finally, there is considerable variation across states. COVID-19 deaths in the four weeks ending September 20 averaged 0.5 per 100 residents across the nation (about 1 out of every 200 residents). At the state level, the death rate was as high as 1.2 per 100 residents (about 1 out of 80), and several states reported no resident deaths in the past month.

Looking at Rhode Island, AARP's first dashboard detailed the following:

- 2.2 COVID cases per 100 residents
- 0.2 COVID deaths per 100 residents
- 1.7 staff cases per 100 residents
- 19.7 percent of nursing homes without a one-week supply of PPE
- 28.9 percent of nursing homes with staffing shortages

AARP's dashboard will be updated every four weeks to track trends over time and will evolve to include more categories to follow other measures of interest.

As Others See It—in Rhode Island

"We have been very clear in our messaging: No state has done a good enough job to protect nursing home residents and staff," said AARP Rhode Island State director Kathleen Connell.

"That said, it is good to see that the first round of data postings on the AARP Nursing Home COVID Dashboard shows Rhode Island in better-than-average shape compared to other states. But to our point, anyone in Rhode Island with a loved one in a nursing home expects—hopes and prays—for more than 'better than average.'

"As we see daily reports of increased cases and deaths, safety concerns for nursing home residents and staff should be increasing as well. The pandemic is far from over, and among many complicated aspects of dealing with it is transparency. The COVID Dashboard provides the public with a benchmark and tracks monthly changes; people need to pay attention and demand action at all levels to make nursing homes safer. These aren't just numbers. These are lives," says Connell.

On the other hand, the Rhode Island Department of Health questions the accuracy of the AARP Nursing Home COVID-19 Dashboard as it relates to its Rhode Island findings. "The data don't accurately reflect the Rhode Island reality in part because of how the questions are phrased," says Joseph Wendelken, RIDOH's public information officer, specifically related to PPE data. "The question asks about PPE in the nursing homes. Nursing homes receive a weekly supply of PPE from their corporate warehouses. The question asks about one point in time. On occasion, reporting happens shortly before facilities receive their re-supply," he says.

"RIDOH has taken several steps to protect nursing home residents," says Wendelken, noting that his department has built Congregate Settings Support Teams targeted to facilities regarding infection control, PPE, testing, and staffing.

"We have weekly contact with facilities. We've worked with facilities to develop creative plans for reopening. We have implemented regular testing of staff every 10 to 14 days. We will take the lessons and experience we've gained from these past seven months and apply them to the increase in cases we see today," adds Wendelken.

According to Scott Fraser, president/CEO, of the Rhode Island Health Care Association (RIHCA), the AARP analysis shows what his organization has been saying in the last few weeks and months—that COVID-19 cases in nursing homes continue to drop. "Rhode Island is below the national average in all categories measured for this dashboard," he says, stressing that the number of cases in nursing homes is dropping as is the number of deaths.

The successful efforts to protect nursing home residents and staff can be directly linked to the measures the facilities have taken since the pandemic first hit, notes Fraser. "We are stocking up on PPE. We initially suspended visitation. We are testing staff regularly and residents when necessary. We are carefully monitoring visitors and vendors who come into our homes. We isolate and quarantine anyone who tests positive or any new resident who moves into our facilities," he says.

Fraser says that RIHCA continues to advocate for regular testing of vendors who come into the state's nursing homes, including ambulance drivers, lab technicians, and hospice workers. RIHCA continues to call on RIDOH to renew the policy of having two negative tests before a hospital patient can be released to a nursing home and to allow those certified nursing assistants who received temporary emergency certifications to obtain their permanent licenses.

A Call to Action

More than 84,000 residents and staff of nursing homes and other long-term care facilities have died from COVID-19, representing 40 percent of all coronavirus fatalities in the US, according to Kaiser Family Foundation's most recent analysis released on October 8. Yet in its statement announcing the release of its dashboard, AARP charges that federal policymakers have been slow to respond to this crisis, and no state has done a good enough job to stem the loss of life.

According to AARP, policymakers have taken some action, such as requiring nursing homes to self-report COVID-19 cases and deaths at the federal level, ordering testing, and providing limited PPE and other resources to nursing homes. But more must be done, says the nation's largest aging advocacy group in its statement urging elected officials "to acknowledge and take action to resolve this national tragedy—and to ensure that public funds provided to nursing homes and other long-term care facilities are used for testing, PPE, staffing, virtual visits and for the health and safety of residents."

COVID-19 cases across the US are again on the rise, and nursing homes remain a hotbed for the virus, says AARP, promising to "continue to shine a light on what's happening in nursing homes so that families have the information they need to make decisions, and lawmakers can be held accountable."

AARP has called for the enactment of the following five-point plan to protect nursing home and long-term care facility residents—and save lives—at the federal and state levels:

- Prioritize regular and ongoing testing and adequate personal protective equipment (PPE) for residents and staff—as well as inspectors and any visitors.

- Improve transparency focused on daily public reporting of cases and deaths in facilities; communication with families about discharges and transfers; and accountability for state and federal funding that goes to facilities.
- Require access to facilitated virtual visitation, and establish timelines, milestones, and accountability for facilities to provide in-person visitation.
- Ensure quality care for residents through adequate staffing, oversight, and access to in-person formal advocates, called long-term care ombudsmen.
- Reject immunity for long-term care facilities related to COVID-19.

To see the AARP Nursing Home COVID-19 Dashboard, go to:

http://www.aarp.org/content/dam/aarp/ppi/pdf/2020/10/ rhodeisland-nursing-home-dashboard-october-2020-aarp.pdf

STUDY CALLS FOR ACTION ON CREATING SENIOR HOUSING FOR MIDDLE-INCOME SENIORS

Published in the *Woonsocket Call* on August 18, 2019

A recently released report sends a stark warning to federal and state policymakers and to the private senior housing sector. The report forewarns that in the coming years, a large number of middle-income seniors, who need assisted living with supportive services, will be priced out of this level of care.

Senior housing in the United States is paid out of pocket by seniors with sufficient assets. A relatively small percentage of Americans have long-term care insurance policies to defray the costs. For seniors with the lowest incomes, Medicaid covers housing only in the skilled nursing setting, but increasingly also covers long-term services and supports in home and community-based settings. Programs such as low-income housing tax credits have helped finance housing for economically-disadvantaged seniors.

The researchers call on the government and the senior housing sector to step up and to assist the projected 14.4 million middle-income people over age 75, many with multiple chronic conditions, who won't be able to afford expensive senior housing.

According to this first-of-its-kind study that appears in the April 24, 2019 edition of *Health Affairs*, 54 percent of middle-income older Americans will not be able to meet yearly costs of $60,000 for assisted living rent and other out-of-pocket medical costs a decade from now, even if they generated equity by selling their home and committing all of their annual financial resources. The figure skyrockets to 81 percent if middle-income seniors in 2019 were to keep the assets they built in their home but commit the rest of their annual financial resources to cover costs associated with senior housing and care.

Accompanying the senior housing study are two perspective pieces in *Health Affairs* on how society can adapt to aging and supporting aging in communities.

The study, *The Forgotten Middle: Many Middle-Income Seniors Will Have Insufficient Resources For Housing And Health Care*, was conducted by researchers at NORC at the University of Chicago, with funding provided by the National Investment Center for Seniors Housing & Care (NIC), with additional support from AARP, the AARP Foundation, the John A. Hartford Foundation, and the SCAN Foundation.

Learning About the Needs of the Emerging 'Middle Market'

"We still have a lot to learn about what the emerging 'middle market' wants from housing and personal care, but we know they don't want to be forced to spend down into poverty, and we know that America cannot currently meet their needs," said Bob Kramer, NIC's founder and strategic adviser in an April 24, 2019, statement. "The future requires developing affordable housing and care options for middle-income seniors. This is a wake-up call to policymakers, real estate operators, and investors," he adds.

The report notes that significant financial challenges are expected to coincide with many middle-income seniors seeking senior housing and care properties due to deteriorating health and other factors, such as whether a family member can serve as a caregiver. The study projects that by 2029, 60 percent of US middle-income seniors over age 75 will have mobility limitations (8.7 million people), 67 percent will have three or more chronic conditions (9.6 million people), and 8 percent will have cognitive impairment (1.2 million people). For middle-income seniors age 85 and older, the prevalence of cognitive impairment nearly doubles.

The researchers say that this "middle market" for senior housing and care in 2029 will be more racially diverse, have higher educational attainment and income, and smaller families to recruit as unpaid caregivers than today's seniors. Over the next 10 years, growth in the number of women will outpace men, with women comprising 58 percent of seniors 75 years old or older in 2029, compared to 56 percent in 2014, they say.

Bringing the Public and Private Sector Together

"In only a decade, the number of middle-income seniors will double, and most will not have the savings needed to meet their housing and personal care needs," said Caroline Pearson, senior vice president at NORC at the University of Chicago and one of the study's lead authors.

"Policymakers and the senior housing community have a tremendous opportunity to develop solutions that benefit millions of middle-income people for years to come," says Pearson.

Researchers say there is an opportunity for policymakers and the senior housing and care sector to create an entirely new housing and care market for an emerging cohort of middle-income seniors not eligible for Medicaid and not able to pay for housing out of pocket in 2029.

The study's analysis suggests that creating a new "middle market" for senior housing and care services will require innovations from the public and private sectors. Researchers say the private sectors can offer more basic housing products, better leverage technology, subsidize "middle-market" residents with higher-paying residents, more robustly engage unpaid caregivers, and develop innovative real estate financing models, among other options.

As to the public sector, the researchers call on government to create incentives to build a robust new market for middle-income seniors by offering tax incentives targeted to the "middle market," expanding subsidy and voucher programs, expanding Medicare coverage of nonmedical services and supports, creating a Medicare benefit to cover long-term care, and broadening Medicaid's coverage of home and community-based services.

"This research sets the stage for needed discussions about how the nation will care for seniors who don't qualify for Medicaid but won't be able to afford senior housing," said Brian Jurutka, NIC's president and chief executive officer. "This discussion needs to include investors, care providers, policymakers, and developers working together to create a viable middle market for senior housing and care," he says.

Adds Lisa Marsh Ryerson, president of AARP's foundation, "All seniors want to live in affordable, safe and supportive housing, and more than 19 million older adults are unable to do so. We must act now to implement innovative solutions—including robust aging-in-community efforts—to accommodate what is sure to be an increasing demand for housing that meets the needs of older adults."

Is Rhode Island prepared to meet the senior housing needs of the state's middle-income seniors in 2029? If not, the state's federal delegation, lawmakers, state policymakers, and the senior housing industry must begin to chip away at this looming policy issue.

To view the study, go to **http://www.healthaffairs.org/doi/full/10.1377/hlthaff.2018.05233**.

CONGRESSMAN CICILLINE POISED FOR LEGACY AS NEXT FIERY ADVOCATE ON AGING

Published in RINewsToday on April 30, 2021

Congressman David Cicilline is poised to offer a resolution to re-establish the House Permanent Select Committee on Aging, whose work came to an end in early January 1993, at the conclusion of the 102nd Congress.

The Washington, DC-based Leadership Council of Aging Organizations (LCAO), a coalition of 69 aging organizations, has recently called on the House to support Cicilline's measure when introduced, "which focuses on the well-being of America's older population and is committed to representing their interests in the policy-making arena."

"Now is the opportune time to reestablish the House Aging Committee," says LCAO chair, Max Richtman, who serves as president and CEO of the National Committee to Protect Social Security and Medicare (NCPSSM), in an endorsement letter sent to the Rhode Island Congressman on March 30, 2021, detailing the graying of America.

"Every day, 12,000 Americans turn 60. By 2030, nearly 75 million people in the US—or 20 percent of the country—will be age 65 or older. As America grows older, the need for support and services provided under programs like Social Security, SSI, Medicare, Medicaid, and the Older Americans Act also increases," he said, stressing the importance of this select committee.

The resolution to approve the House Aging Committee was passed on October 8, 1974, by a 299–44 margin in the House. Its legislative duties expired during the 103rd Congress, as the House leadership was under pressure to reduce its internal costs and to streamline the legislative process. Initially, the House panel had 35 members, but would later grow to 65 members.

Those opposing reauthorizing the House Aging Committee would say that its elimination would slash wasteful spending; after all, the chamber already had 12 standing committees with jurisdiction over aging issues. On the other hand, advocates warned that the staff of these committees did not have time to broadly examine aging issues as the select committee did.

In a March 31, 1993 article published in the *St. Petersburg Times*, reporter Rebecca H. Patterson reported that staff director Brian Lutz of the committee's Subcommittee on Retirement Income and Employment, stated that "during its 18 years of existence the House Aging Committee had been responsible for about 1,000 hearings and reports."

The Fourth Time "Hopefully" is the Charm...

Over 28 years after the House Democratic leadership's belt-tightening efforts to save $1.5 million resulted in the termination of the House Aging Committee, Rhode Island Congressman David N. Cicilline is poised to reintroduce legislation to reestablish the House Aging panel, active from 1974 until 1993.

More than five years ago, Cicilline had introduced H. Res. 758 during the 114th Congress to reestablish the House Aging Committee. Rhode Island Congressman James Langevin and 27 Democratic lawmakers out of 435 House members became co-sponsors. But it caught the eye of the co-chairs of the Seniors Task Force (later renamed the House Democratic Caucus Task Force on Aging & Families), Congresswomen Doris Matsui (D-CA), and Jan Schakowsky (D-IL). The lawmakers also signed onto supporting this resolution.

Correspondence penned by Cicilline urged House Speaker Paul Ryan (R-WI) and House GOP leadership to support House Resolution 758. Ultimately, Ryan blocked the resolution from being considered, and no legislative action was taken in the GOP-controlled House chamber.

With House Speaker Ryan still retaining the control of the House during the 115th Congress, Cicilline's H. Res. 160 would not gain traction. At that time only 27 Democratic lawmakers stepped forward to become co-sponsors, the resolution attracting no support from House GOP lawmakers.

For the third time, during the 116th Congress, Cicilline would again introduce H. Res. 821 to reestablish the House Aging Committee. Even with the Democrats retaking the House and House Speaker Nancy Pelosi taking control of the chamber's legislative agenda, the resolution would not get a committee vote, again blocking it from reaching the floor for a vote.

During the 117th Congress, Cicilline is not taking "no" for an answer, and continues his push to bring back the House Aging Committee. Once his resolution is thrown into the legislative hopper, it will be referred to the House Committee on Rules for mark up and, if passed, will be considered by the full House. It's expected to be just 245 words like the previous ones introduced during the last three Congresses.

The Resolution: Short and Sweet

Cicilline's resolution would reestablish a House Aging Committee without having legislative jurisdiction, this being no different than when the select committee previously existed. It would be authorized to conduct a continuing comprehensive study and review of aging issues, such as income maintenance, poverty, housing, health (including medical research), welfare, employment, education, recreation, and long-term care. These efforts impacted legislation taken up by standing committees.

According to the Congressional Research Service, it is relatively simple to create an ad hoc (temporary) select committee by approving a simple resolution that contains language establishing the committee—giving a purpose, defining membership, and detailing other issues that need to be addressed. Salaries and expenses of standing committees, special and select, are authorized through the Legislative Branch Appropriations bill.

This resolution would also authorize the House Aging Committee to study the use of all practicable means and methods of encouraging the development of public and private programs and policies, which will assist seniors in taking a full part in national life and encourage the utilization of the knowledge, skills, special aptitudes, and abilities of seniors to contribute to a better quality of life for all Americans.

It would also allow the House Aging Committee to develop policies that would encourage the coordination of both governmental and private programs designed to deal with problems of aging and to review any recommendations made by the president or by the White House Conference on Aging in relation to programs or policies affecting seniors.

"After a lifetime of working hard and playing by the rules, Rhode Island seniors should be able to enjoy their retirement years with dignity and peace of mind. Reestablishing the House Aging Committee will help make this goal a reality.

From protecting Social Security and Medicare to lower the costs of housing and prescription drugs, this committee will help ensure we can deliver better results for seniors here in Rhode Island and across America," says Cicilline.

Looking Back

According to NCPSSM's Richtman, who served as staff director for the Senate Special Committee on Aging from 1987 to 1989, the House Aging Committee historically served as a select committee that fostered bipartisan debate from various political and philosophical viewpoints to promote political consensus that, in turn, impacted the legislation that was taken up in authorizing committees. This select committee would have an opportunity to more fully explore a range of aging issues and innovations that cross committee jurisdiction, while holding field hearings, convening remote hearings, engaging communities, and promoting understanding and dialogue.

While seeing the value of the House Aging Committee, Richtman speculates that regardless of which party is in the majority, the challenge of re-establishing the select committee is that the legislative branch appropriation would require that existing House standing committees forgo some funding and staff to create a budget and staff for the Aging Committee. Given that the Aging Committee could have no legislative jurisdiction, the authorizing committees would not lose legislative power.

Robert Blancato, president of Matz, Blancato, and Associates, who was the longest-serving staff person on the original House Aging Committee, from 1977 to 1993, sees the need to bring back the House Aging Committee. "It provided a deeper examination of issues affecting older adults through hearings, investigations, and reports. Every member of the committee was also a member of a standing committee and could take their expertise into that work," he noted.

Blancato, who served with three chairs—Will Randall (D-MO), Claude Pepper (D-FL) and Edward Roybal (D-CA)—warns that a "floodgate problem" may well derail Cicilline's efforts to get his resolution passed. "You create one, and there will be pressure to create more," says Blancato. But, bringing back the House Aging Committee is extremely important because there is no "stated expertise in any current standing committee [to investigate] on aging issues," he adds.

America's aging population warrants re-establishing the House Aging Committee, says Professor Fernando Torres-Gill, M.S.W., Ph.D., social welfare and public policy director, Center for Policy Research on Aging at the UCLA Luskin School of Public Affairs. "By 2029, all 80-plus individuals born between 1946 and 1964 will be 65 years of age and over. These so-called 'aging baby boomers' will create challenges and opportunities that the Congress must examine, understand and respond to with legislation, oversight, and partnerships with government, stakeholders, and advocates," says Torres-Gill, who served as the select committee's staff director from 1985 to 1987.

Under the Chairmanship of Congressman Roybal and the partnership with the ranking minority member, Congressman Rinaldi (R-TX), Torres-Gill saw firsthand the tremendous influence that this select committee had on influencing and motivating House members to promote thoughtful responses to the needs of older Americans, "It served as one of the few venues for bipartisanship and long-term planning on complex issues facing older persons," he stated.

According to Torres-Gill, the complexities of an aging society will increase given the pandemic, the growing voices of immigrants, ethnic and minority groups, and the challenges for ensuring the financial viability of legacy entitlement programs: Social Security, Medicare, Medicaid, and the Older Americans Act. "Now is the time to bring back this vital congressional 'thought leader' on legislative action for the aging and diversity of the United States," he says.

To illustrate the importance of the House Aging Committee, Bill Benson, staff director of the committee's Subcommittee on Housing and Consumer Interests from 1987 to 1990, chaired by Congressmen Don Bonker (D-WA) and later James Florio (D-NJ), points to his subcommittee's work on housing issues. "Both before, during, and after my tenure with the subcommittee, we were able to dig deeply into a multitude of significant housing-related programs and problems facing older Americans. During my tenure alone we conducted at least a dozen hearings just on housing, addressing affordability, quality, and appropriateness, contributing significantly to legislative action," he said.

"I am certain that in just that over-two-year period we held far more hearings on housing and aging than have been conducted, in total, in the nearly three decades since. During this interim, there has been almost no congressional attention to housing for the elderly. It is no surprise that today we see homelessness among older adults increasing rapidly, among many other housing problems facing older Americans," adds Benson, stressing that resurrecting the House Aging Committee is crucial to housing policy for the elderly, along with so many other crucial issues.

Kathleen Gardner served as Claude Pepper's staff director of the Subcommittee on Aging and Long-Term Care from 1984 until his death in 1989, and continued to serve Pepper's successor, Edward Roybal, until the House Aging Committee was abolished. She was the last surviving member of the subcommittee, boxing up and archiving its papers for delivery to the Tallahassee, Florida-based Claude Pepper Foundation.

According to Gardner, few know that it was Pepper who was largely responsible for sponsoring or cosponsoring legislation to establish the majority of the Institutes of Health (including the National Heart and Cancer Institutes, the Deafness and Arthritis Institutes, the National Institute of Mental Health, and six other Institutes). "One of his last legislative improvements to the National Institutes of Health was the establishment of the National Center for Biotechnology Information at the National Library of Medicine—without which the mapping of the human genome—which will unlock so many of the mysteries of disease—would not have been possible," she adds.

Between 1982 and 1990, Melanie Modlin served as a professional staff member for the full committee and ultimately became Gardner's deputy director for the Subcommittee on Health and Long-Term Care. She remembered how the House Aging Committee investigated "diploma mills," by setting up its own diploma mill, then a phony accreditation to give the investigators credence. The select committee also held one of the first hearings on Alzheimer's disease, which was just beginning to become a household word.

Modlin recalled that her subcommittee was tasked with creating a universal health-care bill. "Once more, Pepper and the House Aging Committee was a step ahead of the curve," she says, noting that this debate has come back to Congress.

As newspapers in communities across the nation curtail or jettison their investigative teams, the House Aging Committee has a proven track record and reputation of investigating aging issues, a sound reason as to why the select committee should be reactivated, says Modlin, especially with the rapid growth of America's aging population.

Robert S. Weiner, president of Robert Weiner Associates News, who was a close friend and confidant of Pepper, clearly knew the importance and impact of Pepper's House Aging Committee on the daily quality of life of seniors. Weiner, who served as staff director for the Subcommittee on Health and Long-term Care from 1975 to 1977 and chief of staff of the full Aging Committee from 1976 to 1980, remembered, "I was thunderbolt struck when [GOP House Speaker] Newt Gingrich abolished the Aging Committee—the Senate wisely kept theirs."

"Congressman Claude Pepper used the House Aging Committee as a force for the elderly. Bringing it back would be of immeasurable help regardless of which party has the White House in assuring the best health-care programs possible, stopping any raiding of the Social Security Trust Fund, and protecting seniors," says Weiner.

The House Aging Committee prodded Congress to act in abolishing forced retirement, investigating nursing home abuses, monitoring breast screening for older women, improving elderly housing, and bringing attention to elder abuse by publishing a number of reports, including *Elder Abuse: An Examination of a Hidden Problem,* and *Elder Abuse: A National Disgrace*, and *Elder Abuse: A Decade of Shame and Inaction.* The committee's work would also lead to increased home-care benefits for the aging and establishing research and care centers for Alzheimer's disease.

"One of the best known aging accomplishments of Claude Pepper was to end mandatory retirement by amending the Age Discrimination provision in the Employment Act," remembered Weiner, noting that this would get him the cover of *Time* magazine with the tagline, the "Spokesman for the Elderly."

Kentucky Fried Chicken King Makes His Mark

It was Pepper's idea to bring in Col. Harland Sanders as a witness. "Many still remember the 81-year-old Kentucky Fried Chicken king, wearing his trademark spotless white suit and black string tie, and testifying against mandatory retirement in federal jobs," said Weiner, noting that a few years later it would end up also in the private sector, and the bill would pass 359 to 2 in the House and 89 to 10 in the Senate, with President Jimmy Carter signing the bill despite strong opposition of the Business Roundtable and big labor, he said.

Weiner also noted that among the House Aging Committee's other accomplishments under Pepper's chairmanship was legislation creating standards for supplemental insurance and holding hearings to expose cancer insurance duplication. "Witnesses were literally forced to wear paper bags over their heads to avoid harassment by the insurance companies. That legislation became law," he said.

As a long-time Washington insider, Weiner sees the best avenue of bringing the House Aging Committee back from the dead is to get House Speaker Nancy Pelosi (D-CA) and her leadership team, Congressmen Steny Hoyer (D-MD) and James E. Clyburn (D-SC), to support Cicilline's resolution. "It's not just a matter of getting them to say okay—it's using the right way to do it that works. While you can get groups to support your efforts to bring back the House Aging Committee, you must verbally make the case to House leadership," says Weiner. Looking back, "that's how Pepper always did it—he'd pull people to a place on the floor and talk with them."

"If he gets those three, or even one or two, and they tell the other two—done deal—it goes to the floor of the caucus for a vote," notes Weiner.

In Summary...

Over 30 years after the death of Claude Pepper (D-FL) in 1989, no national advocate has emerged to take the place of the former chairman of the House Aging Committee, who served as its chair for six years. As a result, House Democratic lawmakers and aging advocates are forced every new session of Congress to fend off proposals to cut aging programs, Social Security, and Medicare.

Gardner believes that Cicilline's efforts to re-establish this needed select committee would be a salute to Pepper, the nation's most visible spokesperson for seniors, and more importantly to his desire to establish a "legislative voice" for our nation's most vulnerable population—our senior citizens.

Hopefully House Speaker Nancy Pelosi will agree with Gardner's assessment. If only for the sake of the nation's seniors.

For details about the Claude Pepper Foundation, go to **https://claudepepperfoundation.org/about/claude-pepper-center/.**

DR. TERESA CHOPOORIAN: MCKNIGHT'S WOMEN OF DISTINCTION AWARD-WINNER

Published in the *Pawtucket Times* on February 22, 2021

After reviewing hundreds of submitted entries, an independent panel, composed of two-dozen judges, selected 19 women, including Dr. Teresa J. Chopoorian, to be inducted into the *McKnight's* Women of Distinction Hall of Honor as part of the program's third annual class.

Dr. Chopoorian serves as vice president and administrator of the Central Falls, RI-based Mansion Nursing and Rehabilitation Center, is a former professor of nursing, and chairs the City of Pawtucket Cancer Control Task Force.

According to *McKnight's Long-Term Care News*, the Hall of Honor recognizes executive-level professionals who have made a significant impact in the skilled nursing or senior living industries. Of the 60 women who have been inducted into the Distinction Hall of Honor since its inception in 2019, Dr. Chopoorian is the only Rhode Islander to receive this prestigious recognition.

Considered the hallmark of recognition for women leaders in the seniors' care and living industries, *McKnight's* Women of Distinction honors are given in three categories: Rising Stars, Veteran VIPs, and the Hall of Honor. A Lifetime Achievement Award winner will also be announced in March. The annual awards program is administered jointly by *McKnight's Long-Term Care News* and *McKnight's Senior Living*. The winners will be recognized in editions of the *McKnight's Daily Update* and *McKnight's Daily Briefing* newsletters.

All of this year's honorees, working in the health-care industry, will be celebrated during a May 18 virtual awards event. The ceremony will take place in the evening followed by a special McKnight's educational forum for all professionals in the long-term care and senior living industries the next morning.

The Life and Times of Dr. Chopoorian

Dr. Chopoorian was hired as an instructor at Boston University School of Nursing after completing her master's degree at this university in 1964. She was promoted to assistant professor and recognized as Teacher of the Year in 1968.

She left Boston University in 1970 to accept a professorship at Boston College to co-direct a Macy Foundation graduate program with Harvard Medical School, a novel initiative to prepare clinical nurse specialists. The program was among the first graduate nursing curriculum in the country and served as a critical role model for forthcoming nurse practitioner programs.

In 1974, Dr. Chopoorian joined the faculty of Boston State College Department of Nursing and began doctoral studies at Boston University in 1978. Upon completion of her doctorate in 1982, she accepted a professorship at Northeastern University School of Nursing where she continued to teach and participate in the development of nursing practice.

Coming Back Home to Long-term Care

Dr. Chopoorian joined the Mansion after a 22-year career as a nursing educator. Her career parallels the transformation of nursing home care as it has undergone generational change. As nursing homes evolved from custodial care to a case mix of higher morbidities and a greater need to deal with an increasing population of younger residents and residents with mental illnesses, Dr. Chopoorian's career paralleled this transformation in unique ways.

Starting as a teenager working in her family's business, a 76-bed nursing home on the border of Central Falls and Pawtucket, mill towns emerging from the flight of the textile industry, she was inspired to become a nurse. She then chose the rigor of enrolling at Classical High School in Providence, which laid a strong foundation of scholarship that would serve her well. More importantly, this earliest choice illustrated a characteristic of always taking on the greater challenge.

In 1986, Dr. Chopoorian joined the Mansion staff at a time of family crisis. Her father was retiring as administrator soon after the passing of her mother. At a crossroad of whether to continue the development of a fruitful academic career or apply her clinical knowledge and nursing skills to a family business, she made the critical choice of leading the family's nursing facility while caring for her father. This was a daunting choice on every level: leaving the security of an academic career for a business whose nature and regulatory landscape were dramatically different than two decades earlier when she helped her father as a nursing aide.

Dr. Chopoorian's family crisis thrust her into the role of administrator; she led the Mansion as a quality provider of skilled care and rehabilitation services, consistently a 4- and 5-star rated facility. In 2010, she was recognized as the first recipient of the Nightingale Nurse of the Year Award by the Rhode Island State Nurses Association, as a nurse in the role of nursing home administrator.

Dr. Chopoorian also became active in the greater community and participated in boards such as the Pawtucket YMCA and Samaritans of Rhode Island. But closest to her heart, she has a lifelong commitment to cancer prevention, and has become one of the strongest local voices for cancer prevention in her community. As chair of the Cancer Control Task Force supported by the City of Pawtucket mayor's office, she instituted programs such as a poetry slam that has young local school students writing poems competitively on the theme of smoking cessation or prevention.

A Rising Star in the Nursing Profession

After graduation from the College of Nursing at the University of Rhode Island in 1962, she started as a staff nurse at Children's Hospital Medical Center in Boston. Again, rising to the greater challenge, she enrolled in the nursing master's program at Boston University. It launched a career that would keep her in the mainstream of nursing education and growth, up to the present day to bring her full cycle to administering a family business and the challenges of passing it on to a third generation.

Dr. Chopoorian shared her pioneering work on education for nursing practice through her teaching, publishing, and consulting as these programs became established. She was recognized for her work by the Massachusetts Nurses Association in 1974 – "Recognition of a Nurse Influencing the Directions of Professional Nursing Practice."

Perhaps the most prestigious recognition was her selection as the ninth recipient of the International Council of Nursing (ICN) Fellowship in 1978, the first US candidate to be selected from among its 44 member countries.

Among Dr. Chopoorian's publications, one of special note is her article, "Reconceptualizing the Environment," which called attention to the social, cultural, political, and economic environmental factors that impact the practice of nursing. Published in 1986, it is still heavily cited by scholars in the field and pertinent to the dialogue of nursing practice today.

She was appointed Fellow in the National Academy of Practice, Nursing in 1987.

Meeting the Challenges of COVID-19

Dr. Chopoorian is now practicing what she has preached over the years, applying her knowledge and skills to the practical matters of administering a skilled nursing care facility, and doing it in a manner that has earned her the recognition of her peers as Nightingale Nurse of the Year.

Early in March 2020 as it became clear that nursing homes were ground zero in an epic battle with Covid-19, she consulted with her medical and nursing director and decided to close admission of anyone into the facility who was not already in the facility until October of 2020, when community spread overcame the facility staff's most resolute of defenses. The Mansion is one of only three facilities in Rhode Island with this record in the midst of what was designated as the state's hot zone for the virus. The residents and staff who tested positive have since quickly passed quarantine with no deaths or illnesses. A major practice achievement as we now head into a time of protection with the Pfizer, Moderna, and other versions of the COVID-19 vaccine, and are hopefully home free.

For a listing of winners of the 2021 Women of Distinction Hall of Honor inductees, go to:

https://www.mcknights.com/news/mcknights-unveils-2021-women-of-distinction-hall-of-honor-inductees/

8. MENTAL HEALTH

"The most beautiful people we have known are those who have known defeat, known suffering, known struggle, known loss, and have found their way out of the depths. These persons have an appreciation, a sensitivity, and an understanding of life that fills them with compassion, gentleness, and a deep loving concern. Beautiful people do not just happen."

—Elisabeth Kübler-Ross

REPORT OUTLINES STRATEGY FOR COMBATING SENIORS' SOCIAL ISOLATION AND LONELINESS

Published in the *Woonsocket Call* on March 1, 2020

Nearly one in four older adults residing in the community are socially isolated. Seniors who are experiencing social isolation or loneliness may face a higher risk of mortality, heart disease, and depression, says a newly released report from the National Academies of Sciences, Engineering, and Medicine (NASEM), a Washington, DC-based nonprofit, nongovernmental organization.

For seniors who are homebound, have no family, friends, or do not belong to community or faith groups, a medical appointment or home health visit may be one of the few social interactions they have, notes the NASEM report released on February 27, 2020. "Despite the profound health consequences—and the associated costs—the health-care system remains an underused partner in preventing, identifying, and intervening for social isolation and loneliness among adults over age 50," says the report.

"I'm pleased the AARP Foundation-sponsored study by NASEM confirms the connection between social isolation or loneliness and death, heart disease, and depression for older adults. It also finds that the health-care system and community-based organizations have a critical role to play in intervening," says AARP Foundation president Lisa Marsh Ryerson.

"We also know social isolation, like other social determinants of health, must be addressed to increase economic opportunity and well-being for low-income older adults," says Ryerson.

Addressing Social Isolation and Loneliness

The 266-page NASEM report, *Social Isolation and Loneliness in Older Adults: Opportunities for the Health Care System*, undertaken by the Committee on the Health and Medical Dimensions of Social Isolation and Loneliness in Older

Adults, outlines five goals that the nation's health-care system should adopt to address the health impacts of social isolation and loneliness. It also offers 16 recommendations for strengthening health workforce education and training, leveraging digital health and health technology, improving community partnerships, and funding research in understudied areas.

Although social isolation is defined as an objective lack of social relationships, loneliness is a subjective perception, say the NASEM report's authors. They note that not all older adults are isolated or lonely, but they are more likely to face predisposing factors such as living alone and the loss of loved ones. The issue may be compounded for LGBT, minority, and immigrant older adults, who may already face barriers to care, stigma, and discrimination, the report says.

Social isolation and loneliness may also directly result from chronic illness, hearing or vision loss, or mobility issues. In these instances, health- care providers might be able to help prevent or reduce social isolation and loneliness by directly addressing the underlying health-related causes.

"Loneliness and social isolation aren't just social issues—they can also affect a person's physical and mental health, and the fabric of communities," said Dan Blazer, J.P. Gibbons professor of psychiatry emeritus and professor of community and family medicine at Duke University, and chair of the committee that wrote the report in a statement announcing its release. "Addressing social isolation and loneliness is often the entry point for meeting seniors' other social needs—like food, housing, and transportation," he says.

Providing a Road Map...

The 16 recommendations in this report provide a strategy as to how the health-care system can identify seniors at risk of social isolation and loneliness, intervene, and engage other community partners.

As to improving Clinical Care Delivery, the report calls for conducting assessments to identify at-risk individuals. Using validated tools, health-care providers should perform periodic assessments, particularly after life events that may increase one's risk (such as a geographic move or the loss of a spouse).

The NASEM report also recommends that social isolation be included in electronic health records (EHRs). If a patient is at risk for or already experiencing social isolation, providers should include assessment data in clear locations in the EHR or medical records.

It's important to connect patients with social care or community programs, too. The NASEM report notes that several state Medicaid programs and private insurers already have programs that target the social determinants of health. These programs can be more intentionally designed to address social isolation and loneliness of older recipients. Health-care organizations could also partner with ride-sharing programs to enable older adults to travel to medical appointments and community events, the report recommends.

The NASEM report also suggests that as more evidence becomes available, roles that health-care providers are already performing—such as discharge planning, case management, and transitional care planning—can be modified to directly address social isolation and loneliness in older adults. The report also details other interventions that the health care system might consider, including mindfulness training, cognitive behavioral therapy, and referring patients to peer support groups focused on volunteerism, fitness, or common experiences such as bereavement or widowhood.

Strengthening health professionals' education and training can be another strategy to combating the negative impacts of social isolation and loneliness. The NASEM report calls for schools of health professions and training programs for direct care workers (home health aides, nurse aides, and personal care aides) to incorporate social isolation and loneliness in their curricula. Health professionals need to learn core content in areas such as the health impacts of social isolation and loneliness, assessment strategies, and referral options and processes, say the report's authors.

The NASEM report warns that there are ethical implications for using health technology to reduce social isolation and loneliness. Technologies that are designed to help seniors—including smart home sensors, robots, and handheld devices—might intensify loneliness and increase social isolation if they are not easy to use or attempt to substitute for human contact. Moreover, the report found that 67 percent of the current assistive technologies in dementia care were designed without considering their ethical implications. Developers of technology should properly assess and test new innovations, taking into account privacy, autonomy, and the rural-urban digital divide.

The NASEM report says that more research is needed because of evidence gaps, and calls for more funding of studies to determine the effectiveness of interventions in clinical settings; to develop measures to identify at-risk individuals; and to identify trends among younger adults as they age (such as use of technology and economic trends) that may inform how the healthcare system should target social isolation and loneliness in the future. More research is also needed to identify approaches and interventions that best meet the needs of LGBT and ethnic minority populations.

The National Academies are private, nonprofit institutions that provide independent, objective analysis and advice to the nation to solve complex problems and inform public policy decisions related to science, technology, and medicine. They operate under an 1863 congressional charter to the National Academy of Sciences, signed by President Abraham Lincoln.

For a copy of the NASEM report, go to **http://www.nap.edu/catalog/ 25663/social-isolation-and-loneliness-in-older-adults-opportunities-for-the**.

AAIC 2019 CONCLUDES, RESEARCHERS SHARE FINDINGS TO COMBAT ALZHEIMER'S DISEASE

Published in the *Woonsocket Call* on July 20, 2019

Thousands of the world's leading professionals involved in dementia care and neuroscience research came to the Los Angeles Convention Center from July 13 to July 18, 2019, to attend the Alzheimer's Association International Conference® (AAIC) to learn about the findings of the latest Alzheimer's disease clinical trial and a government-driven public/private initiative to speed them up.

AAIC® is considered to be the largest and most influential international meeting with a mission to advancing dementia research. Every year, AAIC® brings together the world's leading basic science and clinical researchers, next-generation investigators, clinicians, and the care research community, to share research findings that'll lead to methods of preventing, treating, and improving the diagnosis of Alzheimer's disease.

"It is clear, and has been for some years that the (Alzheimer's) field needs to explore other options, and diversify the portfolio of targets. A renewed energy has been brought about by a fivefold increase in Alzheimer's research funding at the federal level. These gains will propel already-established efforts by the National Institute on Aging, Alzheimer's Association, and others to diversify (therapeutic) targets," said Maria C. Carrillo, Ph.D., Alzheimer's Association chief science officer, in a July 17 statement publicizing research findings from the international conference.

Hundreds of Findings of Clinical Trials Shared

According to the Chicago-based Alzheimer's Association, "a record number of scientific abstracts—more than 3,400—were submitted to AAIC this year, including 229 abstracts with results from or descriptions of Alzheimer's clinical trials. AAIC 2019 also spotlighted three clinical trials using innovative methods and targets."

At AAIC 2019, attendees were updated about the activities of the Accelerating Medicine Partnership-Alzheimer's Disease (AMP-AD), a partnership among government, industry, and nonprofit organizations (including the Alzheimer's Association) that focuses on discovering, validating, and accelerating new drug targets. The Alzheimer's Association says that this $225 million research initiative is made possible through the highest-ever levels of US federal funding for research on Alzheimer's and other dementias, approved and allocated in the last five years.

"This is an example of how the government and private entities and researchers can work together [via AMP-AD funded studies] on providing the resources necessary to expand our abilities to test new drugs and find a treatment for Alzheimer's disease and, hopefully find a cure," said Donna M. McGowan, executive director of the Alzheimer's Association, Rhode Island Chapter. "Rhode Island has tremendous researchers, and they are at the forefront of this initiative. They need the tools to increase their scope of work."

Adds Maria C. Carrillo, Ph.D., Alzheimer's Association chief science officer, "It is clear, and has been for some years, that the field needs to explore other options, other avenues, and diversify the portfolio of targets. A renewed energy has been brought about by a fivefold increase in Alzheimer's research funding at the federal level, achieved largely due to efforts by the Alzheimer's Association, the Alzheimer's Impact Movement, and our ferocious advocates. These gains will propel already-established efforts by the National Institute on Aging, Alzheimer's Association, and others to diversify the portfolio of drug targets for the scientific community."

The achievements of the AMP-AD Target Discovery Project were highlighted in a series of presentations by the leading AMP-AD investigators at AAIC 2019.

One study noted, for the first time, 18-month results from an open-label extension of inhaled insulin in mild cognitive impairment and Alzheimer's, including significant benefits for memory and thinking, day-to-day functioning, and biological markers of Alzheimer's.

Another described a newly initiated 48-week Phase 2/3 clinical trial of a drug targeting toxic proteins released in the brain by the bacterium P. gingivalis, generally associated with degenerative gum disease. Previous research findings identified the bacterium in brains of more than 90 percent of people with Alzheimer's across multiple studies and demonstrated that infection may trigger Alzheimer's pathology in the brain.

Can Lifestyle Interventions Promote Brain Health?

There was also an update on the Alzheimer's Association US Study to Protect Brain Health Through Lifestyle Intervention to Reduce Risk (US POINTER) study, now up and running in multiple locations. The US POINTER is a two-year clinical trial to evaluate whether intensive lifestyle interventions that target many risk factors for cognitive decline and dementia can protect cognitive function in older adults at increased risk for cognitive impairment and dementia.

Researchers will compare the effects of two lifestyle interventions on brain health in older adults at risk for memory loss in the future. The US POINTER is the first such study to be conducted in a large group of Americans across the United States.

The researchers say people age 60 to 79 will be randomly assigned to one of two lifestyle interventions. Both groups will be encouraged to include more physical and cognitive activity and a healthier diet into their lives and will receive regular monitoring of blood pressure and other health measurements. Participants in one intervention group will design a lifestyle program that best fits their own needs and schedules. Participants in the other intervention group will follow a specific program that includes weekly healthy lifestyle activities.

Laura Baker, Ph.D., associate professor of gerontology and geriatric medicine at Wake Forest School of Medicine, and one of the principal investigators of the US POINTER study, said, "Lifestyle interventions focused on combining healthy diet, physical activity, and social and intellectual challenges represent a promising therapeutic strategy to protect brain health."

"US POINTER provides an unprecedented opportunity to test whether intensive lifestyle modification can protect cognitive function in older Americans who are at increased risk of cognitive decline and dementia," Baker added.

"We envision a future where we can treat and even prevent Alzheimer's through a combination of brain-healthy lifestyle and targeted medicines, as we do now with heart disease," Carrillo said. "We hope to prevent millions from dying with Alzheimer's and reduce the terrible impact this disease has on families."

For more details about research findings presented at AAIC 2019, go to **http://www.alz.org/aaic**

REPORT: COGNITIVE-STIMULATING ACTIVITIES GOOD FOR YOUR BRAIN'S HEALTH

Published in the *Woonsocket Call* on August 6, 2017

Don't expect playing "brain games" to have the long-term brain health benefits often reported in newspapers. According to a statement released last month by the Global Council on Brain Health (GCBH), the scientific evidence supporting the benefits of "brain games" is at best "weak to non-existent." But, the researchers say you can engage in many stimulating activities to help sharpen your brain as you age.

GCBH's latest statement on "cognitive stimulating activities" follows earlier reports issued by this independent organization created by AARP, advocating on behalf of its 38 million members with the support of Age UK, one of the United Kingdom's largest charities advocating for seniors. Previous areas included: "The Brain Body Connection," "The Brain Sleep Connection," and "The Brain and Social Connectedness."

The 25-page GCBH report, released on July 25, says that while many find "brain games" to be fun and engaging activities, often the claims made by companies touting the game's cognitive benefits are exaggerated. The researchers noted that there are many ways to support and maintain your memory, reasoning skills, and ability to focus, such as engaging in formal or informal educational activities, learning a new language, engaging in work or leisure activities that are mentally challenging, and connecting socially with others.

Keeping Mentally Sharp

The report debunks "brain health" myths, too. Contrary to the many stories told about the brain as we age, the GCBH finds that a person can learn new things, no matter their age. Getting dementia is not an inevitable consequence of growing older. Older persons can learn a second language. And, people should not expect to forget things as they age.

"The GCBH recommends people incorporate cognitively stimulating activities into their lifestyles to help maintain their brain health as they age," said Marilyn Albert, Ph.D., GCBH chair, and professor of neurology and director of the Division of Cognitive Neuroscience at Johns Hopkins University in Baltimore, Maryland. "The sooner you start the better, because what you do now may make you less susceptible to disease-related brain changes later in life."

"We know that the desire to stay mentally sharp is the number-one concern for older adults," said Sarah Lock, AARP senior vice president for policy and GCBH executive director. "Seeking out brain-stimulating activities is a powerful way for a person to positively influence their brain health as they age."

GCBH pulled 13 independent health-care professionals and experts together, who work in the area of brain health related to cognitive functioning, to examine "cognitively stimulating activities." This group crafted the report's consensus statement and recommendations after a close examination of well-designed randomized scientific studies published in peer review journals and studies replicated by other scientists.

Taking Control of Your Brain Health

The report concluded that people have control and influence over their brain changes throughout their lifespan. People can maintain their memory, cognitive thinking, attention, and reasoning skills as they age by doing brain-stimulating activities. There is sufficient evidence that brain-stimulating activities are beneficial to staying mentally sharp over your lifespan

The researchers found through their literature review that training on a specific cognitive ability such as memory may improve that specific ability, but scientific evidence suggests you need to continue to apply that training to maintain or improve the ability over time.

The researchers also found that there is insufficient evidence that getting better at "brain games" will improve a person's overall functioning in everyday life. Maintaining or improving your brain health is tied to the activity being "novel, highly engaging, mentally changing, and enjoyable."

The GCBH report suggested that just by learning a new skill, practicing tai-chi, learning photography, even investigating family history, you can stimulate the brain and challenge the way you think, improving "brain health."

Also, social engagement and having a purpose in life, like "volunteering as a companion and mentoring others in your community," can be mentally stimulating and improve your "brain health."

But, the researchers say don't forget physical activity, such as "dancing and tennis," because the mental engagement and physical exercise can mentally benefit you, too.

The GCBH, founded in 2015, is an independent international group of scientists, health professionals, scholars, and policy experts working on brain health issues. Convened by AARP with support from Age UK, the goal of the GCBH is to review the current scientific evidence and provide recommendations for people so that they can maintain and improve their brain health.

The full GCBH recommendations can be found here: **http://www.globalcouncilonbrainhealth.org**.

Yes, routinely challenging your brain can lead to improved "brain health." As the old adage says, "Use it or lose it."

SPUMONI'S: "WHERE EVERYBODY KNOWS YOUR NAME:" STUDY SAYS BEING SOCIALLY ACTIVE MAY IMPROVE COGNITIVE FUNCTIONING

Published in the *Woonsocket Call* on February 26, 2017

As George M. Cohan's famous musical once lauded, "Just 45 Minutes from Broadway," Mark and Nancy Shorrock have discovered that their "home away from home" is a mere seven minutes away. While some people take to the internet or plug into television, the Shorrocks discovered a long time ago that staying socially engaged with a wide circle of friends and family was their secret to the fountain of youth. Like the fictional Boston bar featured in the television sitcom *Cheers* where "regulars" would gather to share their daily life experiences at that fictional place where "everybody knows your name," this couple found the same camaraderie at Spumoni's Restaurant.

The Shorrocks have been traveling over the Massachusetts state line to Rhode Island for 17 years to dine at the Pawtucket bar and join the regulars at this well-known eatery. And not surprisingly, over the years their social network has drastically expanded, and not shrunk in size. Spumoni's regulars and staff know their names and even the intimacies of their lives.

Good Food, Minutes from Home, and Pac-Man

The Attleboro couple, now in their 70s and married for 52 years, began dining at Spumoni's twice a week with their children in the 1980s, and remember being drawn to the Italian-style restaurant because of its reputation of serving "good food." Over the years, as the Shorrocks' three children became more independent and were "doing things on their own," the couple began increasing their trips to Spumoni's since it was so close by, says Nancy.

Nancy remembers her children playing Pac-Man at Spumoni's, an iconic video game from the 1980s. "The just loved playing that game," she says.

"Coming regularly deepened our relationships with the people we met and our waitresses and staff," she stated.

Prior to retirement, this couple maintained their own busy careers while raising a family. Nancy, a former nurse, worked at special-needs facilities and various hospitals for almost four decades, officially retired in 2000. That year, Mark, who served as manager of materials and properties, retired from Raytheon after 37 years. Soon they began dining at Spumoni's daily, seven days a week, if their schedules permitted.

Today, every night around 7:00 p.m., Nancy and Mark sit at the bar and order individual extra thin pizzas with peppers and onions—one light on cheese and the other four cheeses (in case you're wondering, these pizzas are named after the couple). Pat Maziarz, a bartender for more than 30 years, makes their drinks, "one wine and one martini." And for now they are settled in and will catch up with their extended family of bar regulars, which may last for hours. Mark even plays a little Keno, piling up his tickets on the bar counter.

Even family gatherings with their three children, three grandchildren, and one great grandchild are held at the restaurant. "We don't sit at the bar for these events," quips Nancy.

Richard Veroni, 51, a Pawtucket resident and Spumoni's regular, says that after a long day working at the Massachusetts-based Shaw's Corporate Headquarters, on his way home he will stop off at the restaurant on Newport Avenue if he sees Nancy and Mark's 2005 Toyota Camry in the parking lot. Veroni observes, "They are not lonely, they know so many people here."

Nancy agrees, noting that she and Mark have developed personal relationships with about 30 couples who frequent Spumoni's bar. "Spumoni's is sort of our *Cheers*, and we know everybody's name," she says.

Life milestones are recognized at their favorite restaurant, too. The staff of Spumoni's held a 50th-wedding anniversary party for the Shorrocks. Their children provided enlarged photographs from their parents' wedding and the restaurant even duplicated the couple's wedding cake from a picture.

Dining at Spumoni's is a "shared" activity, says Nancy. If she has to work late at her part-time job at a local funeral home, Mark won't go alone.

Looking at the positive impact of having a regular hangout at Spumoni's, "it's our therapy, and coming here makes us happy," Nancy says. Mark totally agrees.

Hanging Out with Friends May Improve Cognitive Functioning

What the Shorrocks know innately, a 24-page report, *The Brain and Social Connectedness: GCBH Recommendations on Social Engagement and Brain Health*, released by the Global Council on Brain Health in February 14, 2017, spells out. Larger social networks may positively impact your health, well-being, even your cognitive functioning. This report is available at **http://www. GlobalCouncilOnBrainHealth.org**.

"It's not uncommon for our social networks to shrink in size as we get older," said Marilyn Albert, Ph.D., GCBH chair, professor of neurology and director of the Division of Cognitive Neuroscience at Johns Hopkins University in Baltimore, Maryland. "This report provides many helpful suggestions about the things we can do to improve the quality of our relationships with family and friends, which may be beneficial in maintaining our mental abilities."

"We know that loneliness and social isolation can increase physical health risks for older people," said Sarah Lock, AARP senior vice president for policy, and GCBH executive director. "The GCBH's consensus that people who are socially engaged have a lower risk for cognitive decline shows us just how important social connections are to brain health."

The Brain and Social Connectedness report addresses the social benefits of having pets, the role that age-friendly communities play in fostering social ties, and how close relationships promote both physical health and psychological well-being. The report also covers how social media, like Facebook and Skype, helps older adults maintain their social connections.

Strengthening Social Ties Through Volunteerism

"While there are many ways people get involved with AARP, the one thing shared by our volunteers is that their contribution to our mission gets them out and about," said AARP Rhode Island State director Kathleen Connell. "Whether it's a trip to the State House to support age-friendly legislation, staffing a table at a community event or working in support of our Livable

Communities initiative, volunteers are active and engaged with others—fellow volunteers, our community partners, and the public we serve," she says.

"It comes up in conversations as well as volunteer surveys that staying active is one of the added benefits that accompany advocacy and community service," Connell says.

"Also, it is important to know that AARP does more than pay lip service to other organizations that help keep people active," she adds, noting that AARP's Create The Good website (**http://www.createthegood.org**) is an online source to help people find volunteer work at a multitude of organizations and community groups looking for help. You enter your zip code and the distance you're willing to travel, and dozens of various opportunities appear. Another great resource is AARP Staying Sharp (**https://stayingsharp.aarp.org**), which includes a brain health section that features advice and activities as well as an assessment tool that includes active living as an important factor.

NEW REPORT SAYS ALZHEIMER'S DISEASE IS MAJOR PUBLIC-HEALTH ISSUE

Published in the *Woonsocket Call* on March 25, 2018

For the second consecutive year, total payments to care for individuals with Alzheimer's or other dementias will surpass $277 billion, which includes an increase of nearly $20 billion from last year, according to data reported in the Alzheimer's Association *2018 Alzheimer's Disease Facts and Figures* report released last Tuesday.

According to the Alzheimer's Association, the annual report, first released in 2007, is a compilation of state and national specific statistics and information detailing the impact of Alzheimer's disease and related dementias on individuals, families, state and federal government, and the nation's health-care system.

"This year's report illuminates the growing cost and impact of Alzheimer's on the nation's health-care system, and also points to the growing financial, physical, and emotional toll on families facing this disease," said Keith Fargo, Ph.D., director of scientific programs and outreach for the Alzheimer's Association, in a statement. "Soaring prevalence, rising mortality rates, and lack of an effective treatment all lead to enormous costs to society. Alzheimer's is a burden that's only going to get worse. We must continue to attack Alzheimer's through a multidimensional approach that advances research while also improving support for people with the disease and their caregivers," he said.

"Discoveries in science mean fewer people are dying at an early age from heart disease, cancer, and other diseases," adds Fargo. "Similar scientific breakthroughs are needed for Alzheimer's disease, and will only be achieved by making it a national health-care priority and increasing funding for research that can one day lead to early detection, better treatments, and ultimately a cure."

2018 Alzheimer's Facts and Figures

New findings from the 88-page report on March 20, 2017 reveal the growing burden on 16.3 million caregivers providing 18.4 billion hours of care valued at more than $232 billion to 5.7 million people with the devastating mental disorder. By 2050, the report projects that the number of persons with Alzheimer's and other dementias will rise to nearly 14 million, with the total cost of care skyrocketing to more than $1.1 trillion.

Between 2000 and 2015, deaths from health disease nationwide decreased by 11 percent, but deaths from Alzheimer's disease have increased by 123 percent, says the new data in the report, noting that one of three seniors dies with Alzheimer's or another dementia. It kills more than breast cancer and prostate cancer combined. In Rhode Island in 2015, the number of deaths from Alzheimer's disease was 453, making the devastating brain disorder the fifth-leading cause of death in the state.

In 2017, 53,000 Rhode Island caregivers provided an estimated 61 million hours of unpaid physical and emotional care and financial support—a contribution to the nation valued at $768 million dollars. The difficulties associated with providing this level of care are estimated to have resulted in $45 million in additional health-care costs for Alzheimer's and other dementia caregivers in 2017.

State Updates Battle Plan Against Alzheimer's Disease

"The Alzheimer's Association's most recent report about Alzheimer's disease in Rhode Island illustrates the need to take swift action in updating our state plan to ensure Rhode Island is prepared to provide the necessary resources to families, caregivers, and patients who are struggling with the disease," says Lieutenant Governor Dan McKee.

McKee adds that the updated state plan will be a blueprint for how Rhode Island will continue to address the growing Alzheimer's crisis. "It will create the infrastructure necessary to build programs and services for the growing number of Rhode Islanders with the disease. The updated plan will also outline steps the state must take to improve services for people with Alzheimer's and their families. After the update is complete, my Alzheimer's executive board will seek legislative and regulatory changes to carry out the recommendations of the plan and ensure that it is more than just a document," he says.

"One of the many types of caregivers benefiting from AARP's caregiving advocacy in Rhode Island are family members who care for those with Alzheimer's," said AARP Rhode Island State director Kathleen Connell. "They are among the army of 10 million wives, husbands, sons and daughters nationwide. The majority are women and, according to researchers, especially when it comes to dementia and Alzheimer's care. Approximately 40 percent of those caregivers say they have no other options or choices, and a third say they provide care 24/7.

"The latest report indicates what we already know," Connell added. "This will continue to be a rising challenge in Rhode Island as our population ages. The disease will place more stress on our Medicaid-funded nursing home capacity, which should make this a concern for taxpayers. There is a strong case for increasing research funding so that someday we may reverse the tide.

"Our website, **http://www.aarp.org**, provides abundant resources for these dedicated caregivers. AARP in states across the nation, including Rhode Island, have worked to pass legislation that provides paid respite for caregivers who have jobs as well as caregiving obligations. We have supported the Alzheimer's Association here in Rhode Island for many years and, last year, a small team of AARP volunteers participated in the Alzheimer's Walk. Joined by others, they are gearing up for this year's walk."

Increased Research Funding Needed Now

Donna McGowan, Alzheimer's Association Rhode Island Chapter executive director, says that the *2018 Alzheimer's Disease Facts and Figures* report should send a very clear message that Alzheimer's disease is an issue that policymakers cannot ignore. "This is an urgent public-health crisis that must be addressed. Early detection and diagnosis of the disease leads to better planning, avoiding preventable hospitalizations, and overall a better quality of life for the patient and the caregiver," says McGowan.

McGowan warns that the health-care system is not ready to handle the increased cost and number of individuals expected to develop Alzheimer's disease in the coming years. "With a vigorous national plan in place to address the Alzheimer's crisis, and annual budget guidance for Congress, it is essential that the federal government continue its commitment to the fight against Alzheimer's by increasing funding for Alzheimer's research," adds McGowan.

Rhode Island Congressman David Cicilline sees the need for increased funding for direct services for those afflicted with Alzheimer's disease. He voted for H.R.1625, the omnibus spending bill that increases funding for the National Institute of Health's Alzheimer's research by $414 million. And two years ago, Cicilline worked to pass H.R.1559, "The HOPE for Alzheimer's Act," which President Obama signed into law to expand Medicare coverage for Alzheimer's treatment.

If Cicilline succeeds in getting the Republican-controlled Congress to vote on H.Res.160, his bill to reestablish the House Select Committee on Aging, it will allow House lawmakers to hear expert testimony and make new policy recommendations to improve the delivery of care to those afflicted with Alzheimer's and assist caregivers, too.

For details, go to **http://www.alz.org/facts**.

SIMPLE TIPS ON SURVIVING THE HOLIDAYS

Published in RINewsToday on November 26, 2019

The holiday season can be a double-edged sword. For some, it brings feelings of warmth and joy, even closeness and belonging to family and friends, but for others it produces extra stress, anxiety, and feelings of isolation and depression.

Increased demands and family obligations during the holiday season, from last-minute shopping for gifts, baking, cooking, cleaning, and hosting parties, getting the Christmas cards mailed, and even having unrealistic expectations can bring about the holiday blues.

Although holiday stress triggers depression, it can also bring about headaches, excessive drinking, overeating, and even difficulty in sleeping.

During her 24-year career as a licensed behavioral-health therapist, Holly Fitting, LMHC, LCDP, Vice President of Addiction and Residential Services at the Providence-based The Providence Center (TPC), has assisted many of her clients in developing strategies to cope with the holiday blues. Fitting, who oversees more than 20 programs at TPC, says "it's quite common".

Traveling to visit families, flight delays, long check-in lines, and bad weather can add to your stress too--including anticipating topics of conversation that may lead to arguments or events that may not even happen, says Fitting.

Preplanning Potential Family Conflict

Fitting says that preplanning potential issues that you might encounter at a family gathering can be helpful up to a point, if you just don't over plan. "If you try to figure out every possible scenario that might occur, this may only heighten your anxiety," she adds.

So, if you think your sibling will bring up political topics you may not want to discuss, you can plan to say, "Let's talk about this topic after the holidays," suggest Fitting. Or just don't sit near them at the dinner table to avoid the conversation.

It's okay to say "no" if you choose not to attend holiday parties or family gatherings, says Fitting, especially if you feel stressed-out attending. To keep feelings from being hurt and reducing potential problems, it might be better to attend but limit the time there, she says.

Also, you can choose not to take on the responsibility and commitment of bringing trays of treats, says Fitting. But if you choose to bring dessert, take the easy road. Instead of baking everything from scratch, buy a platter of cookies or a store-bought cake to lighten your load.

Combating the Holiday Blues

Maintaining healthy habits can also help you beat the holiday blues. "Try to eat healthy meals before holiday gatherings and minimize sugary desserts and alcohol consumed at the celebrations," states Fitting. During the holidays, "continue your exercise routine, even if it is a scaled-down version, and get plenty of sleep," she suggests, noting that this will help to reduce anxiety and depression, and keep weight off.

Out-of-control holiday spending and last-minute shopping can increase holiday stress, too, says Fitting, who suggests these tips to reduce gift costs: "Stick to your set budget to avoid guilt about buying gifts you cannot afford. Use coupons and attend sales to decrease spending costs. Agree to set the spending limit to no more than $20. Rather than buying presents for ten different people, play Secret Santa, and each family member just has to buy one gift. Set the price and rules ahead of time, and make sure everyone understands them. Or, rather than buying presents, collect cash to donate to an agreed-upon charity," she recommends.

Standing in long lines in the shopping mall can quickly become a source of stress, says Fitting. "One good solution is to double up and invite a family member or friend to shop. Waiting in a long line alone always feels like it takes twice as long as when you have someone to talk to.

You can get into the holiday spirit by starting a new tradition for yourself and your family that you will enjoy, suggests Fitting. "Volunteering to help out with a Toys for Tots Drive, or at a soup kitchen. Giving back by volunteering can really help to boost your spirits," she says.

Finally, Fitting says, "accept the fact that there will be mishaps along the way during the holidays. Try laughing at the unanticipated events certainly will help to reduce the undue stress experienced."

Getting Professional Help When Needed

As Christmas and New Year's approach, and you cannot shake the holiday blues, "it is important to be honest with yourself and your feelings. But, if the feelings of sadness still persist, then you should go speak to a professional. Sometimes going for therapy to talk through your feelings will help to alleviate depression and anxiety. Sometimes prescribed medication along with therapy is necessary to help reduce symptoms."

For those suffering the holiday blues, call The Providence Center at (401) 276-4020 or go to: **http://www.providencecenter.org.**

9. PETS

"Until one has loved an animal, a part of one's soul remains unawakened."

—Anatole France,
French Poet

PETS CAN BRING YOU HEALTH, HAPPINESS

Published in the *Woonsocket Call* on February 4, 2018

My newly adopted three-month-old chocolate Lab, Molly, keeps me on my toes. Literally. My daily walks around the block and playing ball in the backyard equal more than eight-thousand steps calculated by my Fitbit app. Being a pet owner I can certainly vouch for research findings published over the years that indicate that older adults who also are pet owners benefit from the regular exercise and bonds they form with their companion animal.

The Positives of Owning a Pet

According to Dr. William Truesdale, owner of Seekonk, Massachusetts, Central Avenue Veterinary Hospital, "having a companion animal can greatly improve your life. Of course you should always choose the right pet based upon your lifestyle and activity levels," says the veterinarian who has practiced for more than 43 years.

"Studies have demonstrated that having a pet in the home can actually lower a child's likelihood of developing related allergies or asthma. Children exposed early on to animals tend to develop stronger immune systems overall (as published in the *Journal of Allergies and Clinical Immunology*)," says Truesdale.

"The Centers for Disease Control and Prevention (CDC) have conducted heart related studies on people who have pets. The finding showed that pet owners exhibit decreased blood pressure, cholesterol, and triglyceride levels. All of which can ultimately minimize their risk for having a heart attack," adds Dr. Truesdale, noting that people affected by depression, loneliness, or PTSD may find that a companion animal may greatly improve their overall mood.

"As a dog owner myself and knowing so many people who find companionship and just plain fun as a pet owner, I can attest to the many benefits," said AARP Rhode Island State director Kathleen Connell. "While not for everyone, there is an abundance of evidence supporting this. I have heard so many stories about pets in senior living centers and even service pets that provide furry contact for patients in nursing homes and hospitals. I know they can do so much to brighten a day. And when you are on Facebook, you almost expect to see friends' proud dog and cat pictures.

"When it comes to dogs, they need walking. Anything that gets older people up and out of the house is a good thing, even if it requires carrying a supply of clean-up bags. Bending and stretching is exercise, you know. In addition, there inevitably is increased social interaction as people meet and make new pet-owner friends on the sidewalks and at dog parks. It's all good."

Pet-Friendly Policies Abound in Health-Care Settings

Dr. Karl Steinberg, a San Diego-based hospice and nursing home medical director and chief medical officer for Mariner Health Central, has seen the positive impact of pets in patient care settings. For more than twenty years the long-term care geriatrician has taken his own dogs with him to nursing homes, assisted living facilities, and on house calls to hospice patients almost every day. "It generates a lot of happiness," says Steinberg.

Steinberg sees firsthand on a daily basis the joy they bring to the residents, even those with severe dementia. "It slows down the day a little bit, because when you walk past a room and someone shouts, 'Oh! A dog!' you can't just walk on down the hall. You stop and share the unconditional love, and it's so worth it," says the geriatrician and hospice physician.

For years, Administrator Hugh Hall has brought Bella, a Labrador retriever, to visit residents of the West Warwick-based West View Nursing and Rehabilitation. Bella is considered "an important member" of the rehabilitation staff of the 120-bed skilled nursing facility, says Hall, noting the 8-year-old canine is utilized by therapists to assist and motivate patients in their recovery.

"Residents love the ability to interact and hold or cuddle with Bella and visiting pets," observes Hall, noting that his dog is the "official greeter" at the facility's main entrance. "The residents get to pet her and reminisce about their pets of the past, and this memory is warm and happy," he says.

Mike, a 12-year-old Labrador often makes the "rounds" with Geriatrician David A. Smith, MAD, CMD, at facilities in Central Texas. His pet's impact on residents is very positive and improves the quality of his rapport with residents, enabling him to get "better history and better compliance from them," he says.

"In a meta-analysis of non-pharmacologic therapies for behavioral problems in nursing home residents with dementia, pet therapy was one of only a small number of interventions that showed statistical benefit," says Smith, who is a past president of AMA: The Society for Post-Acute and Long-Term Care Medicine.

Smith warns that there is a downside in owning a pet. Frail adults may trip over a pet. Elders may age out of the ability to care for a pet, placing an additional burden on a caregiver who must care for the pet. Plans need to be in place for the placement of a pet in case of a move to an assisted living facility or if an owner passes away.

Lifelike Pets Can Also Bring Benefits to Older Adults

But, for those who find taking care of a living pet taxing because of deceased mobility or memory loss, Hasbro, Inc., has created new realistic pets; an animatronic cat with soft fur, soothing purrs, and pleasant meows; and a barking dog, especially designed to bring companionship to older adults.

In 2015, the Joy For All Companion Pets brand, featuring the animatronic cat, was Hasbro's first foray into products designed specifically for older adults. In addition to captivating older adults, Joy For All Companion Pets can help enhance the interaction between caregivers and their loved ones by incorporating lighthearted fun, joy, and laughter into time spent together.

In 2016, Hasbro's the Joy For All Companion Pet brand included a lifelike pup that sounds and feels like a real dog; when the pup's "owner" speaks, it looks toward him/her and reacts with realistic puppy sounds. That year the Pawtucket-based toy company collaborated with Meals on Wheels America to fight senior isolation and loneliness, which effects one in four seniors across the country. Hasbro donated $100,000 to Meals on Wheels America and provided Joy For All Companion Pets to local Meals on Wheels programs across the country to provide comfort and companionship to the nation's most vulnerable citizens.

"Aging loved ones and their caregivers have been thrilled with the Companion Pet Cats, and we are inspired by their positive feedback and personal stories," said Ted Fischer, vice president of business development at Hasbro in a statement announcing the new lifelike product. "The cat delivers a unique way for all generations to connect deeply through interaction and play, but dog lovers continually asked when we planned to add a dog to the line. We are truly excited for the new Joy For All product—the Companion Pet Pup—to bring even more lighthearted fun and laughter to seniors and their families.

"We heard from seniors across the country that companionship was important to their happiness. Many live alone, miss having a pet, or are no longer able to care for a pet," said Fischer. "While it's not a replacement for a pet, the Joy For All Companion Pet Cat is a lifelike alternative that can provide the joy and companionship of owning a real pet, without the often cumbersome responsibilities," he says.

The Joy For All Companion products are available for purchase on **JoyForAll. com**.

REMEMBERING ABBY

Published in the *Woonsocket Call* on September 4, 2016

I n March 2009, we formally adopted an impaired chocolate Labrador with a host of medical problems. With the signing of legal papers, four-year-old Abby met Murray, her elder adoptive canine sibling, who was also a chocolate Labrador.

Four months earlier Abby had arrived at the Pawtucket Animal Shelter, weak, malnourished, and showing signs of abuse. She appeared to suffer from blindness and a host of other medical ailments. Animal Control Officer John Holmes had sought veterinary care for her, but the medical testing came back inconclusive. It could be a brain tumor or lead poisoning affecting her vision, he would tell us, which for many potential families seeking adoption may be unappealing.

Officially Adopting Abby

According to Holmes, Abby's Labrador retriever breed made her a very popular candidate for adoption, but when people learned about her medical issues they had second thoughts. We thought Abby might just be a good younger companion for our 11-year-old chocolate Lab, Murray. We had good luck with this breed and were looking to adopt another chocolate Lab.

Six months prior to Abby's "official adoption" we made an unusual request from the Pawtucket Animal Shelter asking if a "foster care" arrangement could be made to see how well Abby got along with Murray. Having nothing to lose and everything to gain—they agreed.

When Abby came home our first priority was to try to make her gain some weight, which she eventually did. She adjusted well to Murray and her new surroundings, but during the first week she would have a seizure. We watched helplessly as this four-year-old canine shook all over, with her tongue lolling, her mouth foaming, and her eyes rolling back into her head. It was not pleasant to watch, and we initially thought she was dying. Ultimately, with anti-seizure medication her seizures were under control, and Abby thrived by gaining weight and becoming increasingly playful to the aging Murray.

We were extremely happy with the new addition to the family, even though we were now taking care of two medically needy pets instead of just one. Abby was given her daily pill in peanut butter to control seizures and Murray, a diabetic, was given insulin shots twice a day.

Health issues would force us to put Murray down in 2010. It would take months for Abby to adjust to his passing. She just knew her companion was gone. But, over the years, she adjusted to being the only pet in our household.

Getting Into the Household Routine

A new regimen took over, and every morning, like clockwork, Abby would carefully walk up the stairs, ending up at my bedroom door. The routine shaking of her head, her dog tags would jingle, sending the message to me that it was time to start the day. She was telling me to get up, serve her breakfast, and let her outside. As the years began to pass and she grew older, her medical issues became more prominent, and it was difficult for her to walk those stairs.

Abby's internal clock would also place her at the front door at 9:00 p.m. for her nightly walk, too. She had now become a visible fixture in my neighborhood of Oakhill. Neighbors would see us taking our daily nightly walk, but when I began walking by myself, they hesitated before asking me, "Is Abby okay?" No, I said, she is not.

The Moment of Truth

It happened quickly the day before we were to take her on vacation with us. We came home to find her with legs spread out on the floor with no ability to stand up. Her once healthy appetite suddenly diminished. After almost a week of veterinary care my wife, Patty, and I came to a decision to end the suffering of Abby, our 11-year-old chocolate Labrador. Looking to ease her pain and reduced quality of life, we made the hard and painful decision to put her down. After all, Abby was an integral part of our family.

Pet owners will share the trauma of putting their furry friend to sleep. Many may even tell you they relive their decision for decades, while some vow never to get another pet for fear of reliving the moment.

So as I pen this weekly commentary in a very quiet house, Abby's water and food bowls are put away. Her cremated ashes and collar will be placed next to Murray's wooden box containing his ashes, which sits on the mantel of our fireplace in the living room.

We think about her daily, maybe more than once. But, perhaps there will be a time when we will bring another shelter animal into our house, hopefully a female chocolate Labrador. Maybe even two.

To cope with the loss of your pet go to **https://rainbowsbridge.com/ Poem.htm**.

10. POP CULTURE, ART & MUSIC

"Aging is an extraordinary process where you become the person you always should have been."

—David Bowie

PAWTUCKET CITY HALL TO HOST MAJOR EXHIBIT OF RENOWNED 90-YEAR-OLD SCULPTOR

Published in the *Woonsocket Call* on September 16, 2019

T he City of Pawtucket's Arts and Culture Commission hosts a major exhibition of the work of 90-year-old internationally acclaimed artist Mihail Simeonov, running from September 19-December 31, 2019. An opening reception to meet Mihail will be held at Pawtucket City Hall, Thursday, September 19, 2019, from 4:30 p.m. to 6:30 p.m., 137 Roosevelt Avenue, Pawtucket, RI 02860.

Home to a thriving arts community, the city of Pawtucket is delighted to present this first-time major exhibition by an internationally-acclaimed sculptor and resident, says Mayor Donald R. Grebien. "As a city committed to art, design, and innovation, we are delighted to be able to share the work of such an important artist. Bridging cultures, aesthetic worlds and ideas, Mihail's work is both visually stunning and deeply rooted in history. He is remarkable for his continued innovation and relevance in contemporary art," says the mayor.

"As we celebrate the arts in the city of Pawtucket throughout September, we are honored to have Pawtucket resident Mihail showcase his visionary artwork at a major exhibit in the City Hall Art Gallery," states Miram Plitt, chair of the city's Arts and Culture Commission. "We invite anyone with an interest in art and those who rally to protect the world's wildlife to attend our opening reception to celebrate the lifetime creativity and vision of Mihail, whose extraordinary works of art can be seen at the United Nations," says Plitt.

Cast the Sleeping Elephant

Although the 90-year-old Pawtucket resident has practicing his craft for more than 75 years, with major public monuments in Bulgaria and Tunisia, he is best known for his life-size bull elephant bronze sculpture at the United Nations (UN).

In 1980, after several years of planning and work on a breakthrough idea, Mihail travelled to Kenya where, with the help of the country's Ministry of Wildlife, he took a cast of a live bull elephant in the wild. The elephant survived the 72-minute process completely unharmed. From that live cast, Mihail created the "Cast the Sleeping Elephant" bronze, an over-life-size sculpture. The sculpture was officially inaugurated by Secretary General Kofi Annan and installed at the United Nation's headquarters in New York City in 1998, where it continues to serve as a symbol of man's dedication to preserving all living creatures.

Mihail says his bronze elephant is a symbol of the importance of protecting all wildlife and it is aptly placed at the United Nations, the home of all nations.

The Travels of Mihail

Mihail was born in Bulgaria in 1929, where for seven years he studied philosophy and majored in monumental sculpture at the Academy of Fine Arts in Sofia. When one of his commissioned monuments provoked the wrath of Bulgaria's communist government, Mihail went into exile in Tunisia. In Tunis, enchanted by an exuberance of Mediterranean colors and intense light, the artist embarked on a new aesthetic.

After several years in Tunis, where many of his large-scale monuments continue to stand, Mihail and his wife, Lily, emigrated to the United States in the early 1970s, settling in a loft in New York City. Mihail was granted entry because of his status as an "exceptional artist."

For more than 10 years, Mihail also worked out of a boathouse art studio in Lloyd Harbor, where he was an artist in residence at Friends College, later relocating to Millbrook, New York, and then to Orient, on Long Island. Mihail and Lily raised their daughter, Iana, a filmmaker, who lives in San Francisco with her cinematographer husband.

In 2003, Mihail was looking for a new home and location for his art studio. An article in the travel section of the *New York Times*—picked up at random in an empty train car—that featured the historic Pawtucket mills prompted him to write a letter to Mayor James E. Doyle. Mihail thought he might like to move there. Three days after writing this letter he was contacted by Herb Weiss, the city's economic and cultural affairs officer. Two years later he would become a Pawtucket resident with Lily, living in one of the city's mills.

Extraordinary Impact on Contemporary Art

According to Iana Simeonov, Mihail's daughter and a former art dealer and critic, the Pawtucket exhibition showcases several distinct but related bodies of Mihail's work in a range of media, including bronze, painting, and drawing. The works illustrate how the 90-year-old artist continues to evolve artistically, elaborating on themes which have compelled and fascinated him since the 1960s.

"Mihail's 75 years as artist have not only been prolific, but extraordinary in terms of their contribution to the history and vitality of contemporary art," adds Simeonov. "Mihail's work has been the subject of dozens of solo exhibitions from New York to Chicago, Stockholm, Basel, Geneva to Milan.

"Mihail's work is held in over 100 private and museum collections around the world, and his large-scale public monuments continue to stand in public squares and prominent spaces in the US, Europe, and Africa. His artistic legacy and personal story are uniquely compelling, and at age 90 he continues to innovate with materials and is as freshly obsessed with making art as the day he entered the academy," she adds.

Mihail has not looked back since he relocated to his Pawtucket mill. "I like Pawtucket for its history and old charm, and it's only minutes away from Providence," he says, noting that his artwork now reflects the industrial character of the city.

Mihail acknowledges that he has never had an exhibition at city hall. "It's highly unusual," he says, admitting that he feels "grateful and happy."

RON ST. PIERRE BACK ON-AIR: "RON & JEN'S GREAT ESCAPE" POSITIVE PODCAST

Published in RINewsToday on April 23, 2021

One might say his career has come full circle from its early beginnings on a small radio station in Woonsocket, to programming and performing on-air at popular Rhode Island radio stations, to serving as a sports anchor on television. A familiar morning voice to many listeners, this "seasoned pro" was heard on the local airwaves for years in various capacities—but this past December that sound went silent. But a new venture is about to launch to bring Ron's voice—and that of Jen Brien—back to listeners.

The new podcast will be called "Ron and Jen's Great Escape," and it is set to launch on Monday, May 3. You can listen live on Facebook and wherever you get your podcast.

Reflecting on his time in the past "pandemic" year, St. Pierre reflects on how he had to move his radio show on WHJJ into his home, affectionately called "Chez St. Pierre," with his yellow Lab, Hazel, nearby. He would share the daily news and local happenings often flavored with some Rhode Island humor or memories, which made his style unique and comforting, subtly (or sometimes not so subtly), reminding us of days gone by. But on December 31, 2020, St. Pierre's radio contract ended, and i-Heart Broadcasting chose not to renew.

After decades spent in the radio and television business, this seasoned pro knew this was an all-too-familiar story in the field. He used the time to think about his next steps and new mountains to climb, and set his sight on hosting a podcast. St. Pierre understood that with time being a valuable commodity and people becoming busier, podcasts are becoming extremely popular. Audio content, like radio, allowed the listener to multitask.

Brandastic, a media marketing company, estimates that since 2005, more than 700,000 podcasts have been created, with more than 30 million episodes of content—most of them for free. They say about 24 percent of the US population has listened to a podcast, with more than 155 million people listening to a podcast every week.

St. Pierre says about the impact of podcasts, "AdAge.com says that podcasts are able to engage listeners in a way that traditional media can't. When podcasters speak in a listener's ear, it feels as if they're being spoken to more directly," he said.

St. Pierre will host the newly created podcast with Woonsocket native and long-time good friend Jen Brien, who has co-hosted shows with him on both WPRO and WHJJ. Brien brings years of talk-show hosting to the new podcast. She has hosted talk shows on WRKO and WBZ in Boston and Cape Cod's WXTK.

"Our goal is to provide an escape from the negativity that can overtake conversation about the day's hot topics...an escape from the banal repetition all too often associated with talk radio. Our goal is a positive approach to news and lifestyle topics with an infusion of humor across the board," says St. Pierre.

Hosting a podcast will give St. Pierre greater flexibility with his time and give him more freedom and creativity, he says, noting that "podcasters are by far, the most loyal and engaged audience of any medium out there."

More Than Four Decades of Achievements for St. Pierre

After 43 years in the radio business, St. Pierre, who grew up in the Darlington area of Pawtucket, has been a long-time fixture in the Rhode Island broadcast community.

One of his proudest professional achievements was being inducted into the Rhode Island Radio and Television Hall of Fame in 2010.

In 2017, St. Pierre's hometown embraced his broadcasting accomplishments by inducting him into the Pawtucket Hall of Fame at the Pawtucket Armory Arts Center. This award was given to him for going "above and beyond" in his achievements as the Pawtucket Hall of Fame Committee recognized his outstanding contributions and by "shining a positive light on the community."

Radio started early for St. Pierre, beginning while a student at Rhode Island College, where he learned the ropes of TV production as a weekend cameraman for WJAR-TV-10 in Providence. In 1977, he began his radio career at

WNRI in Woonsocket. His first major position was as program director for 920 WHJJ-AM from 1982 to 1988, now known as NewsRadio 920. He was also part of "The WHJJ Morning Show" at that time, eventually serving as program director for both 920 WHJJ-AM and its sister station, 94 HJY-FM, during the last year of this tenure.

During his time at WHJJ, St. Pierre literally helped revolutionize talk radio in Rhode Island in terms of listenership and ratings. He recruited then-Mayor Vincent "Buddy" Cianci for his first stint as a talk-show host at this time, while working with other local radio stalwarts such as Sherm Strickhouser and Steve Kass. His unassuming, authentic style and natural quick wit were enjoyed daily by tens of thousands of radio listeners in Rhode Island and neighboring Southeastern New England.

In 1988, Cap Cities/ABC hired St. Pierre to "flip" 630 WPRO from a music station to a Newstalk format and take on WHJJ. WPRO passed WHJJ in the Newstalk radio war in less than a year. St. Pierre eventually rose from program director to president and general manager.

In his "spare" time, St. Pierre served as a weekend sports anchor for WPRI-TV-12. During the early and mid-1990s, he managed several stations in Providence before taking a series of management positions in West Palm Beach and the legendary WABC in New York City. He returned to Rhode Island radio in 1997.

He had a highly successful on-air and program-management tenure at WPRO 630-AM, enabling the station to rise to the apex of listenership and ratings in our state's highly competitive radio market. The station's hosts at that time included the legendary Salty Brine, along with the return of Buddy Cianci to the airwaves—with whom he co-hosted a highly successful afternoon drive-time show.

Memories from St. Raphael Academy

Anyone who knew St. Pierre during the days he attended Pawtucket-based Saint Raphael Academy were sure he would end up in the broadcasting business. With his personality, wit, and intelligence, his peers believed he would most likely end up in front of a microphone.

"In his high-school yearbook profile at St. Raphael Academy in 1973, Ron said his life's goal was to become a sportscaster. So that career in the broadcast was always in his mind, but he opened it up a lot wider than any of us could have imagined," says Ron Fournier, an advertising copywriter, who has known St. Pierre for more than 40 years. "Ron is a virtual encyclopedia of comedy who has studied all the greats—from the Marx Brothers to the present day," Fournier added. "That's where his quick wit comes from. On the air, you never know what kind of quip or one-liner is coming next. But you know it'll be a classic in his trademark, tongue-in-cheek style of humor."

St. Pierre lives in East Greenwich with his wife, Patti, and their dog, Hazel.

LONGTIME FANS LOOKING FORWARD TO RIMHOF INDUCTION CEREMONIES

Published in *Woonsocket Call* on April 23, 2017

With extreme regularity, Pawtucket West High School student Steve Cohen arrived every Monday and Tuesday night at Lupo's Heartbreak Hotel in Providence just like clockwork to listen to his two favorite Rhode Island bands, Rizzz and the Wild Turkey Band. Next Sunday, Cohen and hundreds of other people will gather at the Hope Artiste Village mill complex to see Rizzz, Wild Turkey (renamed to Hometown Rockers), and eight other inductees be brought into the Rhode Island Music Hall of Fame's Class of 2017.

The Pawtucket-based RIMHOF, formed in 2011, is a nonprofit organization dedicated to celebrating, honoring, and preserving the musical legacy of Rhode Island musicians, educators, and industry professionals who have made significant contributions to both the national and Ocean State music scene.

Looking Back at More Than Forty Years of Musical Memories

Cohen, 63, who considers himself a music aficionado, remembers going to long-gone Rhode Island music hangouts like The Act, January's, The Edge, and Gulliver's to catch a set or two of Rizzz and the Wild Turkey Band/Hometown Rockers. The native Pawtucket resident says that his love for music began at age 16 and continues to this day.

"I know every original song played by Rizzz and Wild Turkey Band by heart," claims Cohen.

Rick Bellaire, 62, vice chair of RIMHOF, has memories of how Rizzz helped change the course of his musical career. "When I was in my freshman year at Rhode Island College, I was playing in a hard rock cover band to pay my way through school. It was very successful, but I didn't like the music," says

Bellaire. After watching the original six-piece lineup of Rizzz play a song by The Band followed by an original to a packed house at Gulliver's in Smithfield, he said to himself, "Now that's what I want to do."

Bellaire gave notice to his hard rock band the next day and never looked back. "You'll find dozens of musicians in southern New England whose experiences with Rizzz, Wild Turkey and Hometown Rockers were similar," he says.

After the Rizzz and the Wild Turkey Band/Hometown Rockers officially broke up, over the years Cohen and Bellaire regularly attended these bands' reunions. Being by the stage at these reunion shows brought a flood of memories from more than 40 years earlier to Cohen from the days he followed the two local bands as a high school and later a college student.

Cohen is adamant that Rizzz and the Wild Turkey Band/Hometown Rockers were great bands in the '70s and '80s. After attending their recent reunions he says these bands have not lost their "mojo."

Reunions are always special occasions, like anniversaries and fundraisers, and they are never disappointing to Bellaire. "As good as they ever were. So not 'better,' but just as great. Rizzz still has all 10 members from the various lineups—how could it not be great!

"It's the same with Wild Turkey/Hometown Rockers. Although they've lost some important original members—Pat Davis, Paul Gaudette, Kevin Falvey—they always have top-notch players who are also fans sitting in for those guys and they feature the principal frontmen from each configuration, John Baldaia and Tom Keegan. When they get together, it's always incredible," Bellaire says.

With the establishment of the Rhode Island Music Hall of Fame six years ago, through the efforts of Bellaire and others, Rizzz and the Wild Turkey Band/Hometown Rockers and eight other inductees—Artie Cabral, Phil Greene, Dan Moretti, Neutral Nation, Billy Osborne, Plan 9, Frank Potenza, and Throwing Muses—will be inducted in 2017.

Musicians Get Long-Awaited Recognition

"The Music Hall of Fame initiative," says Rick Bellaire, "provides a great opportunity to not only acknowledge Rhode Island's musical greats and celebrate their achievements, but to finally have an organization whose primary goal is to promote and preserve their music and stories. We have in place the tools to curate and showcase the best of Rhode Island's musical artistry."

Adds Robert Billington, chair of RIMHOF, "The Hall of Fame induction ceremony and concerts have become the place to be and be seen at as we continue to showcase the fascinating history of Rhode Island's musical heroes. The events are a virtual 'who's who' of Rhode Island music history."

With 10 inductees in RIMHOF's Class of 2017, organizers split this year's celebration into three separate events, with the jazz and R&B inductions taking place last Sunday at the Greenwich Odeum. There will be two more induction concerts held at The Met next weekend. On Saturday, April 29, at 8:00 p.m., the 2017 RIMHOF Rock Induction Concert—Part I will feature performances by Plan 9, Neutral Nation, and Kristin Hersh, David Narcizo, and Fred Abong of Throwing Muses.

On Sunday, April 30, the unveiling of all 10 RIMHOF Class of 2017 inductee exhibits will take place at 2:00 p.m. at the Pawtucket-based Hope Artiste Village, 999 Main Street, followed by the 2017 RIMHOF Rock Induction Concert – Part II featuring Rizzz, Phil Greene, and the Wild Turkey Band/Hometown Rockers, beginning at 3:00 p.m.

Since its initial induction six years ago, a total of 53 inductee exhibits were produced. Eventually, the Pawtucket museum will hold more than 100 displays as well as assorted Rhode Island musical history memorabilia and interactive components for visitors to enjoy.

ABATE JOINS EXCLUSIVE CLASS OF MUSICIANS

Published in the *Woonsocket Call* on February 28, 2016

S ometimes a simple happenstance can propel a person into life's mission. This happened to nine-year-old Greg Abate, when his mother, Elvira, rented a clarinet from a traveling salesman who just by chance came by their Woonsocket home. A rented instrument led to the youngster joining his school band, where he began playing clarinet and alto sax.

Abate has come a long way from his first music recital to his elementary school classmates. More than 27 years of playing in jazz festivals, jazz societies, and jazz clubs, even being tutored by some of the greatest jazz players, has pushed him to the top of his craft.

Now, in recognition of Abate's long musical career and being a driving force in the world of jazz, in April the Rhode Islander will be among the eight new inductees who are brought into the Rhode Island Music Hall of Fame (RIMHOF). His fellow inductees include: Frankie Carle, Bill Harley, Carl Henry, Carol Sloane, Sugar Ray & The Bluetones, Richard Walton, and The Fabulous Motels/The Young Adults/Rudy Cheeks.

According to Rick Bellaire, Rhode Island Music Hall of Fame (RIMHOF)'s vice chair and archive director, "Greg Abate is one of our state's most popular and successful musicians. He has been well-known in southern New England for 40 years and has been a star on the international stage for the past 30. At the beginning, the board wanted to establish credibility by adhering to chronology and inducting historical figures first in many categories. With the inductions of Bobby Hackett, Dave McKenna, Paul Gonsalves, George Wein, and George Masso, this year's jazz inductions of Frankie Carle, Carol Sloane, and Greg establish an unbroken line which not only stretches all the way from the 1930s to the present, but clearly illustrates Rhode Island's truly important place in jazz history."

Bellaire adds, "Greg is universally recognized as one of the finest players performing and recording today. His massive body of work and international touring history clearly place him on the list of all-time greats." Here's a good example. Greg's new album, Kindred Spirits, recorded with legendary alto saxophonist Phil Woods, has just been released. Although the late Mr. Woods had been recording since the 1940s, Greg has clearly leveled the playing field. In a review of the album for the All About Jazz website, Edward Blanco declared, "...both masters are at their best."

Before he died last September, Phil Woods, considered one of the best alto saxophone players, said, "I sleep a lot better knowing that there are alto players like Greg. It was a joy to make music with him, and he writes good songs that are challenging."

Playing With the Greatest

Upon finishing a four-year program at Berklee College of Music, Abate joined the Los Angeles jazz scene, playing with the David Clark Expedition and other local rhythm and blues groups. An audition led to his first high-profile gig, playing lead alto for the Ray Charles Orchestra from 1973 to 1974. He would record his first record with this group.

Abate came back to the Ocean State in 1976 to launch his career, forming the fusion band Channel One, ultimately releasing his first album, Without Boundaries, in 1981. Playing throughout Connecticut to New York for seven years brought attention to this group and made it a favorite of many New Englanders.

At that time, "I wrote lots of music and did a lot of hard, serious playing," he remembers. The young musician took an opportunity to play tenor sax with the revived Artie Shaw Orchestra under the leadership of Dick Johnson from 1986 to '87. For the next two years he would play with the Providence-based Duke Belaire Jazz Orchestra, honing his musical skills. "I received some of my greatest musical education from some of the greatest players from this band," he says.

Working and learning from the greatest, Abate would begin a solo career showcasing his unique style, bringing him worldwide notice.

Today, Abate, a 66-year-old Coventry resident, is internationally acclaimed for his mastery of jazz. He says, "Music found me, I did not find it." Over his musical career, the jazz saxophonist, flutist, composer, and educator has released 18 recordings.

Last year, Abate traveled more than 200 days playing in jazz festivals, jazz societies, and jazz clubs. He has performed in 30 countries, playing in every state in the nation, except Montana, Alaska, and Oregon.

Looking back at his career, Abate says, "The tradition of jazz is very important to me and I take it very seriously. Jazz is just in my blood."

RIMHOF's Fifth Class of Inductees

Robert Billington, chair of the RIMHOF noted, "This year's class of inductees is especially amazing due to the variety of music styles and musical periods that we are recognizing. The thousand Saturday nights that these musicians spent on the road throughout their careers will be recognized this April as their colleagues throughout Rhode Island stand to applaud their success."

"The Music Hall of Fame initiative," says Rick Bellaire, vice chair of RIMHOF, "provides a great opportunity to not only acknowledge Rhode Island's musical greats and celebrate their achievements, but to finally have an organization whose primary goal is to promote and preserve Rhode Island's rich musical heritage in all its forms. With actual exhibit space, coupled with our planned online digital archive, we will have in place the tools to curate and showcase the best of Rhode Island's musical artists."

11. RELATIONSHIPS

"Relish love in our old age! Aged love is like aged wine; it becomes more satisfying, more refreshing, more valuable, more appreciated, and more intoxicating."

—Leo Buscaglia

NEVER FORGETTING WILL HELP US KEEP THE PROMISE OF "NEVER AGAIN"

Published in RINewsToday on February 1, 2021

D uring a pro-Trump rally, as thousands of rioters swarmed the US Capitol on January 6, Robert Keith Packer, sporting an unkempt beard, came wearing a black hoodie sweatshirt emblazoned with the phrase "Camp Auschwitz," in white letters, the name of the most infamous of the many Nazi concentration camps where 1.1 million people were murdered during World War II. Under a skull and bones at the bottom of his shirt was the phrase, "Work brings Freedom," a loose translation of the phrase "Arbeit macht frei" that was inscribed above the main entrance gate at Auschwitz and other concentration camps' gates.

The 56-year-old former welder and pipefitter's image was circulated widely on social media and by newspapers, evoking shock and disbelief.

Packer, a resident of Newport News, Virginia, was not the only anti-Semitic rioter that day, according to a report released by the Miller Center for Community Protection and Resilience at Rutgers University-New Brunswick and the Network Contagion Research Institute. The report identified at least a half-dozen neo-Nazi or white supremacist groups involved in the failed Capitol insurrection who had also attended President Donald Trump's "Save America" rally speech.

In 2017, the *Providence Journal* reported that the New England chapter of the Anti-Defamation League recorded 13 incidents of anti-Semitism in Rhode Island. Nazi swastikas were painted on a Providence building, at Broad Rock Middle School in North Kingstown, and even at a Pawtucket synagogue.

Anti-Semitism is Nothing New

But anti-Semitism, exhibited at the "Save America" rally, has been in our country since its founding, and in fact, has been around Western societies for centuries. More than three years ago, torch marchers, some wearing Nazi-style helmets, carrying clubs, sticks, and round makeshift shields emblazoned with swastikas and other fascist symbols, and others entered the one-block square in downtown Charlottesville, Virginia, to protect a controversial Confederate monument, chanting "Jews will not replace us" and "Blood and Soil" (a Nazi rallying cry).

The Anti-Defamation League's (ADL) 2014 Global Index of Anti-Semitism documented world-wide anti-Semitism. The survey found that more than 1 billion people—nearly one in eight—around the world harbor anti-Semitic attitudes. Carried out by First International Resources and commissioned by the ADL, this landmark survey included 53,100 adults in 102 countries, representing 88 percent of the world's adult population.

More than 30 percent of those surveyed said it was "probably true" that Jews have too much control over financial markets, that Jews think they are better than other people, that Jews are disloyal to their country, and that people hate Jews because of the way that Jews behave.

Most troubling, the ADL study found a large gap between seniors who know and lived through the horrendous events of World War II, and younger adults who, some 75 years after the Holocaust, are more likely to have heard of or learned that six million Jews were exterminated by the Nazis' "Final Solution." Nearly half of those surveyed claim to have never heard of the Holocaust and only a third believe historical accounts are accurate.

Gearing Up to Fight Anti-Semitism

On January 14, the American Jewish Congress (AJC), a global Jewish advocacy organization, briefed the FBI on the continuing threats of anti-Semitism to the nation.

"Anti-Semitism fundamentally is not only a Jewish problem; it is a societal one. It is a reflection on the declining health of our society," Holly Huffnagle, AJC's US director for Combating Anti-Semitism, told FBI officials on a video conference briefing. "Education is essential to clarify what constitutes anti-Semitism, the various sources of this hatred, and what effective tools are available for law enforcement to fight anti-Semitism," she said.

The presentation of AJC's second annual report on anti-Semitism in the US took place in the wake of the January 6 assault on Capitol Hill, where anti-Semitic images and threats were openly conveyed by some of the rioters.

AJC's 2020 report, based on parallel surveys of the American Jewish and general populations, revealed that 88 percent of Jews considered anti-Semitism a problem today in the US, 37 percent had personally been victims of anti-Semitism over the past five years, and 31 percent had taken measures to conceal their Jewishness in public.

In the first-ever survey of the general US population on anti-Semitism, AJC found a stunning lack of awareness of it. Nearly half of all Americans said they had either never heard the term "anti-Semitism" (21 percent) or are familiar with the word but not sure what it means (25 percent).

The AJC experts praised the FBI for its annual Hate Crimes Statistics report, which provides vital data on anti-Semitism. The latest report found 60.2 percent of religious bias hate crimes targeted Jews in 2019. But the report historically has not provided a full picture of the extent of hate crimes, since reporting by local law enforcement agencies is not mandatory.

To improve the monitoring and reporting of hate crimes, AJC continues to advocate for passage of the Jabara-Heyer National Opposition to Hate, Assaults, and Threats to Equality (NO HATE) Act. This measure will incentivize state and local law enforcement authorities to improve hate crime reporting by making grants available, managed through the Department of Justice.

In addition, AJC is asking the FBI to use the International Holocaust Remembrance Alliance's (IHRA) working definition of anti-Semitism as an educational tool. The definition offers a clear and comprehensive description of anti-Semitism in its various forms, including hatred and discrimination against Jews and Holocaust denial.

FBI officials in the Bureau's Civil Rights Unit, Intelligence Division, and Community Outreach Program, among others, participated in the AJC briefing.

Keeping the memory alive about the Holocaust is key to fighting anti-Semitism, says Andy Hollinger, director of communications for the United States Holocaust Memorial Museum (USHMM). "We are seeing a disturbing trend in the rise of anti-Semitism and the open display of neo-Nazi symbols, most recently at the attack on the US Capitol. This is a long-time problem requiring a long-time solution. We must remember. Education is key. We must learn from this history—learn about the dangers of unchecked hatred and anti-Semitism. And we must not be silent," he says.

Bill Benson, who has interviewed Holocaust survivors before live audiences at the USHMM's *First Person* program for more than two decades, observes that the majority of those visiting the museum are not Jewish and many have little familiarity with the Holocaust, and as a result of their visit are profoundly affected by their experience. "The USHMM provides an extraordinary avenue for educating the general public about the Holocaust and anti-Semitism for those millions who visit it, but it is essential that many millions more learn the truth about anti-Semitism and that must be done through our educational systems," he notes.

"The USHMM does an incredible job of educating and assisting teachers who want to teach about the Holocaust, but far too many school systems do not teach about the Holocaust, without which the gulf in knowledge and awareness may only grow as we lose that firsthand knowledge of the Holocaust," says Benson.

A 2009 report, *Jewish Survivors of the Holocaust Residing in the United States Estimates & Projections: 2010 – 2030*, prepared by the Berman Institute-North American Jewish DataBank for the Conference on Jewish Material Claims Against Germany, estimated that 36,800 Holocaust survivors would still be living by 2025. As the number of survivors who witnessed the horrors of genocide and the Holocaust during World War II continues to dwindle, a growing number of states, including Alabama, Florida, Georgia, Illinois, New Jersey, Ohio, and Texas, have established commissions to keep this knowledge alive to Millennials, Gen Z, and younger generations through educational programming. The commissions raise awareness through public education and community events to provide appropriate memorialization of the Holocaust on a regular basis throughout their respective states.

If the Rhode Island General Assembly legislates the establishment of a Rhode Island Genocide and Holocaust Education Commission, its motto might just be, "*Never forgetting* will help us keep the promise of '*never again*'."

ON TAKING A STAND AGAINST RACISM AND ANTI-SEMITISM

Published in the *Woonsocket Call* on August 27, 2017

Morris Nathanson, an 89-year-old who served in the United States Navy in World War II, was outraged at President Donald Trump's failure to strongly speak out against the hateful philosophy of neo-Nazis, white nationalists, Ku Klux Klan (KKK) and militia groups exhibited at a violent protest that escalated out of control in the streets around the University of Virginia campus in Charlottesville, Virginia.

Growing up Jewish, Nathanson is horrified about the growing racism and anti-Semitism so visibly flaunted at the Charlottesville rally and seen throughout the nation. Before the Second World War, his parents had escaped the violent pogroms in Russia, ultimately settling in a three-decker house with relatives in Pawtucket. Family members who remained in Europe were killed, victims of the Holocaust, he said.

"It's indefensible," says Nathanson, an Eastside resident who is an internationally acclaimed artist and semi-retired restaurant designer, for Trump not to outright denounce the neo-Nazi groups. He warns, "We must recognize the growth of the neo-Nazi movement for what it is, a terrible disease that must be eliminated."

The jarring historical imagery of the torchlight procession of supporters of Adolf Hitler moving through the Wilhelmstrasse in Berlin on the evening of January 30, 1933, came to life for Nathanson and millions of Americans last weekend when hundreds of neo-Nazis, white nationalists, KKK, militia members, and other right-wing groups gathered for a "Unite the Right" rally in Charlottesville, Virginia. Carrying tiki torches, flags with swastikas, and Confederate flags, they came to the city's Emancipation Park to ostensibly support a protest against the removal of a statue of Civil War Confederate General Robert E. Lee. But it was really an opportunity to display their strength.

Battle Lines Drawn

On the evening of Friday, August 11 at 10:00 p.m., the torch-bearing marchers, some wearing Nazi-style helmets, carrying clubs, sticks, and round makeshift shields emblazoned with swastikas and other fascist symbols, and others entered the one-block square in downtown Charlottesville, the site of the controversial monument, chanting "Jews will not replace us," "Blood and Soil" (a Nazi rallying cry), "White Lives Matter," along with homophobic, racist, and misogynistic slurs. Heavily armed militia members, carrying semi-automatic weapons and dressed in camouflage military fatigues, came to support and embolden their fellow extremist groups that identify as the "alt-right."

At the site of the controversial monument in the city's park and surrounding streets, throughout Friday evening and Saturday, August 12, members of alt-right groups opposed counter-protestors, including Antifa, a far-left militant political movement that opposes fascist groups; members of Black Lives Matter; church groups; and others who oppose racial bigotry and anti-Semitism. During the weekend rally, it was reported that 15 people were injured. On Saturday, James Alex Fields, Jr., a 20-year-old, drove his gray Dodge Challenger into a group of counter-protesters, killing 32-year-old Heather Heyer and injuring 19 other counter-protesters.

Two Virginia State Police officers, monitoring the protests, died when their helicopter crashed.

Immediately following the rally on Saturday and the death of Heyer, Trump went to Twitter and posted an open-ended statement, calling the nation to "condemn all that hate stands for."

Following this tweet, on Sunday, August 13, he issued a statement at his golf club in Bedford New Jersey, stating, "We condemn in the strongest possible terms this egregious display of hatred, bigotry, and violence on many sides."

Trump Vacillates on Who's To Blame

On Monday, August 14, intense political pressure would force Trump to make a statement at the White House to strongly condemn KKK and neo-Nazi groups after he blamed the violence at Charlottesville, Virginia, two days earlier in a tweet on "many sides."

By Tuesday, August 15, Trump had backed off his public scolding of America's hate groups. At an impromptu press conference held at Trump Tower, he cast blame for Charlottesville's violence equally on the "alt-right" and "alt-left" counter-protesters. "You had a group on one side that was bad, and you had a group on the other side that was also very violent," Trump said, noting that, "Nobody wants to say that, but I say it.

"Not all of those people were neo-Nazis and white supremacists, believe me," says the president, noting that some protestors wanted to stop the removal of the Robert E. Lee statue. Some were "nice people," he stated.

"So this week, it's Robert E. Lee. I noticed that Stonewall Jackson's coming down. I wonder, is it George Washington next week? And is it Thomas Jefferson the week after? You know, you really do have to ask yourself, where does it stop?" said Trump.

Trump's comments that not all rally marchers were neo-Nazis or white supremacists caused a political tsunami, with critics pointing out that these individuals marching with the neo-Nazis were not "nice people." It was guilt by association.

The two former Bush presidents joined world leaders, GOP and Democratic senators, governors, rank-and-file members of both parties; and Fortune 500 executives to chastise Trump for his failure to speak out against Nazi and white supremacist ideology, declaring that his comments trivialized the anti-Semitism and racism of these extremist alt-right groups.

Even the members of the Joint Chiefs of Staff, the senior uniformed military leaders in the United States Department of Defense who advise the president, posted tweets denouncing the alt-right extremists and blaming them for Saturday's bloody violence in Charlottesville.

However, white supremacists took Trump's Charlottesville statements as an endorsement to their legitimacy and acceptance to allow their members to become more visible in society. David Duke, a white nationalist and former Imperial Wizard of the KKK, tweeted, "Thank You Mr. President Trump; God Bless You for setting the record straight for All Americans." The Daily Stormer, a neo-Nazi website, quickly called Trump's statements on blaming both sides a sign that he implicitly supported their goals and objectives.

The Increasing Visibility of Racism and Anti-Semitism

Ray Rickman, 65, executive director of the nonprofit Stages of Freedom, says, "I am deeply worried about the piercing images of men marching with Nazi torchlights on the University of Virginia campus. These men were screaming, 'Jews won't replace us.' It was Nazi Germany all over again. The idea of seeing a Nazi flag, the most vicious symbol of anti-Semitism on American soil, is almost unbelievable to me. All of this is followed by the deeply divisive comments from Mr. Trump," says the long-time Rhode Island activist.

"This man in the White House has shown total disrespect for the millions of American soldiers both living and dead who died to save the world from the Nazis," adds Rickman, noting that, "It's the first time since Woodrow Wilson that a president has refused to condemn racism after such an act of violence."

Rickman says that the neo-Nazi groups used the Charlottesville gathering as a public show of force and to promote hatred. "Maintaining the Robert E. Lee monument was just an excuse to attack Jews and Blacks," he says, noting that the three-day protest was planned as a "hateful rally by people who hate people of color and Jews. It is as simple as that."

One of the most interesting aspects of beliefs held by General Lee was that he was not in favor of raising Confederate monuments, says Rickman, noting that in 1869 he wrote that it would be wiser "not to keep open the sores of war but to follow those nations who endeavored to obliterate the mark of civil strife."

Combating Intolerance and Hatred

While both GOP and Democrat lawmakers lambasted Trump's choice of words for laying the blame of violence at the Charlottesville rally on both the far right demonstrators and counter-protesters, there were some who remained silent or defended his comments, saying his words were adequate.

With the increased public visibility of the neo-Nazis, white supremacist, and other hate groups, if Trump fails to use his national bully pulpit and the moral authority of the office of the presidency to steadfastly condemn hate groups, national and state elected officials and Americans from all walks of life must take on this responsibility.

In response to the violent weekend in Charlottesville, the Illinois Senate adopted a resolution, sponsored by Senator Don Harmon, (D-Oak Park), urging law officials to recognize white nationalists and neo-Nazi groups as terrorist organizations.

Nathanson, who in 1965 marched with Martin Luther King in Selma, Alabama to fight racism, calls for organizing rallies at the state and national level to "reduce the damage of Trump's comments."

It would be an appropriate time to remember the speech given by Martin Niemoller, a German Lutheran minister who opposed the Nazis and was sent to several concentration camps. He survived the war and explained:

> First they came for the Jews. I was silent. I was not a Jew.
> Then they came for the Communists. I was silent. I was not a Communist.
> Then they came for the trade unionists. I was silent. I was not a trade unionist.
> Then they came for me. There was no one left to speak for me.

SAVE THE ROSES AND TRY THESE TIPS: SIX WAYS OF IMPROVING COMMUNICATION AT HOME

Published in the *Woonsocket Call* on February 5, 2017

Effective communication at home with your husband, wife, or partner is key to maintaining a meaningful, healthy environment and thriving family. With Valentine's Day fast approaching, author Donna Mac, a well-known corporate trainer, based in South Easton, Massachusetts, with 25 years of experience in the broadcasting industry, translates effective corporate communication into tips for use in enhancing communication with your loved ones.

According to Mac, sexual infidelity, commonly linked to divorce, is not the leading cause for couples separating. The corporate communications expert notes that a recent article in *Psychology Today* says that whether a partner's communication "lifts you up or brings you down" is the single largest predictor of divorce.

So, mastering your communication skills may be the best Valentine's Day gift you can give, much better than a dozen roses. Mac, founder and president of Rehoboth, Massachusetts-based DMacVoice Communications, explains her Six Pillars Of Effective Communication, which can bring healthy energy into an ailing relationship and bring you closer together with your loved one.

Six Pillars of Effective Communication

"The first pillar in becoming a more effective communicator," says Mac, noting this "is tied to 'knowing and owning who you are.' That means your strengths and vulnerabilities. You must be comfortable with who you are and understand that you have a right to communicate what you are thinking and feeling." She cautions us to be careful to always communicate as calmly and respectfully as possible. Don't wait to communicate until emotions build up to the point where that is not possible.

"Also, get a sense for whether you are an extrovert or an introvert." Mac notes that this will influence how you interact with your partner. According to Mac, communication flows more easily for extroverts. Introverts need more time to process before they speak, but they are usually better listeners.

She also cautions against being a passive, or even a passive-aggressive communicator. Both of these styles are non-productive but they are easy to fall into. Often it feels easier to be a passive communicator because being an effective communicator takes courage and work. "These days, it's easy to hide behind our computer screens," she says.

The second Pillar calls for the need to understand your partner. "Understand how your personality and communication style differs from that of your loved one," suggests Mac, who says that there are differences as well as varying points of view in every relationship. "When you disagree, be open to the possibility that either of you may be 'right' or 'wrong' or a bit of both.

"Be open to learning something new. It is also important to make it easy for your partner to share his or her vulnerabilities and ask for your help. Create a safe space for communications by allowing and encouraging your partner to communicate often and to be authentic," she adds.

To use a phrase from her book, you can continue to "understand your audience" over the years by listening intently and often.

Pillar three encourages you to "master the content of the conversation" you are about to have. She stresses the need to be clear on what it is you would like to say, especially if you have to have a challenging conversation.

Mac says, "You may need to practice how you are going to broach an extremely difficult topic. Do your best to speak in a way that is compelling but concise and has the best interest of both of you. Instead of accusing your partner of something, talk about the way that issue has affected you. Remember, they might not know if you don't tell them. Also, try not to ramble. Instead, state your case with clarity and the most positive energy you can muster. If their actions are unacceptable, know where your boundaries lie and clearly and calmly state them."

Put Yourself Into Their Shoes

Pillar four calls for you to "anticipate questions and reactions to conversations." Mac recommends, while you want to make sure you get your point across, ensure that you've taken time to put yourself into your partner's shoes. "Life isn't easy for anyone. But if you take time to think about and anticipate how they may feel or react to your topic you won't be so quick to react emotionally and with harsh words and energy."

By anticipating reaction you will be able to become more proactive in your relationship, she says, noting that, "your partner will appreciate it."

"Remember, effective communication in a trusted relationship takes time, thought, and occasional discomfort," says Mac.

Pillar five suggests that you "speak to serve" in your conversations. "When you 'serve' the person you're speaking with, you are taking time to make sure that the conversation is not 'all about you.' It's for the benefit of you, for them, and for the greater good of the relationship or even the entire family!" says Mac. "When you serve while speaking, you are making sure that understanding is taking place. If you're not sure that it is, you might want to say something like, 'Is this making sense to you?'"

Finally, Pillar six calls for you to "detach from the outcome" of the conversation. "If you follow the first five Pillars of Effective Communication you will be well on your way to becoming a highly effective communicator. But you aren't quite there yet!" states Mac. "It is very important that you don't try to control your partner's reaction.

"Instead of concerning yourself with perfection, remain flexible and detached, knowing that total agreement is never possible. Plus, it's really unimportant. What is important is the health and strength of your relationship and two powerful voices, even if they don't always see eye to eye," she adds.

Don't Try to Change Others, Change Yourself

Mac suggests that if you want to become an effective communicator, don't focus on changing the other person. We have no control over other people, only ourselves. "So work on changing what you can change in your communication style so that you can communicate in compelling and influential ways."

While Mac's Six Pillars of Effective Communication can be directed to couples, look at the recommendations and try replacing "romantic" partner with "business" partner or someone you're collaborating with at work. And replace "the entire family" with "the entire department or company" in Pillar five.

"These communication tips are universal and are the foundation for healthy professional AND personal relationships. They are not easy to integrate into our lives, but the more you use them, the quicker they'll become part of who you are and how you communicate."

Donna Mac is author of *Guide to a Richer Life–Know Your Worth, Find Your Voice, Speak Your Mind* and creator of The Six Pillars of Effective Communication. She is also a keynote speaker and private coach.

To contact Donna Mac, go to:
www.ivoicecommunication.com/donna-rustigian-mac

NEW AARP STUDY TAKES A CLOSE LOOK AT AMERICA'S GRANDPARENTS

Published in the *Woonsocket Call*, April 14, 2019

A ARP's newest research study, highlighting the latest trends, gives us a peek into the world of grandparenting, a role that millions of Americans now take on in their later years. This number has steadily grown, from 56 million in 2001 to a whopping 70 million today.

The youngest grandparent is about 38 years old, with 50 being the average age of becoming a first-time grandparent, notes Brittne Nelson-Kakulla, AARP Research's senior researcher. For those with children, by age 65, 96 percent of Americans are grandparents, she says.

"Today's grandparents are an economic force that cannot be ignored," said Alison Bryant, senior vice president of research, AARP, in an April 8 statement with the release of this 40-page report.

"They are living longer, working longer, shattering stereotypes and supporting their grandchildren in a variety of ways, including financially and culturally. Nearly all grandparents are providing some sort of financial support, helping to ease the costs of raising kids," notes Bryant.

Grandparents Pump Billions into Nation's Economy

According to AARP's study, 70 million grandparents can have a major impact on the nation's economy. Grandparents spend money on their grandchildren, an average of $2,562 annually, this equaling approximately $179 billion dollars per year. Those dollars are spent supporting their grandchildren in a variety of ways, from helping to pay day-to-day expenses (meals, groceries, etc.) allowances, vacations, and school/college tuition costs.

The study found that grandparents have, on average, four to five grandchildren, down from six to seven in 2011. The number of grandparents in the workforce has increased in the past seven years, with 40 percent of grandparents currently employed up from 24 percent in 2011.

Grandparents enjoy the positive aspects of grandparenting such as supporting dreams and sharing roots, history and culture, and experiences, says the AARP study, but they face financial challenges, too. Thirteen percent of grandparents struggle with the financial expectations of being a grandparent, including the cost of education and traveling to see the grandchildren.

Seven percent of grandparents have taken on debt to help their grandchildren pay for college and one in four of those grandparents have even cosigned private student loans for their grandchildren and/or incurred credit card debt that has not yet been paid back in full.

Over the decades, the role of grandparenting has remained consistent, observes the AARP study. Grandchildren continue to refer to grandparents as "grandma" or "grandpa" (70 percent to 60 percent respectively). But 1 in 20 of the grandparent respondents prefer to be called by their first name.

Serving as a Source of Wisdom

Eighty-one percent of the grandparent respondents say they play a key role in their grandchildren's lives. More than half say that they serve as a "moral compass" to the grandchildren on a variety of issues ranging from education to morals and values. But they say that discussing topics on sexuality and politics are way "out of their comfort zone."

Grandparents also see the importance of teaching gender equality and the rise of the strong, independent woman, too, says the AARP study.

Thirty-four percent of the grandparents say they have grandchildren of mixed or difference races or ethnicities. Nearly all of the respondents believe it is important that these grandchildren know about the heritage they share. Seven in ten make an effort to help their grandchildren learn about the heritage they do not share, says Nelson-Kakulla.

Sixty-eight percent say that distance is the biggest obstacle that keeps them from getting enough one-on-one time with their grandchildren. Fifty-two percent of the survey respondents have at least one grandchild who lives more than 200 miles away, while 29 percent live more than 50 miles from the closest grandchild, up from 19 percent in 2011. Like distance, busy full- or part-time work schedules, as well as schedules of their children and grandchildren, keep them from connecting.

Grandparents are turning away from making phone calls to maintain contact with their grandchildren, and toward new technologies like email, Facebook, video chat, and texting to bridge the mileage gap. Forty-seven percent "like" the idea of group texting messages to chat with their grandchildren and 67 percent "like" the idea of using online video chatting to keep in touch.

Finally, 89 percent of the grandparent respondents say their relationship with their grandchildren is good for their well-being and 67 percent believe this role makes them more sociable. Sixty-six percent say having grandchildren makes them more active, too.

AARP's 21-minute online survey of 2,654 grandparents ages 38 and up was conducted between August 20 and September 4, 2018 by Hotspex, Inc.

WOMEN CAPABLE OF CHANGING CORPORATE CULTURE WITH EFFECTIVE COMMUNICATION

Published in the *Woonsocket Call* on March 11, 2018

Effective communication is a major factor for women executives to be successful on the job and for having healthy personal relationships, says author Donna Mac, a well-known corporate communications trainer and keynote speaker. Ms. Mac is based in southeastern Massachusetts, with 30 years of experience in the communications industry.

The corporate communications expert notes that a recent article in *Psychology Today* says that whether a partner's communication "lifts you up or brings you down" is the single largest predictor of divorce. "That one trait can also translate into work too," observes Mac. "Often, a company's greatest talent leaves a job because of miscommunication or a lack of communication and limited trust," she says.

"Our society is changing at an incredible pace, so we often fail to have those vital conversations or to take time to ensure that understanding has taken place. Details fall through the cracks, and we spend more time picking up the pieces than if we had taken a few moments to communicate effectively in the first place," says Mac.

Western Women Will Save The World

In 2012, Mac said, the Dali Lama was quoted as saying, "Western women will save the world." "I agree and disagree," says Mac. "I believe His Holiness saw the importance of bringing softer, more nurturing communication skills into the workplace. It's clear he was talking about the skills that prove to people that you've taken the time to think and care about them," she says.

Mac says, "Empathetic communication skills are more important now than ever. But the workplace also needs employees who have thick skin; professionals who are able to articulate the rules, regulations, and take a firm stand on issues. Those skills," Mac says, "are the kind that will get you noticed by upper management. They come from someone not afraid to do and say the right thing at the right time, even if discomforting," she says.

"I see it all the time. Like when a boss doesn't provide her employees constructive feedback for fear of how that worker will feel," says Mac, noting that when this happens it can be a great disservice to the employee and the organization because you've lost an opportunity for everyone to maximize the potential of the company and its people.

Speaking & Communicating Mindfully

Even with three decades of communication experience under her belt, Mac doesn't lose sight of the fact that she still has more to learn. "I learn new modalities all the time. These days, I'm helping people become more mindful of how they communicate and what they can and cannot control. I've sharpened these skills through some recent mindfulness training. That means shutting down our noisy, overstimulated brains by sitting in silence, noticing our biases, and doing breathing exercises."

"It's amazing," Mac says, "how communicating mindfully helps with the fear of speaking. We fear speaking at the podium and we also fear having challenging conversations. Being more mindful helps you feel more confident as you acquire the tools necessary to communicate.

"We've been taught not to focus on our weaknesses," Mac says, "but if you want to communicate more effectively, it's vital that you know what they are. This way, if you are more reserved, you are not overpowered by colleagues or partners who are more outgoing. If your communication skills are more boisterous, you can learn the virtues of slowing down, judging less and listening better.

"I help people understand people, so they're able to tune in and relate better. Email and texting is not going away but I think everyone knows that our society can be healthier with more human-to-human interaction and less time on our cellphones! We will also have a more balanced society when communicators are able to be kind and to speak with certainty."

Mac suggests that if you want to become a more effective communicator, don't focus on changing others. "When you begin to find your voice after being more introverted, you can actually become more influential pretty quickly. If you've been a very communicative person and begin to ask more questions and listen, those around you will notice.

"It takes time, energy, and effort to become a more effective communicator but the benefits at work and at home are well worth it. Plus, the time for all people to acquire the confidence and ability to speak is long overdue. So, ask yourself," Mac suggests, "are you ready and able to take on the challenge?"

With the #MeToo movement and growing number of incidents of sexual harassment being reported daily, she spends more time looking forward than to the past. "Just about every woman has a story of being or feeling intimidated. And it's a different world now. Thanks to the many women who have come forward, it's a perfect time to learn how to shut down someone who is seeking to take advantage."

Mac says, "I can't help with the current laws of the land or regulations in various businesses. But everyone in the workplace, women and men, need the courage and ability to tell an abuser to stop...to say statements like, 'I find that comment way out of line and I am asking you to stop now,' or, 'Help me understand what you mean by that. I'm sure you realize that I don't stand for any type of intimidation.'

"Give them eye contact and stand in your powerful silence. It's quite effective."

This month we celebrate Women's History Month, to showcase the contribution women have made throughout society. Yes, history can be made in corporate American when women stop apologizing for speaking directly. You can do this while still being kind and respectful. It's like blending traditionally male and female communication traits when you are able to speak using both your brain and your intuition.

Donna Mac is author of *Guide to a Richer Life–Know Your Worth, Find Your Voice & Speak Your Mind*, and creator of The Six Pillars of Effective Communication. She is also a keynote speaker and private coach.

To contact Donna Mac, go to:
www.ivoicecommunication.com/donna-rustigian-mac

YOU ARE NEVER TOO OLD FOR ROMANCE

Published in the *Pawtucket Times*, February 13, 2015

Packing your bags can simply become the first step you take toward rekindling your relationship. Last week, with Valentine's Day fast approaching, Love and Relationships Ambassador Dr. Pepper Schwartz weighed in on a recently released AARP Travel study that reveals that 85 percent of Americans 45-plus have not taken a romantic vacation in the past two years.

For Dr. Schwartz, Ph.D., a sociologist and sexologist teaching at the University of Washington Seattle Washington; an author or co-author of 19 books, magazines, website columns; and a television personality on the subject of sexuality, the findings reveal a need for couples to plan romantic getaways as a way to spend quality time with their partner and bolster their relationship.

Make Time for Love

In a release, Dr. Schwartz, co-author of the newly released book *Places for Passion*, says, "There is every indication that romantic travel really does refresh a couple's relationship, makes them feel more in love, and makes them crave each other's company...And there is also research, which indicates that trying something new is the best bonding mechanism of all."

"I wish we could be as romantic at home as we can on a trip—but there is something about getting away that lets us forget about our daily stuff and instead, fully concentrate on each other," says Dr. Schwartz. "When we stay at home, it's hard not to answer the phone or try and answer one more email—but in fact, we seem to need to get away—to have a new stage setting for romance to bring out the best in us," she adds.

"That of course goes double if you have children at home; even a short getaway without them is a great romantic boost," notes Schwartz.

But, if a vacation can be healthy for your relationship, why are the numbers of those who have taken romantic vacations so low? According to AARP Travel research, people most often cite busy schedules and tight budgets as the primary reasons to not pack their bags, forgoing a needed vacation. However, Dr. Schwartz says that with smart and easy-to-use tools and resources, the perfect romantic vacation can be just as relaxing to plan as it is to enjoy, and affordable too.

Creating New Memories, Igniting Passions

Dr. Schwartz's book, *Places for Passion*, co-written with Dr. Janet Lever, Ph.D., a sociology professor at California State University in Los Angeles, who led teams of researchers who designed three of the largest sex surveys ever tabulated (also coauthoring *Glamour's* Sex and Health column), outlines 75 destinations across the world for couples to explore and create new memories. Because people have such different preferences, Dr. Schwartz and Lever's 416-page book, published in December 2014, identifies romantic destinations in urban areas, around beaches, in places that offer national wonders, or those places for the adventurous.

"However, whether we are recommending Santa Fe, Bali, Zion or Capetown, there are certain romantic 'must-haves' that are specified in the book," says Dr. Schwartz. She also urges aging travelers to avoid "convention hotels" which can ruin a romantic mood. "We don't like bed-and-breakfast inns unless they are built for privacy and still provide private, luxurious bathrooms," adds Dr. Schwartz, noting she and Lever provide the reader with a full listing of hotels, restaurants, and attractions—all geared for romance.

Creating the Mood

Get expert advice to create the romantic mood, says Lever, suggesting that the hotel concierge or manager be approached for interesting ideas or help in creating dinners in unexpected places. "We've heard of people placed at the side of waterfalls, alone in front of the fireplace, or even loaned the balcony in an unused suite," she says, stressing, "You won't know what your options might be if you don't ask."

Lever says, "If you are already on vacation, splurge on a room service dinner. If you're not, look to the future and create an 'I Owe You' for a future travel getaway. Set your date, so it really happens, then enjoy a nice dinner and ponder the choices for your promised vacation."

Book reviewers are raving about *Places for Passion*, too. Dr. Helen Fisher, Ph.D., anthropologist at Rutgers University, says, "Travel is the liquor of romance. Novelty triggers the brain's dopamine system to sustain romantic passion. This surge soon fires up testosterone to tickle your sex drive. And as you hug and kiss, you feel the oxytocin system—ushering in feelings of deep attachment." So Pepper Schwartz and Janet Lever have it right with this charming book. It's full of great ideas on how to keep love alive.

"As for spice, we are the same authors who wrote *The Getaway Guide to the Great Sex Weekend*! It's a much different type of book with a lot of tips for providing more eroticism and sexual playfulness," adds Dr. Schwartz. "But for starters people could make sure they brought sexier clothes to sleep in (or even take off), and maybe rent an erotic movie or read a sexy book. Giving each other a shampoo and head rub in the shower, a foot or hand massage afterwards, also helps heat up the evening," she says.

AARP Travel (**http://www.aarp.org/romantictravel**) includes information about most of those destinations on the website alongside other planning guides, which can be valuable tools for couples looking to enhance their relationship this Valentine's Day weekend.

12. RETIREMENT & LEISURE

"Retirement is not the end of the road. It is the beginning of the open highway."

—Unknown

AARP SAYS AGE DISCRIMINATION ROBS $850 BILLION FROM NATION'S ECONOMY

Published in the *Woonsocket Call* on February 9, 2020

I n 1985, my 71-year-old father was ready to leave his job, looking for greener pastures. After working for Dallas, Texas-based Colbert-Volks for over 33 years as vice president, general merchandise manager, he knew it was time for a job change.

After telling me of his desire to find new employment, I told my father that he would bring more than three decades of experience in the retail sector to a new company along with a vast network he had accumulated. I remember saying, "You would be a great catch." His curt response: "Nobody will hire me at my age."

Thirty-five years after this conversation, AARP released a report charging that age discrimination is still running rampant in America's workplaces and it even negatively impacts the nation's economy, too.

Last month, AARP and the Economist Intelligence Unit released a report, *The Economic Impact of Age Discrimination*, reporting that the age-50-and-over population contributed 40 percent of the US Gross Domestic Product (GDP) in 2018, creating 88.6 million jobs and generating $5.7 trillion in wages and salaries through jobs held directly or indirectly.

But older workers would have contributed a massive $850 billion more to the GDP in 2018 if they could have remained in or re-entered the labor force, switched jobs, or been promoted internally, notes the AARP study.

AARP's new study shows that the elimination of that bias in 2018 would have increased the contribution of the 50-plus cohort to the GDP from $8.3 trillion to $9.2 trillion. It also projects that the potential contribution of the older population could increase by $3.9 trillion in a 'no age bias' economy, which would mean a total contribution of $32.1 trillion to the GDP in 2050.

"This important report shows the cost to the entire economy of discriminating against older workers," said Debra Whitman, AARP's executive vice president and chief public policy officer in a January 30, 2020 statement announcing the release of the 22-page report. "The economy in 2018 could have been 4 percent larger if workers did not face barriers to working longer," says Whitman.

"Studies have shown that older workers are highly engaged, with low turnover, and often serve an important role as mentors," Whitman added. "Their expertise helps businesses and pays big dividends for the economy as a whole. Employers who embrace age diversity will be at an advantage," she says.

House Moves to Combat Age Discrimination

The groundbreaking AARP report comes on the heels of the House of Representative's recent passage of HR 2030, "Protecting Older Workers Against Discrimination Act," to combat age discrimination.

The House chamber's action comes as older workers play an increasingly important role in the workforce. Estimates are that by 2024, 41 million people ages 55 and older will be in the labor force, nearly an 8 percent increase from the current number. In addition, next year the oldest Millennials will start turning 40 and then will be covered by the Age Discrimination in Employment Act (ADEA).

The legislation, passing with a bipartisan vote of 261-155, restores anti-discrimination protections under the ADEA that were weakened by the Supreme Court's 2009 decision in *Gross v. FBL Financial Services, Inc.* The decision changed the burden of proof for workers to be the sole motivating factor for the employer's adverse action, making it much harder for workers to prove age discrimination.

In the Senate, the bipartisan companion legislation (S.485) is sponsored by Senators Chuck Grassley (R-IA) and Bob Casey (D-PA).

"The House vote sends a strong bipartisan message that age bias has to be treated as seriously as other forms of workplace discrimination," said Nancy LeaMond, AARP executive vice president and chief advocacy & engagement officer. "Age discrimination is widespread, but it frequently goes unreported and unaddressed," charges LeaMond.

Thoughts on Age Discrimination

AARP's new report includes survey findings gleaned from a study conducted last July and August, interviewing 5,000 people age 50-plus to identify how they have experienced age discrimination at work or while looking for work.

The researchers analyzed: involuntary retirement due to age bias; age 50-plus workers involuntarily in part-time jobs; missed opportunities for wage growth; lost earnings following involuntary job separation; longer periods of unemployment compared to younger workers; and people age 50 and older who dropped out of the labor force, but want to continue working.

The study's findings indicate that the age-50-and-over labor force has grown by 80 percent since 1998; about 40 percent of workers age 65 and over intend to continue working into their 70s. While 80 percent of employers support employees working into their later years, nearly two-thirds of older workers say they have experienced or seen age discrimination in the workplace.

As to gender, the study's findings note that men who retire between ages 50 and 64 are most likely to feel that they are being forced into retirement because of their age. Older women bear the double burden of age and gender discrimination, say the researchers. Those age 50-64, especially women, experience longer unemployment than other groups.

The study also found that lower-income workers are more likely to feel trapped in their present role as a result of age discrimination.

AARP's report warns that "in order to benefit from age 'inclusion,' employers need not only to recognize age bias, but actually 'actively' stop it; they need to 'bust myths' about older workers, be it that they cost too much or are not tech-savvy; they need to recognize the value that experienced workers bring to the workplace, like their dependability and ability to problem-solve and remain calm under pressure, and they must build and support a multigenerational workforce."

Final Thoughts

We have worked for years to raise awareness of valuing people in the workforce, regardless of age," said AARP Rhode Island State director Kathleen Connell. "This isn't AARP rhetoric. Data repeatedly proves that age discrimination is not only unfair to older workers, but something that also has a negative impact on the economy.

"Employers should take advantage of the best talent available without dismissing equally capable employees at a certain age or by choosing not to hire new workers simply because of their age," Connell added. "Companies with a diverse culture often laud that as a business asset. That philosophy should not exclude older workers. They can bring experience and wisdom into the mix and should be judged only on their performance."

For information on AARP workforce-related resources, go to **https://www. aarp.org/work/employers/**.

For a copy of AARP's report, go to **http://www.aarp.org/content/dam/ aarp/research/surveys_statistics/econ/2020/impact-of-age-discrimination.doi.10.26419-2Fint.00042.003.pdf**.

STUDY: COVID-19 CHANGES WAY AMERICANS THINK ABOUT RETIREMENT

Published in RINewsToday on November 27, 2020

The raging coronavirus pandemic is changing the fundamental way working adults think, plan, and save for their retirement, underscoring the important role Social Security and Medicare play for retirees, according to the *2020 Wells Fargo Retirement Study* conducted by The Harris Poll in August. The annual research report examines the attitudes and savings of working adults, taking a look this year at the impact of the COVID-19 pandemic on retirees.

For those workers whose jobs were negatively impacted by COVID-19 over the last eight months, the Wells Fargo study found that planning for retirement has become even more challenging, with many survey respondents expressing "pessimism" about their life in retirement—or worried if they can even retire.

This year's Harris Poll conducted 4,590 online interviews, from August 3–24, including 2,660 working Americans age 18-76 whose employment was not impacted by COVID-19, 725 Americans age 18-76 whose employment was impacted by the coronavirus pandemic, 200 high-net worth American workers age 18-76, and 1,005 retired Americans, surveying attitudes and behaviors around planning their finances, saving, and investing for retirement.

According to the Wells Fargo study's findings, 58 percent of workers impacted by the pandemic say they now don't know if they have enough savings for retirement because of COVID-19, compared to 37 percent of all workers. Moreover, among workers impacted by the coronavirus, 70 percent say they are worried about running out of money during their retirement while 61 percent say they are much more afraid of life in retirement, and 61 percent note the pandemic took the joy out of looking forward to retirement.

The study, released October 21, found that COVID-19 has driven some workers even further behind in saving for retirement: Working men reported median retirement savings of $120,000, which compares to $60,000 for working women, say the researchers. Yet for those impacted by COVID-19, men report median retirement savings of $60,000, which compares to $21,000 for women.

"With individual investors now largely responsible for saving and funding their own retirement, disruptive events and economic downturns can have an outsized impact on their outlook," said Nate Miles, head of retirement for Wells Fargo Asset Management, in a statement releasing the findings of this study. "Our study shows that even for the most disciplined savers, working Americans are not saving enough for retirement. The good news is that for many of today's workers, there is still time to save and prepare," he says.

Taking a Close Look at Retirement Savings

The Wells Fargo study also found that women and younger generations are falling behind, too. Women are less sure if they will be able to save enough for retirement, and appear to be in a more precarious financial situation than men. The study findings indicate that almost half of working women (51 percent) say they are saving enough for retirement, or that they are confident they will have enough savings to live comfortably in retirement (51 percent). Those impacted by COVID-19 have saved less than half for retirement than men and are much more pessimistic about their financial lives. In addition, women impacted by COVID-19 are less likely to have access to an employer-sponsored retirement savings plan (59 percent), and are less likely to participate (77 percent).

According to the researchers, Generation Z workers (born between 1997 to 2012) started saving at an earlier age and are participating in employer-based savings programs at a greater rate than other generations. They are nonetheless worried about their future. Fifty-two percent of Generation Z workers say they don't know if they'll be able to save enough to retire because of COVID-19, 50 percent say they are much more afraid of life in retirement due to COVID-19, and 52 percent say the pandemic took the joy out of looking forward to retirement.

Remaining Optimistic

"The study found incredible optimism and resiliency among American workers and retirees, which is remarkable in the current [pandemic] environment," said Kim Ta, head of client service and advice for Wells Fargo Advisors. "As an industry, we must help more investors make a plan for their future so that optimism becomes a reality in retirement," she said.

The Wells Fargo study findings showed that despite a challenging economy, many American workers and retirees remain optimistic about their current life, their future. The majority of workers (79 percent) say they are very or somewhat satisfied with their current life, in control of their financial life (79 percent), and are able to pay their monthly bills (95 percent). Eighty-six percent say they are still able to manage their finances.

The study's findings indicate that 69 percent of workers and 73 percent of retirees feel in control and/or happy about their financial situation. Ninety-two percent of the workers and 91 percent of retirees say they can positively affect their financial situation, and 90 percent of workers and 88 percent of retirees say they can positively affect how their debt situation progresses.

The researchers noted that 83 percent of workers say they could pay for a financial emergency of $1,000 without having to borrow money from friends or family. However, the respondents acknowledged they could improve their financial planning. Slightly more than half—54 percent of workers and 50 percent of retirees—say they have a detailed financial plan, and just 27 percent of workers and 29 percent of retirees have a financial advisor.

Social Security and Medicare Key to Retiree's Financial Security

The Wells Fargo study noted that despite an increasing shift to a self-funded retirement, in the midst of the pandemic, nearly all workers and retirees believe that Social Security and Medicare play or will play a significant role in their retirement. According to the study, 71 percent of workers, 81 percent of those negatively impacted by COVID-19, and 85 percent of retirees say that COVID-19 reinforced how important Social Security and Medicare will be for their retirement. Sixty-seven percent of workers say they have no idea what out-of-pocket health-care costs will be in retirement, say the researchers.

The researchers say that workers expect that Social Security will make up approximately one-third of their monthly budget (30 percent median) in retirement. And even those high-net workers believe that Social Security and Medicare factor significantly into their retirement plans, expecting that the retirement program will cover 20 percent (median) of their monthly expenses.

The majority of the study's respondents expressed concerns that the programs will not be available when they need them and worry that the government won't protect them. Specifically, 76 percent of workers are concerned Social Security will be raided to pay government debt, and 72 percent of workers are afraid that Social Security won't be available when they retire.

The Wells Fargo study also found that 90 percent of workers would feel betrayed if the money they paid into Social Security is lost and not available when they retire, and that 45 percent of workers are optimistic that Congress will make changes to secure the future of Social Security.

JENKINS: WORKING SENIORS PRIMING THE NATION'S ECONOMIC ENGINE

Published in the *Woonsocket Call* on December 22, 2019

In recent years, Senate Majority Leader Mitch McConnell of Kentucky, Senator Marco Rubio of Florida, and even former House Speaker Paul Ryan of Wisconsin, have warned that the growing number of seniors is fast becoming an economic drag to the nation's economic growth, citing the spiraling costs of Social Security and Medicare. As the 2020 presidential election looms, GOP candidates are calling for reining in the skyrocketing federal budget deficit by slashing these popular domestic programs.

In 2015, President Donald Trump declared that he would not touch Social Security and Medicare. But now some GOP insiders are saying he may cut these programs during his second term, if he wins.

But after you read the newly released AARP report, *The Longevity Economy Outlook*, you may just want to consider these comments about seniors being a drain on the economy as false and misleading claims, just "fake news."

AARP's *Longevity Economy Outlook* report pulls from national data detailing how much people age 50 and older spend, earn working, and pay in taxes.

Just days ago, AARP CEO Jo Ann Jenkins penned a blog article on the Washington, DC-based aging group's website highlighting the findings of this major report. AARP's top senior executive strongly disputes the myth that people age 50 and over are an economic drain on society. Rather, the report's findings indicate that older workers, who are getting a monthly Social Security check and receiving Medicare benefits, are priming the nation's economic engine, she says.

"As the number of people over 50 grows, this cohort group is transforming America's economic markets and sparking fresh ideas, and the demand for new products and services across our economy," says Jenkins.

Jenkins notes that when older workers delay their retirement they continue to impact the economy by earning a paycheck, purchasing goods and services, and generating tax revenues for local, state, and federal government.

"The economic activity of people 50-plus supports 88.6 million jobs in the US, generates $5.7 trillion in wages and salaries, and accounts for $2.1 trillion in combined taxes," says Jenkins.

AARP's economic impact study, released on December 19, reports that people age 50 and older contribute a whopping $8.3 trillion to the US economy, putting this age group just behind the US as a whole ($20.5 trillion) and China ($13.4 trillion) when measured by gross domestic product. They also create an additional $745 billion in value through being unpaid family caregivers (see my commentary in the November 17/18 issues of the *Woonsocket Call* and *Pawtucket Times*).

Jenkins says AARP 's major report also projects the economic impact of older works to continue in the coming decades, tripling to more than $28 trillion by 2050 as younger generations (Millennials and Generation Z) turn age 50 in 2031 and 2047, respectively.

With the graying of the nation's population (predicted to be 157 million by 2050), the AARP report predicts that older persons will have more collective spending power, too, says Jenkins. "Fifty-six cents of every dollar spent in the United States in 2018 came from someone 50 or older," she says, adding that by 2050 this amount is expected to jump to 61 cents of every dollar.

For more than six years, AARP has been tracking the economic impact of older adults on the nation's economy, Jenkins penned in her recently published blog article. It's growing steadily over the years, she says.

"When AARP began researching the economic power of people 50 and older in 2013, we found that they generated $7.1 trillion in economic activity," says Jenkins, noting that three years later it had grown to $7.5 trillion. "The 2019 report reflects an 11 percent growth in economic impact, a 6 percent growth in jobs created, and a 12 percent growth in wages and salaries over the most recent three-year period," adds Jenkins.

Older Rhode Islanders and the State's Economy

"By virtue of Rhode Island being one of the oldest states per capita in the country we have long been aware of the contribution and buying power older people contribute to the state's economy," said AARP Rhode Island State director Kathleen Connell. "When you add in those 50-64 it becomes a big and powerful percentage of the population," she says.

Over the years, Connell has observed more engagement with AARP in the younger end of the demographic spectrum because people in their 50s have justifiable concerns about their future. They wonder: "Will they outspend their savings? Will Social Security change in ways that will reduce their benefits? Will out-of-pocket prescription drug expenses sink the savings they hope to put away for retirement?," she says.

"Waiting for retirement to think about these issues could well be too late," warns Connell. "This is creating greater interest in government and politics and magnifies the importance of their vote," she adds.

"At the same time, as older Rhode Islanders remain in the workforce longer, they keep paying taxes—a sizable plus for the state's economy," observes Connell. "With their extensive experience, many continue to be movers and shakers, innovators and professionals lending guidance that helps fuel economic growth," she states.

Connell adds, "Outside the workplace, they are connected in new ways via technology and social media. The great thing is that across the range of 50 and older workers it can be said that more people are sharing the workplace, adding to our cultural development, and participating in civic engagement more than ever before."

Wake-Up Call to Businesses, Congress

AARP's report should be a "wake-up call" to businesses and federal and state policymakers to rethink their attitudes, warns Jenkins in the conclusion of her blog article. She calls on business leaders to "build strategies for marketing their products and services to older Americans and to embrace a multi-generational workforce." Jenkins also urges Congress and state lawmakers to develop policies to support the growing number of uncompensated caregivers.

NCPSSM SAYS IT PAYS OFF TO DELAY CLAIMING SOCIAL SECURITY BENEFITS

Published in the *Woonsocket Call* on April 28, 2019

You have an eight-year window to choose to sign up for Social Security to collect your monthly benefit check. Some may be forced to collect Social Security at age 62, because of their finances, health, and lifestyle. Others make a decision to wait until either age 66 (if you were born after 1954) or 67 (if born in 1960 or after) to collect full monthly benefits. While some even choose to wait until age 70, if they financially can, to get the maximum program benefits.

For this age 64-year-old writer and many of my older peers in their 60s, determining the right age to collect Social Security can be confusing at best. Will my decision, to make less by collecting at age 62, or more by waiting until full benefits are paid at age 66 or 67, or waiting to receive maximum benefits at age 70, provide me with adequate retirement income to pay my bills into my 80s or even 90s? The National Committee to Preserve Social Security and Medicare (NCPSSM) hopes to assist older workers to make the right decision for them through a new educational campaign, Delay & Gain.

Educational Campaign Kicks Off in Five Cities

This month, the NCPSSM kicks off a new educational campaign, Delay & Gain, to urge workers in their 60s to opt for more money, up to thousands of dollars per year in additional Social Security benefits, by working at least until their normal retirement age: 66 or 67. Filing for Social Security at age 62 locks you into a lower benefit, permanently. You are not entitled to 100 percent of the benefit calculated from your earnings history unless you apply at age 66 or 67.

Launched by the Washington, DC-based NCPSSM, Delay & Gain includes a six-figure ad campaign targeting five US cities where workforce participation is high, but too many workers are losing money by choosing to retire early.

According to NCPSSM, more than one-third of American workers claim Social Security at the early retirement age of 62, lowering their monthly benefits for the rest of their lives. In a recent survey of American workers, nearly half of respondents did not know that their monthly Social Security benefits will be reduced by claiming at the earliest eligible age of 62—and boosted up to 25 percent for waiting until the full retirement age of 66. Seniors who delay claiming until age 70 receive an even larger financial bump—up to 44 percent more than if they had filed for benefits early. For the average beneficiary that can mean a difference of roughly $1,000 per month in extra income.

"We understand that not all workers have the option of working longer due to poor health, caregiving demands, age discrimination, or physically demanding work. But we consistently hear from seniors who retired early because they were sick and tired of working, who soon discovered that they were more sick and tired of not having enough money in retirement," says Max Richtman, NCPSSM's president and CEO in an April 8 statement announcing this new initiative.

Many Benefits of Working Longer

The risks of running out of money in later life are very evident, says NCPSSM. "Some 8 percent of seniors under 70 live in poverty. But the poverty rate jumps to 12 percent for those over 85. Older women are in greater jeopardy than men, because they tend to live longer, saved less for retirement, and get lower Social Security benefits. Some 11 percent of all elderly women live in poverty compared to 8 percent of older men," says NCPSSM, whose chief mission is to protect Social Security and Medicare.

"Because Social Security helps keep seniors out of poverty—and because benefits are adjusted for inflation—it's imperative that workers maximize their future benefits," says NCPSSM in its statement. "Retirees rely more and more on Social Security as they age. One-half of all retirees receive most of their income from Social Security. But 42 percent of seniors over age 80 depend on Social Security for almost all their cash income. With one in four 65-year-olds expected to live past 90, it's evident why workers should try to reap the highest possible monthly benefits." As they say, "you can outlive other sources of income, but not Social Security," notes the aging-advocacy group.

The Delay & Gain campaign was rolled out in Baltimore, Maryland; Davenport, Iowa; Detroit, Michigan; Louisville, Kentucky; and Pittsburgh, Pennsylvania, on April 8, 2019. NCPSSM's campaign will reach out to older workers through radio ads, videos, social media, and mobile billboards while providing educational material for distribution and publication to human-resource departments, community centers and libraries, and financial institutions. The campaign website, **https://www.ncpssm.org/delay-and-gain/** offers additional resources including Ask Us, a free service where Social Security experts answer personal questions about benefits, filing a claim and more.

"We want seniors to be able to pursue a comfortable retirement, with the least amount of stress about paying the bills," says Richtman. "This campaign will show older workers how to get there," he notes.

Simply put, NCPSSM's Delay & Gain initiative can provide older workers with a simple strategy for planning their retirement, one that just might make their retirement years more comfortable.

A COUPLE'S UNOFFICIAL GUIDE TO (SURVIVING) RETIREMENT

Published in the *Woonsocket Call* on December 18, 2016

Some people will tell you that nothing is for certain in life but death and taxes. But, author Nora Hall adds another truism for us to think about. That is, retirement guarantees that couples are going to face new issues in their relationship. No ifs, ands, or buts.

Hall, a 72-year-old North Kingston resident, recalls, "We were surprised that retirement was a bigger adjustment than we thought it would be."

The freelance writer began researching the joys and frustrations of retirement when her husband, Art, a former president of a manufacturing company, retired, and they saw the need for major adjustments in their relationship.

Sharing Retirement Woes

As a new retiree, Hall admitted she was unsure of how to deal with these life-stage changes and immediately began to seek information on adjusting to a retirement marriage. Since she found no book or articles on the topic, Hall began to interview other retirees. As she learned from their personal experiences, she realized that there was a need for a book.

"I never thought that I would ever write this book," says Hall. But she ultimately penned the 113-page paperback book, entitled *Survive Your Husband's Retirement*, published by Narragansett-based EBook Bakery.

"This book was just the natural extension of my freelance writing," she notes, adding that it took more than three years to write and publish the first edition of her book. The second edition only took one year to produce because she had already accumulated a lot of the research.

However, Hall admitted, "I was a lot fussier about the look and feel of this book."

Hall notes that her skills in interviewing others and writing about their messages and concerns came from jobs throughout her professional career where she wrote copy for appeal letters sent to potential donors to the New England Colleges Fund and then the VNA in Massachusetts. She began her career as an elementary school teacher before moving to arts administration, where she coordinated the Artist in Residence and the Boston Globe Scholastic Art Award Programs in Massachusetts.

In the process of talking with hundreds of retired women, and sometimes even their husbands, Hall gleaned from these interviews five areas (a husband's tendency to be bossy, always there, dependent, angry, or to never listen) that caused conflict in the retirement relationship along with solutions that these couples discovered that ultimately would maintain harmony in marriage. She decided that she would share this information with other retired couples by writing a book.

Tips to Fix Your Relationship

Hall's first edition released in 2013 (along with a second edition, published last month, which provides more stories and couple coping tips) goes far beyond simple identification of issues. In addition, she provides reasons behind the common feelings many men experience when they first leave their life's work and the potential conflicts many couples face.

In her books, she also offers the solutions older couples shared with her that provide examples for newly retired couples to implement as they struggle to find harmony in this new life stage.

Most of all Hall strives to help couples see that they are not alone and that laughter is the best solution for all of us, and details some quirks that need to be tolerated, ignored, or altered.

Hall observes, "A lot of people initially dread retirement but when they work at making it a positive experience it can really be a wonderful time in your life. The more we develop our companionship as a couple, the difficulties we face are more manageable."

So, what is the secret for older couples ultimately having a fulfilling relationship?

"Communication and compromising" can be key to fixing a retiree's relationship difficulties, says Hall.

Spreading the Gospel

Hall is focused on getting the word out about her book by speaking at libraries, churches, women's groups, and Rotary Clubs throughout the Ocean State and even at the Osher Lifelong Learning Institute, an adult learning program based at the University of Rhode Island. The Rhode Island author is even planning a trip to Anchorage, Alaska, to spread the gospel that a couple's retirement "can be an exciting new chapter in their life."

Hall received her undergraduate degree from Dunbarton College, Washington, DC and a master's degree in education from Boston University. In addition to *Survive Your Husband's Retirement*, Hall blogs regularly on her website, and offers workshops on adjusting to retirement.

Her family consists of two children and their spouses, six grandchildren, and one, now seasoned, retired husband. She and her husband, Art, moved to Wickford, Rhode Island in 2000.

Contact Nora to schedule workshops or raise a retirement question via email at **nora@surviveyourhusbandsretirement.com**. To purchase a copy of the second edition of *Survive Your Husband's Retirement*, go to **amazon.com**.

SURVIVAL STORY: FORMER BUSINESS OWNER OVERCOMES DEVASTATING SETBACKS

Published in *Senior Digest* on April 2016

I f you are in pursuit of the American Dream, you probably weren't given a roadmap that would guarantee a successful journey. Ask the average man or woman on the street today what immediate thoughts come to mind about owning your own business, and you'll probably hear "being your own boss," and "working your own hours" that top the list of perceptions. But when opening your own business becomes the alternative to unemployment in your later years, as Donald Russell, Jr. found out, it may not be what you expected or even planned. Like millions of middle-aged workers in the early 1990s, a severe economic downturn forced this Central Falls resident to make choices that ultimately would financially hit his pocketbook as he approached retirement.

Donald Russell had worked his way up from stock boy to manager at F.W. Woolworth Co., one of the area's original five-and-dime stores. During his 33-year career with this large big-box retail company, what was at the time the fourth-largest retailer in the world operating more than 5,000 stores, he eventually managed seven of the retail company's stores, one located in Providence (at Westminster and Dorrance Streets), and the others in Massachusetts, Vermont, and New York.

But everything changed in the late 1990s, when this 117-year-old company struggled to compete with the growing big discount stores. F.W. Woolworth filed for bankruptcy protection, and Russell, facing unemployment, had to quickly make major career decisions. He knew that, "at age 52, big-box competitors don't want you," or if he was offered a position, the salary would be much lower than what he was used to. "I could not take less because I had to pay for my daughter's college education," he added.

Russell credits "courses he took at Boston College" for teaching him valuable lessons on how to open a small business, and with knowledge in hand, he was ready to take that leap of faith and open his own business. Russell decided to cash out his $80,000 pension (less penalties) and combined with a loan from the US Small Business Administration, he would have enough capital to open a small retail business.

Getting into the Pet Business

Russell spent time researching a market niche, searching for one that would not put him in direct competition with the chain store. He discovered that the pet business was not really sought after by "big box retailers" and at that time "there were only 30,000 pet stores throughout the country.

Today the number has decreased to 6,000." Now Russell found his niche, and in 1997 opened his business, Dr. Doolittle's Pets & More, a small pet store in an East Providence shopping plaza. Though situated between two large Petco stores—one in Rumford, Rhode Island and the other in North Attleboro, Massachusetts—Russell did not view the large chain stores as competition, for he knew his prices were better. In 1997 when Russell opened his store, small business accounted for about 85 percent of the nation's economy, he states, noting that today this percentage has dropped to 70 percent.

Business was strong when Dr. Doolittle's first opened and for more than 13 years, Russell employed seven full- and part-time employees. However, by 2004 "the economy began to take a dive" and juggling the monthly rent, utilities, and employee salaries became difficult when his cash flow slowed. Russell began to lose money.

By 2006 his revenue had dropped 30 percent from the previous year, and neighboring big stores located in the plaza, like Ocean State Job Lot, began to close. In an effort to trim expenses, Russell was able to renegotiate his rent to a lower amount, however "losing the Stop & Shop supermarket in the next plaza, which was a main draw to the area, was ultimately the straw that broke the camel's back."

Taking from Peter to Pay Paul

Like thousands of small-business owners in the Ocean State, Russell had to juggle each month to meet his expenses, which included his Rhode Island sales tax. Choosing to pay his monthly sales tax or paying his employees salary was not an easy choice to make, but he could not pay both. "I chose to pay my employees first, with the plan to make up my [delinquent] sales tax later," he stated, noting however, that the "economy put the brakes to that. I could not even borrow a dime even with an excellent credit rating of 750," added Russell. The poor economy had forced banks to cut off credit to small businesses—period.

In 2009, the Rhode Island Department of Taxation came knocking on his door, and the 65-year-old pet-store owner was forced to close his business because he was in arrears on his payment of sales taxes. While his business was his sole source of income, the forced closing of the business put him in a "catch-22" situation—blocking any attempt to rescue his business and pay off the remaining sales tax owed, which had grown to thousands of dollars. Rather than padlock the door, the State did allow him access to the store to feed and maintain the animals until other arrangements were made.

Two weeks after his closing, Russell hammered out an agreeable payment plan with the State of Rhode Island for back taxes, but the economy never recovered, and by September 2010 the doors closed for the final time. In a valiant effort, Russell paid off $18,500 of the $20,000 owed before he closed, but two years later to his surprise, he was blocked from registering his car because of the remaining taxes (and penalties) still owed. A dispute as to the amount of sales taxes paid (plus penalties and interest) ultimately ended with the state's tax agency backing off and allowing him to register his vehicle.

Russell's forced closing and ultimately his bankruptcy caught the eye of both statewide and national media. Two radio talk shows and television coverage brought the news of his closure to the public. Even the nation's most popular website, The Drudge Report, posted articles. Amazingly, he says that more than 100 pages of blog posting were also generated, too.

Making Ends Meet

Today, Russell, 72, is collecting Social Security supplemented by a part-time job delivering pizzas. He notes that beneficiaries will not receive cost of living increases this year. Like millions of Social Security beneficiaries, Russell feels the impact of inflation. "There is no extra money to buy groceries after paying my rent and utilities," he says. Local food pantries provide additional food, and the Pawtucket-based Blackstone Valley Community Action Program pays for some of his heating bills.

Reflecting on the lay-off in his 50s that led to the opening of his small business and ultimately its closing as he reached his mid-60s because of an ailing economy, Russell admits he did not have a strategy for getting through the tough times in his later years.

"I just coped," says Russell. The former business owner has a strong opinion on opening a small business in Rhode Island. "Never," he says.

GERRITT IS GREEN WITH COMMITMENT

Published in *Senior Digest* on January 2016

Some people ease into retirement, traveling to exotic locales, catching up with friends at the neighborhood supermarket, or fixing up the homestead, long put off because of time constraints. Not so for 62-year-old Greg Gerritt, who still sees many years of work ahead of him to make Rhode Island economically sustainable through protecting the environment and advocating for the poor and downtrodden.

When Gerritt was 14 years old, he remembers reading a book on endangered species. At that young age, he would intuitively know that environmental advocacy would become his life's mission. Three years later he would create the first Earth Day celebration at his high school in Teaneck, New Jersey. Later he would relocate to Maine to attend college, ultimately receiving his bachelor's degree in anthropology in 1974 from the University of Maine. With degree in hand, the college graduate hitchhiked across the country before returning to Maine.

As a self-taught carpenter, Gerritt was able to make a living on his 10 acres of land. He offered low-cost work to seniors. During his 25 years in Maine, he worked to create a sustainable economy by growing a garden and putting up solar panels on his house along with creating an organic homestead.

Gerritt and his wife, Kathleen Rourke, met in 1991 through a personal ad placed in *The Maine Times*. The couple got married at town hall in Industry, Maine, and would later relocate to Rhode Island to be close to Kathleen's family.

His passion for protecting the environment is "on and off the clock," notes Gerritt. During the day, the Providence resident works as an administrator for the Environment Council of Rhode Island and leads the nonprofit group's Rhode Island Compost Initiative. In 2012, he received a Merit Award from the Environmental Protection Agency Region I for advancing the cause of compost in the state.

Gerritt gives countless hours of his work off time to environmental causes. As the founder of Friends of the Moshassuck, he promotes using sound ecological principles to enhance the community. He even took his environmental advocacy into the political sphere, where he helped to found the Green Party of the United States and ran for mayor of Providence as a Green Party candidate in 2002. He admits, "There's just no way to distinguish where my time goes because everything I do is interconnected."

Through his love for the environment, Gerritt has learned to shoot videos and has become an expert on amphibians in the North Burial Ground in Providence. He has shot "countless hours of video showing the development, feeding habits, and behavior of fowler toads," he says.

However, Gerritt may be better known in the Ocean State for establishing the "Buy Nothing Day Winter Coat Exchange" in 1997. According to Gerritt, the idea of giving substance to an already existing "Buy Nothing Day" created by consumer advocates came out of a meeting at the Rochambeau Library in Providence. The initiative had to be "better than a protest," with the goal of helping the poor, he says.

Gerritt estimates that in its first year, more than 250 coats were given away at the site of the GTECH building. "We just put a piece of plastic on the ground to keep the coats dry, and people came to get their coats," he remembers. The second year the half-day event was relocated. "It was so symbolic placing it between the Statehouse and the newly built Providence Mall. You have 'big government' and 'large corporations' with the poor in between," he says.

Gerritt has announced his retirement from the successful coat giveaway initiative held the day after Thanksgiving. Thousands of coats were given to needy Rhode Islanders at 10 sites throughout the state, he says.

It was the perfect time to leave, notes Gerritt. "It's grown big enough and should not depend on just me to keep it going. It's time to pass it on to another person when it's thriving," he says.

In Rhode Island for more than 20 years, Gerritt has published two books and scores of articles in newspapers, magazines, and on his blog, **www.prosperityforri.com**. He writes to advocate for a sustainable economy, social justice, and protecting the environment, and he does not expect to retire in the near future from his job or other volunteer efforts.

"The work never ends," he said, noting that there always will be a need for advocates. "I will actually continue my work until I can't physically do it," he added.

Looking back at his life as an environmental and social advocate Gerritt has some insight to pass on to those who will listen. "Do what you want to do. Look to see if you are doing what really brings you joy and makes the world a better place to be in. That's what you should be doing," he said.

WE HAVEN'T YET TURNED THE PAGE ON READING

Published in the *Woonsocket Call* on September 11, 2016

I n May 1897, the great American humorist, novelist, publisher, and lecturer Samuel Clemens—whom we all know as Mark Twain—was in London on a worldwide speaking tour. In this city someone had started a rumor that he was gravely ill, and ultimately the rumor changed to him having died.

When Twain was told that one major American newspaper actually printed his obituary, he quipped: "The reports of my death are greatly exaggerated."

As the rumor about Twain's death was "greatly exaggerated," those lamenting the decreasing number of Americans who read print books, even predicting its demise with the advent of e-books, audio books, and computer tablets is not correct, says a new Pew Research Center Survey released. Researcher Andrew Perrin notes in his study, *Book Reading 2016* that printed books remain more popular than books in digital formats for American readers.

Americans Love Print Books

According to the survey findings, released on September 1, 65 percent of Americans have read a print book in the last year, more than double the share that has read an e-book (28 percent) and more than four times' the share that have listened to an audio book (14 percent).

While the total share of Americans who have read a book in the last 12 months (73 percent) has remained consistent since 2012, nearly four in ten Americans read print books exclusively. Just 6 percent of Americans are digital-only book readers, adds the Pew Research Center Survey findings.

Although print remains the most popular book format, Americans who read e-books are increasingly turning to multipurpose devices such as smartphones and tablet computers, says Pew Research Center Survey findings. The share of e-book readers on tablets has more than tripled since 2011, and the number of readers on phones has more than doubled over that time.

Perrin's 9-page report also details other key findings.

The study found that 84 percent of American adults read to research specific topics of interest, while 82 percent read to keep up with current events, 80 percent read for pleasure, and 57 percent read for work or school. Also, 19 percent of Americans under the age of 50 have used a cellphone to read e-books, and cellphones play a relatively prominent role in the e-reading habits of Blacks (16 percent), and those who have not attended college (11 percent).

As to education, the study found that college graduates are nearly four times' as likely to read books—and twice as likely to read print books and listen to audio books—compared with those who have not graduated high school. In addition, Americans read an average, or mean, of 12 books per year; however, the typical, or median, American has read 4 books in the last 12 months.

Finally women (77 percent) are more likely than men (68 percent) to read books in general, and they are also more likely to read print books (70 percent). However, men and women are equally likely to read digital-format books such as e-books and audio books.

Book-Buying Strong in Rhode Island

Jennifer Massotti, who manages both the Barrington and Cranston locations for Barrington Books, has some thoughts about the recently released report. "The survey findings support the reading style and buying trends that we have seen from our loyal customer base for years. The majority of our customers prefer to read from a physical book. Even those who use their smartphones to research titles, still come in looking to buy the book instead of ordering it online or downloading. This could be personal reading preference or in support of the localism movement. Either way, book-buying is strong," she says.

Massotti does not see bookstores becoming obsolete because of today's digital age. "While the advent of e-readers and online buying options certainly altered the book industry several years back, it has not been the nail in the proverbial coffin that everyone predicted...If anything, there has been a resurgence in the independent bookstore industry, specifically. Brick-and-mortar stores that are supported by and steeped within their communities are thriving," she says.

Massotti says, "In fact, in the last year, Rhode Island and neighboring Massachusetts have seen that growth firsthand with the highly anticipated opening of three new bookstores. It's a feel-good time in our industry."

The general manager of Barrington Books notes, "downloading a book to your smartphone is convenient and serves a purpose to some. But it doesn't come close to replicating the authentic experience one finds when perusing the carefully curated stacks in a bookstore, or engaging in a conversation with a like-minded bookseller."

According to Massotti, bookstores aren't like most other retail outlets that are in the business of selling goods; bookstores, and books, are the original social media. "It's a sharable experience; it's about community. You can't get that delivered to your door or your phone."

As to the future of reading, Massotti firmly says that e-books and digital formats will never replace print books.

Self-Publishing Leaves a Legacy

Author Steven R. Porter, a publisher and president of the Association of Rhode Island Authors (ARIA), representing more than 260 independent and traditionally published authors who live and write in Rhode Island, says that Rhode Islanders love to read locally written books and to chat with the authors. "Readers also find great value in a signed book. There is something special about reading and sharing a book that the author held in their hands. The bottom line is that people who love to read are voracious. They can't get enough. And we can't write them fast enough," he says.

Porter has seen an "explosion of self-published books" in the last five years, but more recently, the rate has leveled off. "I think most of the leveling has to do with the fact that there were thousands of frustrated writers in the world and when the gates finally opened, they all rushed through at the same time," he says, noting that improved information and technology has efficiently assisted authors getting their books to market.

"Seniors are publishing more and more every day. I think there is an inherent need in all of us to have some sort of legacy. That legacy for many may be achieved through your life's work, or through your family," says Porter. It is the "ultimate expression of immortality," he says.

Like Massotti, Porter agrees with the findings of the Pew Research Center's report on book reading in America. "More people are writing than ever before, and reading than ever before. It's a great time to be a writer and a reader!," he says.

To read the report, go to **http://www.pewinternet.org/2016/09/01/ book-reading-2016/**.

13. SAGE ADVICE

"Aging is not 'lost youth,' but a new stage of opportunity and strength."

—Betty Friedan

SOME TIPS FOR GRADUATING SENIORS

Published in the *Woonsocket Call* on June 2, 2019

Throughout May and June, robed college graduates at Rhode Island's 11 colleges and universities listened to commencement speeches delivered by well-known lawmakers, judges, television personalities, actors, and chief executive officers of businesses. These included: former Congressman Patrick J. Kennedy at the University of Rhode Island; Bryan Stevenson, a widely acclaimed public interest lawyer, at Rhode Island School of Design; and actor and director John Krasinski, at Brown University. Many of the orators advised the young adults on how to create a more rewarding personal and professional life in their later years.

Members of the Association of Rhode Island Authors (ARIA), from their life experiences, also have insightful tips on aging gracefully in a very challenging and constantly changing world to give to the Class of 2019, and some of what the authors would have said if they had been invited to speak follows.

Co-authors **VICTORIA CORLISS**, (a resident of Cumberland) and **LEIGH BROWN**, (from Warwick) have written three books. The newest book, *The Pendulum's Truth*, published in 2018, is a story of Ava Dell, a protagonist with a twist. Like many people, Ava firmly believes that everything happens for a reason; but unlike her friends and family, she also believes she knows why they happen. She happily shares her intuitive insights with the people she loves, providing them guidance and affirmations until the day her awareness fails her. When tragedy results, Ava suddenly finds herself in a moral and emotional dilemma. For details, go to **http://www.browncorlissbooks.com**.

Commencement Tips: "Sometimes, when you think things are falling apart, they're really just falling into place. So, in times of chaos, of which there will be many, take a deep breath, a step back and be still; it will help you to see the sense of things. One more piece of advice: 'It's not what happens to you that matters most, but how you react to it.' Taking things in stride is a skill that keeps on giving."

DANA GAMBARDELLA, 42, a reading specialist, resides in North Providence. She has written two children's books, *Mama Bear's Magic* and *Grandma's House*, published in 2018. In *Mama Bear's Magic*, Tiny Bear realizes that bath time is "bear-y" fun! This humorous, truth-telling tale illustrates how Mama Bear embraces Tiny Bear's process so he can overcome his apprehension for the bath and discover that bathing is enjoyable. With Brother Bear's modeling and Mama Bear's clever approach, it's like magic! Savor the sounds, tastes, smells, and feelings that come alive only at *Grandma's House*. The illustrations in this book replicate the author's grandmother's house that still stands in Providence, Rhode Island. Vivid memories come alive through the light, impressionistic watercolor techniques on each page that evoke feelings of nostalgia for readers of all ages.

For details, go to **http://www.literacychefpublishing.com**.

Commencement Tips: "Always savor your own story. It's made up of the best ingredients. My two passions, literacy and culinary arts, have nurtured my story since graduating college. Being a reading specialist educating the highest priority reader is not that different from being a chef enthusiast. Experts in both areas must combine the right ingredients and practices to create a successful recipe that reaches many individual learners and palettes. Embrace Literacy. Live to Learn. Love Your Process."

GLEDÉ BROWNE KABONGO, 45, is an author and marketing consultant, living in North Attleboro, Massachusetts. She has written four novels, the latest, the award-winning *Autumn of Fear*, published in 2018. In her tome, college student Abbie Cooper's dream of becoming a surgeon is shattered when she wakes up in the hospital after a violent assault with no memory of the attack. To uncover the truth of what happened that night, Abbie must confront a stunning web of lies that stretch back decades, and a vicious predator who is willing to kill to protect his secret.

For details, go to **http://www.gledekabongo.com**.

Commencement Tips: "If you live for the approval of others, you will die by their criticism. So, take your time and figure out who you are and what you want in life. It's OK if it takes a while, the journey is as important as the destination. You will have many failures and make many mistakes. Don't hide from them. It's part of the journey. Be kind to yourself and others. Kindness is powerful and can change the world."

SHERYL LYNN KIMBALL, 51, is a resident of North Smithfield and owner of Kimball Property Maintenance. In 2019, she published *The Witches' Antidote: Abigail's*. In this book, when best friends Evan and Valarie hear that a tiny island on the Blackstone River is haunted, they have to see it for themselves. Once there, they discover an enchanted book instructing them how to put Salem Witch Trials victim Abigail Carver to rest. The teens will have to draw on all their strength if they are to survive the night and bring peace to a tortured soul.

For details, go to **http://www.amazon.com**.

Commencement Tips: "Follow your dreams. Many things will come along to throw you off your intended path. You'll tell yourself you're only taking a short detour but suddenly you've become just another hamster on the wheel. Understand that a few tiny steps in the direction of your heart are so much more valuable than any strides you make that go against your grain."

RICHARD T. ROOK, 71, is a lawyer from Wrentham, Massachusetts. The basic plot of his book, *Tiernan's Wake*, is a real-life historical mystery. An unlikely team apply their different skills to locate the only identifiable portrait, and maybe the missing treasure, of the iconic 16th-century Irish Pirate Queen (and political operative) Grace O'Malley. But it's also a story of damaged adults confronting their mortality and looking for the "missing portraits" of themselves. Sometimes the important messages are delivered by ancestral spirits, if we're smart enough to listen.

Commencement Tips: "Advice: Congratulations! You've accomplished a great deal, but not enough. Savor it, then start thinking about your obituary. By that I mean your legacy, how you want to be remembered. If you're not careful, life will eat your dreams one small bite at a time, and you won't even notice. I put off writing for 50 years, one day at a time. Be smarter. Draft your legacy now, then go make it happen."

ANGELINA SINGER, 22, an entrepreneur and crochet artist, lives in Boson, Massachusetts. She is author of *The Sorting* (Book 1 of the Upperworld Series), published in 2017. When asked to describe her book, Singer says: "Who decides where we are born and whom we love? Luna is an immortal entity in the Upperworld learning how to assign human souls to bodies. Everything goes well until Luna's friend makes a major mistake and Luna is sent to Earth after covering for her."

For details, go to **http://angelinasingerauthor.wordpress.com.**

Commencement Tip: "Life is a lot like writing a book. Even if you haven't formally published anything in the literal sense (or even want to), everyone has the power to write their own life story. This is both equal parts exciting and scary, but that's why I write—to make sense of everything I can't understand or even to get a second chance at something I'd like to redo."

DANA VACCA, a college instructor, resides in Narragansett. Her historical-fiction tome, *A Civil War Slave Escapes by Sea,* was published in 2018. When asked to describe this book, she says: "A storm at sea, a voyage aboard a whaling ship, the battlefields of Virginia, the Great Dismal Swamp, perilous escapes, and a forbidden romance change the life of a runaway slave forever. This epic journey to freedom in the midst of the Civil War is an unforgettable story of strength, determination, and love. Historically accurate, action-packed adventure."

For details, go to **http://www.amazon.com.**

Commencement Tips: "You have come of age with purpose, with desires, with resolve and probably, also with fears. Do not be ashamed of those fears. Do not merely react to them letting them dictate your journey or paralyze you into stasis. But, do not expect to find a magic potion to make them disappear. Instead, dominate fear—take up the reins and steer your life, in spite of it. The face of fear may change with age, but it will always be your traveling companion. If you keep your eyes on what is honest, what is just, and forge ahead, you can be its master."

MARY CATHERINE VOLK, over age 55, is a life coach residing in Narragansett. In her book, *Believe in Forever: How to Recognize Signs from Departed Loved Ones,* published in 2015, she details firsthand experiences of people being contacted by their deceased family members and friends. She says that the humorous and heartwarming stories will give you chills as they touch your heart; teaching you to trust your own intuition. It was not just your imagination or an odd coincidence. Our loved ones are near shortly after passing to help us with our grief and to let us know their consciousness and love for us is eternal.

For details, go to **http://www.marycatherinevolk.com.**

Commencement Tips: "What did you enjoy playing as a child in the third or fourth grade? What gave you joy? Your answer holds a valuable key to your unique gift. Embrace your uniqueness! Follow your dreams, you will have support along the way. It's all part of the journey to discover you and your special gifts. Don't be afraid to share your gift with the world. Humanity needs you!"

For more information about the ARIA go to **http://www.riauthors.org**.

CARVELLI: MAKING LEMONADE OUT OF LIFE'S LEMONS

Published in the *Woonsocket Call* on April 9, 2017

A uthor and life coach Linda Carvelli believes that everything in life has a purpose and that resilience will get you through any obstacle in your path. She succinctly illustrates this philosophy in her 340-page memoir, *Perfectly Negative: How I Learned to Embrace Life's Lemons Lessons*. The self-published book details how she faced personal and family tragedy over a decade of deep emotional pain only to realize that each devastating life experience gave her more courage and strength to face the next one.

Carvelli dedicated more than 20 years of her professional career to computer technology and project management before writing her first full-length memoir, published in 2016, that reveals how she ultimately came to terms with her life's mission. That is, helping people overcome and learn from the challenges in their daily lives. As a board-certified life coach, she brings lessons from her book to people to help them regain control of their lives, discover new perspectives, create more options, and move forward with confidence and courage.

Facing Your Own Life Lemons Lessons

Perfectly Negative introduces a cast of real, relatable characters who will have you crying, laughing, and ultimately rejoicing in Carvelli's triumph and determination to make sense of the overwhelming heartbreak she endured. This insightful memoir reveals nuggets of wisdom to reassure you as you face your own life lemons lessons.

The inspirational tome follows Carvelli's 46 years, through her idyllic childhood growing up in a close-knit Italian household into her later years where she faced a decade's worth of personal and professional losses. It begins when the native Cranston resident was focused on planning her first marriage in 1996 and received the news of her mother being re-diagnosed with breast cancer, ultimately leading to her death two years later.

Six months later, the memoir details her sister's diagnosis of breast cancer and how she lived with this devastating disease for seven years. Like her mother and sister, Carvelli was also diagnosed with breast cancer, although she ultimately made a decision to have a double mastectomy. She also experienced a divorce, left a long-term relationship shortly before her father died, and finally was laid off from her job.

This book is for all ages and anyone who is overcoming obstacles. Carvellli's first full-length book, detailing her overcoming life challenges, is getting rave reviews, too.

Here's a review from a judge at the 24th Annual Writer's Digest Self-Published Book Awards:

"It's unputdownable! From the first paragraph, author Linda Carvelli draws in the reader with tightly focused, well-written scenes and immediately identifiable characters. Even though this family is well-to-do with all the material trappings, they have heartbreak galore with 'four cancer diagnoses, three deaths, two divorces and a significant other turned not-so-significant' not to mention job and friendship upheavals and a medium who helps provide some much-needed spiritual anchoring. These can be anyone's friends, family and significant others, regardless of race, creed or socioeconomic status."

The judge adds, "By interweaving several plotlines and balancing suspense—and using plain but powerful language with a much-needed dollop of objectivity—this book avoids the mawkish self-pity and excessive detail that can be the undoing of similar attempts. It's like sitting down with a best friend and catching up on the latest news—before one knows it two hours have passed and there's still more to discuss."

Another reviewer said, "I thought this was going to be depressing but boy was I wrong."

A Decade Worth of Learning

Looking back, "my life was a mess," said Carvelli. What surprised the 14-year cancer survivor the most was that when she eventually reflected on that most painful decade of her life, she realized that each tragic event gave her more courage and strength to successfully face the next one, she says.

Carvelli remembers that after ending a seven-year relationship she took a solo vacation to Jamaica to just refocus and stabilize her life. She rediscovered journaling, a healing activity that she took up earlier in her life to detail the decade of upheavals. An audio book, *The Shack*, an inspirational story where the protagonist overcomes personal tragedy and finds faith again, gave Carvelli food for thought and insight on her life's journey.

"I realized that when I was in the midst of each tragedy I just did what I had to do to get through it," says Carvelli, noting that "I lived in the present moment." But, looking back, she found herself surprised with the realization that she survived some tough events. "Only then did I realize the intensity," of the experiences.

Carvelli's personal life stabilized a bit when she got engaged in 2011. Although she had found her true love, a lump in her breast discovered a week before being let go from her job brought back anxiety and fear she remembered when being initially diagnosed with cancer. It was losing her job and the result of the medical test that inspired her to write the book.

"At first I was angry about losing my job because I was really good at what I did," said Carvelli, who quickly acknowledged the job loss and accepted it when she realized, "It gave me time to begin writing the book I always wanted to," she said.

With a supportive fiancé and all that free time Carvelli began the writing process. With the help of a writing coach, using old journals of the tragic decade and recent writings, a book slowly took shape. Over four years, four completed drafts combined with a final edit would lead to her self-published memoir released last year.

The Power of Resilience

"When I finished writing the last chapter of my memoir, the reason for my existence stared me in the eyes and ignited a fire in my heart. My life's purpose is to serve as an example of resilience," says Carvelli.

Author Carvelli has added certified life coach to her professional skillset to bring the insights and tips from her book to people, helping them move forward in the midst of life's tragedies. Carvelli, 51, says that her life journey has given her clarity about her purpose on earth.

"Coaching and managing people through business and personal changes is why I was put here, it is my life's purpose," she says.

Lemons can be a great teacher in your life. Carvelli shares these lessons in her memoir and also on her blog (**http://www.lindacarvelli.com/blog/**).

The Rhode Island author has also published a short story, "I Miss My Breasts" in *Chicken Soup for the Soul: Hope and Healing for Your Breast Cancer Journey*. She co-facilitates an informal support group, Sisters in Survival, for cancer survivors and their caregivers. She lives in Warren with her husband, two step-teens, and Enzo Vino, the family dog who follows Carvelli everywhere.

Perfectly Negative is available online at **amazon.com**. To arrange an interview or schedule a book signing or inspirational talk, visit **http://www. lindacarvelli.com** or email **linda@lindacarvelli.com**.

RHODE ISLANDERS GIVE TIPS TO GRADUATES

Published in the *Woonsocket Call* on May 14, 2017

During the month of May, commencement speakers will be addressing the graduating Class of 2017 at colleges, universities, and higher-learning institutions in Rhode Island and throughout the nation. Robed graduating seniors will listen attentively to these 10-minute speeches usually given by well-known lawmakers, judges, television personalities, and business CEOs who offer tips on how the graduate can live a successful and fulfilling life. The graduate can only hope that this advice might just propel them into a more rewarding personal and professional life.

Traditionally this notable, successful, and stimulating figure is often well-known in the community. Larger institutions may choose speakers of national or international renown, but sometimes this recognition comes at a great cost, commanding high speaking fees. Locally, Brown University, unique among Ivy League institutions, features graduating seniors, rather than out-side dignitaries, as their commencement speakers.

So, I suggest to presidents of colleges and universities, with your tight oper-ating budgets, you can save a little money by not bringing in high-paid com-mencement speakers with another alternative. As can be seen below, there are many potential candidates in Rhode Island communities that fly below the selection committee's radar screen and can give college graduates very sound strategies for success gleaned from their everyday life experiences. The mes-sages gleaned from average everyday Rhode Islanders will most surely give a road map on how the graduating senior can reach their potential in a very challenging world.

ERIC J. AUGER, 48, Pawtucket, co-founder/creative director for TEN21 Pro-ductions: "Having been an active artist and exhibiting my work since the age of 4, I can look back at 44 years of trials and errors that have influenced me to become the artist that I am today. My advice to anyone starting out is to follow your intuition and embrace all the success and failures that it may bring you. Living through and learning from these experiences is what opens your eyes to your true potential."

MICHAEL BILOW, Providence, writer at *Motif Magazine*: "Only you are the ultimate judge of what you want. Take advice from people who want to help you, but don't worry about pleasing them. Money is important to have enough to be independent, but not as an end in itself. Never take a job or a romantic partner just because others expect it of you. Be nice, but not too nice. Don't lie to yourself. Worry less. You have a right to be happy."

NATELIE CARTER, 73, Cumberland, director of operations for Blackstone Valley Tourism Council: "One of the oldest pieces of wisdom ever dispensed is one that has guided my life: 'Know Thyself.' It still directs my life that has been filled with remarkable events and few regrets. However, there is the wisdom of Edna St. Vincent Millay to learn from: 'I am glad that I paid so little attention to good advice; had I abided by it I might have been saved from some of my most valuable mistakes.'"

GREG GERRITT, 63, Providence, head of research for ProsperityForRI.com: "Climate change is the existential crisis of our time. Be ready to resist the oligarchy when they seek to prevent protest and work to protect their fortunes. Be ready to resist the oligarchy when they crank up the false news and the war machine. If you shut down the war machine and truly stop climate change, your lives will be better. If you do not, get ready for a hot and violent planet and community."

MAUREEN O'GORMAN, Warwick, adult correctional-institute GED teacher: "Meredith Grey, fictional philosophizing doctor said: 'The story of our evolution is the story of what we leave behind.' Human tails no longer exist and the appendix isn't functional. Every choice we make comes at the cost of choices we didn't make. Reinventing ourselves can't happen without discarding something behind as we move forward. Honor the past, but do not live in it."

NORA HALL, 72, North Kingston, freelance writer: "Empathy may be the most important life skill you can develop. It enables you to 'put yourself in another's shoes' and makes you a great leader."

EVERETT HOAG, 63, North Providence, president of Fountain Street Creative: "Advice to new artists—Believe in yourself and your work. Explore as many forms as you can. Discover art comes from inside and, as long as you have the skills, true art will emerge. Keep creating and create what is true to you, never stop or be discouraged by what others say...Designers—we make the world more beautiful. More functional. Safer. More special. The more of 'you' that goes into your work, the more original it becomes; there's something magical about that."

JOHN KEVORKIAN, 63, East Greenwich, management psychologist/business coach: "Over the years, I've noticed that so much of success comes from simply showing up. Be aware, get involved, get engaged with what is important to you. Be there and be! Be truly interested in understanding the other's viewpoint and situation. Ask questions and listen to learn what you don't know and then you will be well prepared to confidently voice opinions and be helpful. Be a catalyst. It is easier to make things happen if you don't care who gets the credit."

LARRY MONASTESSE, 65, Pawtucket, director of administration, Coastline Employee Assistant Program (EAP): "Passion and education is the key. Mistakes happen—learn from them but do not quit. Keep your goals front and center. Have the courage to follow you heart, it is the true measure of your success. Time is limited, share with family and friends. They will be with you on your lifelong journey. Make time for yourself and give back to society in some form that you are comfortable with and enjoy. Do dream and enjoy the ride."

STEVEN R. PORTER, 52, Glocester: "A college diploma is treated like the end of an educational learning journey, but truthfully, it's just the start. Those who will be the most successful in life never stop reading, studying, or acquiring new skills. The world is a rapidly changing place, and higher education does a good job of preparing you for what the world was like, not what the world is going to be. Stay positive and aggressive."

DEBRA ROSSETTI, over 50, Central Falls, staff developer/literacy, New York City Department of Education: "You can and will make a difference in our society and world. This day is a special and important milestone in your life. You have accomplished much to be standing where you are now, but your journey has just begun. You have much more to do and challenges to bear in your years ahead. Transform yourself into the person you aspire to be, be ready for change, think forward and move forward. Continue to educate yourself. Life is a journey with lessons to learn at every corner. Take advantage of opportunities to grow your mind and pursue your dreams. Believe in yourself, believe in others, always be humble and kind."

RANDY SACILOTTO, 55, Cumberland, Navigant Credit Union, vice president of community development: "My mom told me to remember to love people and use things, never the other way around. This may seem pretty simple and logical. Yet there are times we may want to do the reverse. Remember that it is by genuine caring interaction with another human soul that we learn and laugh and grow. And nothing you will own will ever visit you when you're sick, hold you when you're sad, or celebrate your accomplishments."

SUSAN SWEET, 75, Rumford, former state employee: "Make your own trail and avoid the well-worn path. Find interests and passions and live them. Create purpose in your life. Do something good, something useful in your life. Contribute to the happiness and well-being of other beings. Let Death be your advisor."

PATRICIA ZACKS, 63, Pawtucket, owner of Camera Werks: "Never be afraid of trying new things. Hardships and setbacks are part of life, but it is how we deal with them that can make all the difference. Obstacles may be opportunities in disguise, and change often leads to new roads, exciting journeys, and a time of self-discovery. Follow your bliss."

PAUSCH'S *THE LAST LECTURE* IS A MUST-READ

Published in the *Pawtucket Times*, January 30, 2015

Sometimes you may just pick up a good book to read, especially during a storm with the governor's call for a State of Emergency three days ago because of the blizzard. Yes, being homebound because of bad weather does have its advantages. It gives you time to read books, especially if you still have electricity.

For years, my wife has gently suggested that I read a book, lying on her nightstand. She told me that "it'll help you put life's priorities in order." But, I never did, until this week when I finally picked up that nationally acclaimed book, *The Last Lecture*, coauthored by Randy Pausch and Jeffrey Zaslow. I quickly devoured the 206-page book, published by Hyperion in 2008, in just one day.

Thoughts of a Dying Professor

Doctors gave Pausch, a 47-year-old father of three, from three to six more months of "good health" when they diagnosed him with pancreatic cancer in August 2007. Just one month later, the dying Carnegie Mellon University (CMU) professor would address a packed auditorium for his afternoon lecture, addressing more than 400 students, colleagues, and friends. His talk was part of an ongoing CMU lecture series where top academics gave their "final talk," revealing what really matters to them and the insights gleaned over their life if it was their last opportunity.

Sadly, Pausch literally got his last chance.

Pausch was an award-winning professor and researcher in computer science, human-computer interaction, and design at CMU in Pittsburg, Pennsylvania. He passed away from complications from his disease on July 25, 2008. Zaslow, a columnist for the *Wall Street Journal*, attended the last lecture, and wrote the story that helped fuel worldwide interest in it.

According to Wikipedia, "*The Last Lecture* became a New York Times bestseller in 2008, and remained on the prestigious list for 112 weeks, continuing into the summer of 2011. The book [ISBN: 978-1-4013-2325-7] has been translated into 48 languages [including Italian, German, Chinese, Arabic and more] and has sold more than 5 million copies in the United States alone."

The CMU shot a video (1 hour and 16 minutes in length) of Pausch's last lecture—and soon the footage began spreading across the internet, on YouTube, popping up in tens of thousands of websites. Pausch's inspirational talk, which has been viewed today by more than 17 million people today on YouTube, can now be seen on CMU's website, at **http://www.cmu.edu/randyslecture/**. His book and e-book can also be purchased on this website or at any bookstore, including your favorite neighborhood store.

Pausch's Last Hurrah

Pausch's lecture, "Really Achieving Your Childhood Dreams" wasn't about his dying. But, he freely admitted that he would rather have terminal cancer than be hit by a bus and suddenly killed because if he was hit by a sudden accident he would not have time to spend with his family or get his house in order. He moved from Southern Virginia to Pittsburg so his wife, Jai, and his children could be near family.

Meanwhile, the CMU lecturer humorously begins by noting that while he had cancerous lesions throughout his body, outwardly he looked healthy. At one point, to prove his point, he dropped down to the floor and did push-ups on stage.

Throughout his talk, Pausch reeled off his unique insights gained from his four-plus decades of life experience, specifically surmounting the challenges in your life he calls "brick walls." He says, "Brick walls are there for a reason. They give us a chance to show how badly we want something," he said. Seize the moment, he adds, because, "time is all you have...and you may find one day that you have less than you think."

One of his dreams was becoming a Disney Imagineer. Three rejection letters and a dean who attempted to block his efforts were an insurmountable "brick wall." He ultimately would accomplish that childhood dream. He met William Shatner, won large stuffed animals, floated in zero gravity, and even authored an article in the World Book encyclopedia. Although he never played for the NFL, he learned about life from his football coaches in his early school years.

So, while Professor Pausch stresses his talk was about achieving childhood dreams, it's really about how to lead your life, he admits. "If you live your life the right way, the karma will take care of itself," he believes. Often he refers to "head fake" throughout the lecture, meaning we tend to gain the most experience or lesson when it's disguised by something else. But, at the lecture's conclusion, Pausch freely admits the "last lecture" was the biggest head fake of them all—for it wasn't for those in the room but for his children, all under 7 years old. His talk is sprinkled with things he wants his children to learn and wants them to know about him, including personal stories of his growing up, his courtship with their mother, and ways to succeed in life. So, there are many levels and points Pausch gets across in his lecture, detailed in his bestselling book.

Pausch practiced what he preached, telling the packed auditorium to enjoy life and just have fun, like he did. Live life to the fullest because one never knows when it might be taken away, the terminally ill professor warns, who has just months to live.

Loyalty is important so "dance with the one who brings you," says Pausch. He quotes Seneca, the Roman philosopher born in 5 B.C., "Luck is what happens when preparation meets opportunity." With this quote, "Other than that, Mrs. Lincoln, how was the play?" he reminds us not to focus on the little issues while ignoring the big ones. "We cannot change the cards we are dealt, just how we play the hand," he says.

Pausch tells a story of his father's "heroic achievement" for bravery awarded to him by the commanding general of the 7th Infantry Division in World War II. The 22-year-old-solider, like many of the Greatest Generation, never mentioned his Bronze Star, which Pausch only discovered after his death. It just never came up, stated Pausch, but revealed volumes about the importance of being touted their awards, never revealed to his mother.

The CMU professor would even award the "First Penguin" to students who failed to achieve their goals in his "Building Virtual Worlds" course, because they took a risk using new technology or ideas in their design. He says this award was for "glorious failure" and "out-of-the-box thinking and using imagination in a daring way."

The Last Lecture is a great read for those who seek a road map for living a better, more productive life. It's jam-packed with Pausch's wisdom that will certainly come in handy throughout one's journey in life, especially when you confront the "brick walls" or challenges in your personal and professional careers. Take time to live your dreams, to cross them off your bucket list. Sometimes life can be unexpectedly too short, just as Pausch ultimately found out.

GRADUATING COLLEGE SENIORS GET SOME ADVICE FROM RHODE ISLAND'S AUTHORS

Published in the *Woonsocket Call* on July 1, 2018

Throughout May and June, robed college graduates listened to commencement speeches delivered by well-known lawmakers, judges, television personalities, actors, and chief executive officers of businesses. Many of the orators advised the young adults on how to create a more rewarding personal and professional life in their later years.

Members of the Association of Rhode Island Authors (ARIA) also have insightful advice on aging gracefully in a challenging and changing world to give to the Class of 2018, and some of what the authors would have said if they had been invited to speak follows.

Hopefully, all readers will benefit from the commencement tips and find time to take a look at the authors' books.

The ABCs of Aging Gracefully

NORMAN DESMARAIS, 71, professor emeritus at Providence College, lives in Lincoln and is an active re-enactor and a former librarian. He is the author of *The Guide to the American Revolutionary War in Canada and New England*, *The Guide to the American Revolutionary War in New York*, and *The Guide to the American Revolutionary War in New Jersey*. These books intend to provide comprehensive coverage of the confrontations of the American War of Independence and to serve as a guide to the sites.

For book details, go to **http://www.revolutionaryimprints.net**.

Commencement tips: "It's nice to be important but more important to be nice. Remember that the people you pass climbing the ladder of success will be the same people you meet on the way down. They will often be the people you will need to be successful."

RICK BILLINGS, 59, a retired firefighter and emergency management technician lives in Barrington. He authored and illustrated two children's books, *The Tragic Tale of Mr. Moofs*, a story about the changing relationship between a stuffed toy and a boy's older sister, and more recently *Melba Blue*, a light introduction for children on the works of Edgar Allen Poe and William Shakespeare.

For book details, go to **http://www.reddogart.com.**

Commencement tips: "What are you waiting for? This is my mantra. I became a firefighter at age 35. I wrote, illustrated, and self-published my first book 19 years later. Today, I cycle between 40 and 80 miles each week. I travel. I laugh. I love. Embrace family, nature, health, spirituality, peace, creativity, and the purity of the new. What are you waiting for?"

***

PATRICIA HINKLEY, 73, a former holistic counselor and journey practitioner in private practice, lives in Wakefield. She authored *Chasing Sleep/Lonely Tussles in the Dark*, a book that explores the issues and challenges surrounding sleep deprivation and how to overcome them by changing attitudes and behaviors and *Claiming Space/Finding Stillness that Inspires Action*, a book that invites you to step back from the busy world to uncover the peaceful intelligence, genuine happiness, and capabilities within.

For book details, go to **http://www.patriciahinkley.com.**

Commencement tips: "Find what you love and do it. Learn about your world and become a part of positive change. Respect and peacefully negotiate with people who differ from you. Know history, government, and civics. Involve yourself to make a better world. Trust your heart's wisdom when deciding what is right. Speak up for it."

***

HANK ELLIS, 69, formerly employed by the Rhode Island Department of Environmental Management, lives in Exeter. He authored *The Promise: A Perilous Journey*, a book appealing to all ages and a must-read for those who love the magic of a childhood adventure.

Commencement tips: "Know what is important to you: happiness or wealth. You can have both, but it can be more difficult. Be open to change, roll with the punches and don't punch back. Always be kind. Be brave and stretch yourself. The greatest advice I can give is to give of yourself. Serve others in all you do. I guarantee amazing results."

BARBARA ANN WHITMAN, 62, a family support specialist, lives in Johnston. She authored *Have Mercy*, a book about the effects foster care can have on a child.

For book details, go to **http://www.facebook.com/ BarbaraAnnWhitmanAuthor.**

Commencement tips: "Before you can be kind to others, you must first be kind to yourself. If you want to be honest, start with the person in the mirror. The same principle applies to being authentic, loyal, and loving. Being selfless is overrated. Indulge and invest in knowing yourself. Only then will you be ready to share your gifts with the world."

ETTA ZASLOFF, 70, lives in Hope Valley. She published an alphabet book for all ages on her 70th birthday, *Beginning with Xs and Os: The Evolution of Alphabet*. It's a child's first chapter book! Personified letters change, rearrange, and interchange in rhyming stories of origin.

For book details, go to **http://ettazasloff.com.**

Commencement tips: "Live, really live. Look out the window more than in the mirror or at your phone. Explore the world. Engage with people beyond your immediate circle. Pursue your passion with education, experience and practice to mastery. Have the courage to forge your own path and leave a trail for others to follow. Always think of those who follow."

HARRIS N. ("HERSHEY") ROSEN, 85, ran a Pawtucket-based candy company for 40 years before retiring. He lives in Providence, and he authored *My Family Record Book*, providing easy tips on organizing personal information, financial plans, and final wishes for seniors, caregivers, estate executors, etc.

For book details, go to **myfamilyrecordbook.com.**

Commencement tips: "Achievement is 90 percent perspiration and 10 percent inspiration. So in life, find your purpose in something you enjoy and don't be afraid to aim high. Look around for help and value the network of friends you made in college. Persist in realizing your goal, knowing that it's OK to fail (you will) but not to quit. You'll get there; I promise."

BJ KNAPP, 44, a former college radio station disc jockey, lives in Coventry. She authored *Beside the Music*. Imagine if a washed-up 80s metal band moved in to your house. It happens to Brenda and Time in *Besides the Music*. Can Brenda be one man's wife and another man's muse?

For book details, go to **http://www.bjknapp.com**.

Commencement tips: "Never forget how to laugh at yourself, how to be silly and how to make others laugh. Laughter is great for your abs, for your soul, and for your relationships. And it's not all about you. Don't turn every situation around so it's about you. Most of the time it's about someone else, and it's up to you to be supportive of that person. They will do the same for you when it really is all about you."

ALISON O'DONNELL, 52, a freelance editor, proofreader, and ghostwriter, lives in Pawtucket. She authored *Stupid Cupid: A Survivor's Guide to Online Dating*. The book has a sarcastic slant toward online dating, chronicling 100 really bad dates followed by a moral learned from each experience.

For book details, go to **http://www.facebook.com/AuthorAlisonODonnell**.

Commencement tips: "Do not fear your own power! There are people who will try to beat you down; rise above it. There are people who will use their power to beat you down. Go around it. Then, mentally thank them for the life lesson. There are people who will support you. Show gratitude. Your success will have been earned. Embrace it."

MICHAEL A. BATTEY, 65, a podiatrist, lives in East Greenwich. He authored *The Parent Trap, Vol. 1*, the first of a two-volume collection of humorous and insightful observations on contemporary teen parenting.

For book details, go to **http://www.parenttrapcolumns.com**.

Commencement tips: "There is a power to kindness. There is no act, which you can choose, which will be more powerful. It is stronger than the most reasoned logic. It can vanquish the sharpest wit. Deceptive at times and pre-ternaturally puzzling, it is your best ally. It elevates discussions and makes you a better person. It is defining, and it is memorable."

L. A. JACOB, 50, a government claims auditor for CVS, lives in Central Falls. She authored *Grimaulkin*, a book about a young wizard who was sent to prison for summoning demons. Now he's out trying to be a better man, but others want to use his knowledge and abilities—against his parole.

Commencement tips: "I published my first book at 48, but I've been writing since I was 15. Why did I wait so long? Because I was afraid. Afraid of what my family would say about me, of how the book would be received. Here's my advice: Don't wait. Life is too short. Buy the darn shoes you love."

PHYLLIS CALVEY, 68, an educator and storyteller who lives in Bellingham, Massachusetts. Her latest book, *The Butterfly Club*, presents real people's stories of how God can, and does, use signs to communicate His presence to those in need.

For book details, go to **http://www.butterflyclubbook.com.**

Commencement Tips: "The odds were probably a thousand to one to be published, and yet I quit my job to be a writer. My dad said, "You could be the one. How much does a book sell for these days? $6.95? When you sell a million, that's..." But all I heard was the word "when;" it immediately seemed to change the odds!"

For more information about the ARIA, go to **http://www.riauthors.org**.

RHODE ISLAND AUTHORS REFLECT ON THEIR PUBLISHED TOMES AND NEW YEAR'S RESOLUTIONS

Published in the *Woonsocket Call* on December 30, 2018

A ccording to a YouGov, an internet company that conducts polls on politics, public affairs, products and brands, the most common New Year's Resolutions in 2018 were to eat healthier, get more exercise, and to save money. With New Year's just days away, seven members of the Association of Rhode Island Authors (ARIA), give us their literary aspirations and self-improvement resolutions for 2019, many of them mirroring YouGov's poll findings last year while sharing details about their published tomes.

JULIEN AYOTTE, 77, of Cumberland, wrote *Code Name Lily*, a book about a young Belgian nurse who becomes a key leader in the Comet Line escape network during World War II. Through clever and persuasive ways, she aids more than 250 downed airmen in escaping the Germans.

Publisher: Kindle Digital Publishing.
Price: $16 (soft cover).
For details go to **http://www.julienayotte.com**

New Year's Resolution: Improving my eating habits to maintain a healthier weight in the coming year and to keep moving. My philosophy has always been, "it's harder to hit a moving target." Walk at least a mile a day, and lift weights. Continued good health will allow me to write my sixth novel in 2019. And all I need to do to make *Code Name Lily* a blockbuster bestseller and major film by building my reader audience. My goal is still to write 10 books in 10 years, and I am halfway there.

PHYLLIS CALVEY, 68, of Bellingham, Massachusetts, wrote *The Butterfly Club: "Is That You?"* One component of the book is the butterfly phenomenon; the intriguing fact that God has used the perfect timing of the appearance of this spiritual sign to comfort innumerable people after a loved one has died.

But the signs are not only butterflies or signs connected to a death experience. Each of the true-life stories in the book focuses on an incredible sign God used to communicate with someone. *The Butterfly Club* is for all who have experienced or would like to be inspired by a sign that is undoubtedly more than just a coincidence!

Publisher: Createspace Independent Publishing Platform.
Price: $10 (soft cover).
For details, go to **http://www.butterflyclubbook.com.**

New Year's Resolution: I believe it is the combination of nearing age 70 and having friends around me tragically dying of cancer that echoed these words of wisdom in my heart: "All we have to decide is what to do with the time that is given." It brought to mind when our two children were young. We made a difficult decision to put the television away, which allowed us the time to joyfully discover the wondrous gifts that had truly been given to each of us! This year I am resurrecting the spirit of using the time given to focus on writing what I believe has been imparted to me. And hopefully that same discovered joy from years' past will be found and kept all year!

HANK ELLIS, 70, of Saunderstown, wrote *The Promise: A Perilous Journey*. One afternoon in late June, two adventurous, adolescent brothers stumble upon a huge mysterious cavern protected from the elements for centuries. Using dreams and deciphering riddles, they travel through underground passageways to meet a man named Eli. Through a series of strange and supernatural encounters, the two boys rely on resourcefulness, perseverance, and love to lead them to an opportunity they could never have imagined and make a decision that will change their lives forever.

Publisher: Archway Publishing.
Price: $21.99 (soft cover); $39.99 (hard cover); $2.99 (e-book).
For details, go to **http://www.archwaypublishing.com**

New Year's Resolution: My biggest resolution is to finish writing my second book (sequel to *The Promise*). But with advancing age, and more important than any book, I want to pay more attention to the needs of those around me. At the same time, I want to simplify my life, eliminate clutter, and give things away. I am blessed.

DR. KAREN PETIT, 67, of Cranston, wrote: *Banking on Dreams, Mayflower Dreams, Roger Williams in an Elevator, Unhidden Pilgrims*, and *Holidays Amaze*. Her five books have Christian content, historic elements, suspenseful action, dream/reality sections, romance, pictures, and methods of dealing with such problems as losing weight, fighting, quitting smoking, nightmares, writer's block, anxiety, and separation.

Publisher: WestBow Press.
Price: $11.95 to $24.95 (soft cover) depending on the book; $28.95 to $39.95 (hard cover) depending on the book; $3.95 (e-books for each book). For a specific listing of book prices and details on books, go to **http://www. drkarenpetit.com**.

New Year's Resolution: To lose weight by substitution and exercise. Because I love to munch on chocolate, I'll substitute most of my chocolate items with low-calorie hard candy. I'll also be substituting vegetables for half of my carbohydrates. After still enjoying a little bit of the sweetness of my favorite foods, I'll be exercising while watching TV. Being healthier will mean a sweeter, longer life. In my book *Holidays Amaze*, the last two lines of my maze poem titled "A Maze of Choices for New Year's Day" are: "A resolution opens new doorways / for new years of fun with amazing days."

STEVEN PORTER, 53, of Harmony and owner of Pawtucket, Rhode Island-based Stillwater Books, wrote: *Confessions of the Meek and the Valiant*, a South Boston crime saga; *Mantises*, an adventure novel set against the mysterious history and legends of Block Island; *Scared to Death... Do it Anyway*, the story of Brian Beneduce and his lifelong work to overcome panic and anxiety attacks.

Publisher: Stillwater River Publications.
Prices: $18 each (soft cover); $ 5.99 each (e-books). For more details go to **http://www.stevenporter.com.**

New Year's Resolution: My wife, Dawn, and I have been crazy-busy these past 12 months setting up our new bookstore. We've basically been working around the clock. Our New Year's Resolution is to simply find more time this year to relax and spend quality time at home.

As 2019 approaches, Porter has three-and-a-half new books written and a fourth book of shorter works and essays ready to go. "My resolution is to have at least two books finished and ready for the 2019 holiday season," he says.

RICHARD T. ROOK, of Wrentham, Massachusetts, wrote *Tiernan's Wake*. The book is a historical mystery about a search for the "missing portrait" of the Irish Pirate Queen Grace O'Malley, but more importantly, it's about how relationships and priorities change as we age.

Publisher: Lulu.com.
Price: $15.97 (soft cover).
For details go to **http://www.amazon.com** and search "Tiernan's Wake," or google "Tiernan's Wake."

New Year's Resolution: Never to forget that the most important things in life are health, family, and friends. If we have those, we don't really need much else. To finish at least one sequel, listen more and talk less, and to keep my brain and body moving as much as possible.

RAYMOND A. WOLF, 76, of Hope, wrote a three-volume set, *Rhode Island Outhouses Today*, detailing exterior and interior color photographs of 469 outhouses discovered throughout the Ocean State, including details such as when each was built and number of holes. A second five-volume set (cars from 1905 to 1949, the 1950s, the 1960s the 1970s and trucks from 1921 to 1979) identifies more than 1,100 cars and trucks photographed (in color) at Rhode Island cruise nights, car shows, and private collections. Photo captions explain when the vehicle was purchased, in or out of state, did the owner restore it or was it completely restored already, and identifies the owner, too.

Publisher: Wolf Publishing.
Prices: $21.99 for each book (soft cover).
For more details go to **http://www.raywolfbooks.com.**

New Year's Resolution: Like previous years, his 2019 resolution is "never give up my dreams."

The Association of Rhode Island Authors (ARIA) is a 501(c)(3) non-profit organization of local, published writers of both fiction and non-fiction committed to raising awareness of the outstanding written works crafted by writers in Rhode Island and other nearby communities. For details about ARIA's 340 authors or to join the organization, go to **http://www.riauthors.org.**

REGULAR FOLKS GIVE SOUND ADVICE TO CLASS OF 2016 FOR FUTURE SUCCESS

Published in the *Pawtucket Times* on June 6, 2016

A s in previous years, high-profile commencement speakers are coming to Rhode Island's colleges and universities, selected to give to the robed 2016 graduates unique practical tips as to how one can have a rewarding personal and professional career. As I mentioned last May in my weekly commentary, these widely-recognized speakers can quickly bring prestige to the educational institution but they often command big bucks for a brief appearance.

Like last year, this writer calls for choosing regular folks to give commencement speeches to graduating college seniors. Their practical tips, suggestions, and "words of wisdom" are honed each and every day at work and through their personal intimate relationships with family and friends, and by the challenges faced throughout their life's journey.

The following advice from these Rhode Islanders can be especially helpful to those graduating to cope in a complex and changing world.

DOUG ALLEN, 53, Douglas, Massachusetts (formerly from Lincoln, Rhode Island), owner of Lincoln Associates: "Look around at your fellow graduates. There is at least one person here that you never spoke to, nor socialized with, that will someday become extremely successful. And they, unfortunately, will remember how they were treated in high school. Don't make this mistake again. Every person you come in contact with could be that person who changes your life. Make it a point to say a kind word to everyone. Otherwise, you will never know if the next Mark Zuckerberg sat beside you in math class your sophomore year."

RICHARD BLOCKSON, 61, Providence, former general manager of the *Pawtucket Times* and *Woonsocket Call*, who currently works in the financial service sector: "Striving to be a person of sound character is an admirable goal. It cannot be bought, given to you, or taken away. It levels the playing field between privileged and underprivileged. It will help guide you through troubled waters and grant you a path of good decisions during your lifetime."

CAROL CONLEY, 60, Pawtucket, assistant to the executive director, Rhode Island Film Office, Rhode Island: "Be grateful. Be kind. Karma is a real thing. Give to others what you would like to receive, and it will eventually come back to you. Wait for it; trust the universe's timing. Challenge yourself. Conquer your fears. Never, ever give up."

MICHELLE DEPLANTE, 29, Cumberland, director of programs, Leadership Rhode Island: "Discover who you are and what strengths you bring to the table. Engage with people who seem the least like you and listen to them to understand, not simply to reply. Become comfortable with the uncomfortable—you'll grow as a person, and life will never be boring. Get to know your neighbors and be accountable to your community."

DIANE DUFRESNE, 63, Pawtucket, director at Pawtucket Prevention Coalition: "Take the knowledge and experience of those who have mentored you and invested in you, those who have helped mold your life and use that to become the best version of yourself that you can be... use what you have gained and contribute to make society better... one day you will have the opportunity to mentor others, and you will impact another person to do the same."

PAUL C. HARDEN, 56, Newport, director of transportation technology at New England Institute of Technology: "As a college graduate, take every opportunity to learn, consider new ideas, and develop new skills. You do not have to go back to school and get another degree. Try reading books, taking a free online course, or finding a mentor who can give you sound counsel."

MIKE LYONS, 73, East Providence, corporate and community partnerships, Pawtucket Red Sox Baseball Club: "Henry David Thoreau is the author of one of my favorite quotes: 'To affect the quality of the day, that is the highest of the arts.' College graduates in particular have both the opportunity and responsibility that their education has afforded them to make each day matter."

JOHN RESNICK, 52, Cranston, entrepreneur: "I have learned that your parents may try to live their lives through you and your career choice. Never give up your own dreams to follow the dreams and plans your parents may have for you. The only thing that you owe your parents is the promise that you continually pursue happiness throughout the course of your life."

WAYNE ROSENBERG, 60, Providence, real estate broker and construction manager: "Most college degrees are not going to be your ticket to financial freedom. Your most important challenge you will face is finding meaningful work. You must realize that no one can do this for you but yourself. Take charge. If you cannot find employment, consider becoming your own boss and employ yourself."

JOYCE SILVESTRI, 62, Seekonk, Massachusetts, former banquet director at Twelve Acres: "As you are entering upon your post-graduation experience, it is important to remember that as much as you are all vying for possible jobs or post-graduate education, the competition will be even greater than you have experienced so far. Reflecting on what you have heard and seen in this election year, you would be wise to entertain this workplace or educational competition without losing sight of civility. That would be your true success."

JIM TIERNAN, 55, Hamilton, owner of 80 Fountain Street, LLC, a Pawtucket mill that houses artists and creative sector companies: "It is important for graduating seniors to realize that not many people know what they want to be when they 'grow up.' Don't fret about making that perfect choice or worry that you don't have a passion for your chosen field of education. You won't always make perfect choices, but with a little thought and feedback from your friends and those older, your choice will lead you in a positive direction. Wherever you land, learn from those around you with more experience and become as fully engaged in life as you possibly can. You only go around once."

RICO VOTA, 34, Cranston, communications & constituent affairs officer, City of Pawtucket. "You never know when the last time you talked to someone is going to be the last time you talk to someone. Make every interaction you have with people count for something."

And this writer concludes with his favorite quote from the Roman poet Horace's Odes: "Carpe Diem, Quam Minimum Credula Postero." Translation: "Seize the day, put very little trust in tomorrow."

14. SPIRITUALITY & HELPING OTHERS

"Aging is a stage in life that's especially ripe for us to get free."

—Ram Dass in *One-Liners*

BUTTERFLIES BRING COMFORT IN TIME OF GRIEVING

Published in RINewsToday on June 25, 2020

Susan feels "joy in her heart and complete happiness" whenever she sees a butterfly. A butterfly came into her life as she mourned her brother's death in 1990. Before he died, she remembers her brother saying that he would come back as a butterfly. The 62-year-old Pawtucket resident says "he meant it," and she believes he has sent messages to her through butterflies each year for more than 30 years.

She believes the butterflies that play in the garden during the late spring and summer every year could possibly be other family members (deceased husband and father) and friends that have departed. "Most of them knew the story of the butterfly, and perhaps they too wished to come back as a beautiful butterfly. I know I would love to come back as a beautiful butterfly if I had the chance," she says.

Significance of Butterflies Brings Sign from Beyond

Looking back, Susan remembers meeting her future husband, Stephen, after the death of her first husband. She was introduced to him by her close friend Jackie. As the three dined at an outdoor restaurant in Tiverton, Jackie quickly pointed at a beautiful monarch butterfly sitting on a purple butterfly bush not far from their table. As they gazed at the lovely sight, a text message came into Susan's cellphone from her next-door neighbor who had sent a photo of a monarch butterfly sitting on a purple butterfly bush in Susan's backyard in Pawtucket. Both sightings of the monarch butterfly were at the same time of day, both directed to Susan—one in Pawtucket and one in Tiverton.

"I knew what was happening here. My brother, maybe my husband and my dad (both deceased) were telling me that Stephen is the man for me. That's why I married him! Well, besides, he's a good man too," said Susan.

Like Susan, Phyllis Calvey, 68, a writer, speaker, educator, and storyteller, sees the significance of the butterfly and how it can bring comfort in one's darkest hours after the death of a loved one. In *The Butterfly Club: "Is That You?"* the Bellingham, Massachusetts writer shares her inspirational true-life stories of how God can, and does, use signs to communicate His presence to "those in need." "It's a book that people can pass on to someone they know who has lost a loved one," she says.

"My book has brought comfort to many who had not yet found the closure they were hoping for. And still, for some, the age-old question persists, 'Was it a sign or just a coincidence?'

"Their underlying need bleeds through—I need more proof! I believe I have found 'more proof' in the butterfly phenomenon," she says. When Calvey began hearing from others who crossed her path about how God used the sign of a butterfly to comfort those grieving the loss of a loved one, she began to explore these occurrences, becoming more aware of their frequency of happening. Calvey began to hear about other "sign stories"—red cardinals, dragonflies, feathers, music, flowers, and even a "divine fortune cookie," to name a few.

The 136-page nonfiction book of inspirational stories detailing the butterfly phenomenon brings up the age-old debate for discussion, "Are these signs, or merely coincidences, or an incidental occurrence?" For Calvey they are not coincidental. As a caregiver for parents who were allowed to die in their own homes, there are always "great matters of life and death," to deal with, says Calvey in writing her book. "Two people in the equation—one wondering if their loved one will be okay, along with the finality of facing if they truly believe there is an afterlife. And one soon to be on the other side wondering the same. Both hoping to somehow be able to communicate that answer. *The Butterfly Club* is the communication of their answer," she says.

Calvey recounts a story told her by Jackie, her cousin, who attended the wake of her brother. She had met a man wearing a butterfly pin on his lapel. In conversation, he mentioned that his daughter, AnneMarie, had died of leukemia in 1997. It seems that the 17-year-old had clearly found a way to send a signal to her father that she was okay, through a butterfly. When asked about the lapel pin, he smiled and said, "Welcome to the Butterfly Club," and then walked away.

"There wasn't a name for this experience, but in talking to people, you learn just how many people share it," Calvey said, thus—naming her tome, "Welcome to the Butterfly Club." Calvey herself had shared in a butterfly encounter many years before she wrote *The Butterfly Club* when Danny, an 18-year-old outgoing, charismatic, loved-by-everyone boy from her church community was killed by a hit-and-run driver after leaving for college three weeks earlier.

"His mother, Nancy, was at a point where she felt she couldn't bear to go on," Calvey explained. "She took a walk in the woods and sat on a fallen log wanting to bury herself in her grief, when a monarch butterfly alighted on a small stick near her feet. Danny's mother bent down to pick it up and sensed that the butterfly would not fly away. She looked at it in her hands and described this feeling to me, that it was as if her son were speaking the words to her himself, 'Mom, it's okay. I'm all right.'

"The transformation I saw in her and the healing that followed was no less than miraculous," Calvey said. Now, when people ask her if they could have real proof that a butterfly can be a sign from God or a loved one, she tells them "people like Nancy are all the real proof I need!"

Fortune Cookies Bring Messages Too

At a Cranston book signing event, Calvey told this writer a story from her book, describing a divine sign that came through a message from a fortune cookie, delivered in perfect timing, one that brought comfort to her and was an "undeniable message" from her deceased father that he "was okay, and with God." As her father was dying, Calvey sensed his fear of dying and the unknown and sought to comfort him by saying, "You do know that you are going to heaven?" She stressed that he had lived his whole life as an example of the Good Samaritan in the parable that Jesus told. Calling him a "Good Samaritan" she recounted all the people throughout his life that he had helped. The day after he died, Chinese food was brought in, and Calvey's mother opened a fortune cookie, receiving this message: "The Good Samaritan did not get his name through good intentions."

"The sign of the fortune cookie could not have been a more perfect communication to deliver the message to our family that our father was indeed in heaven," Calvey explained.

Calvey has heard from readers from all over the world who found comfort and closure by knowing a loved one can still communicate through signs across the veil by reading her book. Their shared experience is the key for those who haven't seen their sign as of yet and, perhaps, will help them learn how to recognize their own encounter.

"A sign is undeniable. It's making the connection of the perfect timing of a loved one delivering a message to you that constitutes the difference," adds Calvey. "But through the years, I've found it never works to ask God for a sign. Signs come to you only in God's perfect timing," she says.

Calvey's book details stories of people who experience universal signs. "They don't know they are part of a club," she says. "But they are." Readers can share their views or tell their own "sign story" or purchase, *The Butterfly Club: "Is That You?"* by going to **http://www.butterflyclubbook.com**. To order, go to **pcalvey@hotmail.com**. Or call (617) 869-2576.

"BOSOM BUDDIES" BRINGS HEALING TO BREAST–CANCER SURVIVORS

Published in the *Woonsocket Call* on November 26, 2017

Sometimes a personal health-related issue and one's professional life experiences blend together almost seamlessly to create an opportunity to help others in similar situations. It took more than 20 years for Mary Jane Condon Bohlen, a Cranston resident, professional photographer, artist, former teacher, and breast-cancer survivor, to do just that, achieving her dream of publishing her book, *Bosom Buddies*.

Each photograph of the 29 women posing in *Bosom Buddies* reveals the scars of breast reconstruction and the coffee-table book also features an essay, poem, or other writing from the model on the opposite page, providing further insight into the journey through breast cancer.

"I chose the name *Bosom Buddies* as the title of this book and photographed my 'buddies' kayaking, riding horses, working in their gardens, singing, doing yoga and other loves," says Bohlen. "I sought to reveal the thoughts, fears, inner spirit, and especially the hopes of those brave enough to bare their bodies and show their beauty," in a book that took two years to complete.

In May 2008, after living with a mastectomy of her right breast for 16 years, she was told that cancer had returned to her left side. Now with two mastectomies breast cancer gave her the insight and wisdom to photograph women in a vulnerable health state to appear in *Bosom Buddies*. The women photographed are typical of women who "battle breast cancer every day." Bohlen says.

"They have taken their bravery one step further by allowing themselves to be photographed in subtle and delicate settings," says Bohlen.

The Inspiration

As a fourth-grader, Bohlen began taking pictures with a camera that her parents gave her. In later years, as a medical photographer working in hospitals all over the city of Boston she photographed artificial hearts being implanted in pigs and cows, cutting-edge surgeries on humans, a 16mm movie of a lung transplant in a rat photographed through a microscope, social events that included dignitaries, film, TV, and Broadway stars, weddings, bar mitzvahs, and PR work, in addition to her own fine art photography, including *Bosom Buddies*.

Bohlen, 73, remembers that her desire to publish *Bosom Buddies* began in 1993 in Ledyard, Connecticut, one year after she was diagnosed and treated for breast cancer. Standing by a magnificent tree more than 400 years old, 90 feet high with a circumference of about 26 feet, where Native Americans had gathered to vote on tribal issues, Bohlen began snapping photos of the remains of the dead tree damaged by gypsy moths over the centuries. Upon close inspection of the printed images she saw a one-breasted figure that immediately inspired her to create an aquatint etching, which she would call *Bosom Buddy*.

"The Ledyard Oak became my 'Bosom Buddy' and helped me to relate to my inner beauty that was so much more meaningful than what was found beneath my clothing," says Bohlen.

Ultimately her etching would lead to the publishing of a coffee-table book including photos and essays of breast-cancer survivors expressing how breast cancer has affected their lives. A short biography about what they are now doing with their life is also included. "I wanted the world to know that there is life after breast cancer. Life goes on, and it isn't always a death sentence," she says.

Reflections from "Bosom Buddies"

Sharyn Vicente, 52, of Cumberland, was photographed at a spa in Arizona during a special trip. In 2008, Vicente was diagnosed with cancer at the age of 41. Initially she did not wish to be photographed but went outside of her comfort level to participate in the project.

Vicente details in her essay in *Bosom Buddies* how breast cancer impacted her life. "It was a long road with many unexpected bumps along the way. In three short years, I had both breasts removed, half of my right kidney, my uterus and both ovaries. While I felt that my body was systematically being hollowed out, I thought that I really didn't deserve yet another escape from the grim reaper. This all also made me feel as though I was no longer a woman."

"Cancer did not and will not rule my life," says a reflective Vicente in her biography, noting that she spends time fundraising for the Gloria Gemma Breast Cancer Resource Foundation (GGBCRF) and mentoring woman going through the diagnosis and treatment of breast cancer. Participating in this book project began the healing process.

Nicole Bourget-Brien, 47, a two-time breast-cancer survivor celebrating a decade of being cancer-free, was photographed lifting hand weights in her brother-in-law's gym. The photograph captured how she felt that day: "strong."

The Woonsocket resident was warned that after the mastectomy she might not be able to exercise at the same level as before the surgery. "I have proven that to be false. I am working out more vigorously now than I did when I was in my 20s," she says.

In her biography in the book, Bourget-Brien says, "I have made a choice to live and not just exist after my cancer diagnosis. I have learned to breathe—to remember that the rearview mirror is smaller because it is where we have been and to look through the windshield to enjoy what lies ahead."

Tracey Donahue Henebury, 48, sits on a rock by a pond sunning herself. She urges readers of *Bosom Buddies* to "look beyond the scars and nudity and read each and every heart-warming story which describes the strength, sacrifices, and fears each one of us has faced." The book is just "breathtaking," she says.

Over the last couple of years, she has been on "an emotional rollercoaster due to the complications of her mastectomy," admits Henebury. In *Bosom Buddies*, she states, "Nothing has knocked me down where I don't get back up on my feet." Support from family and friends and The Gloria Gemma Foundation "enhanced my scars as beauty and strength."

Of course, you will find a self-portrait showing Bohlen wearing boxing gloves, ready to fight a battle against cancer. After her second mastectomy, neither her friends nor family "got it." "No one to tell me they knew what I was going through, no one to ask questions about what to expect. I knew no one else with breast cancer, it was a lonely journey," she says in her essay in *Bosom Buddies*.

Relocating to Rhode Island and connecting with the Pawtucket-based GGBCRF changed her life, providing her with a support system and friends. She supports the nonprofit by donating 50 percent of the profits of her $40 book to the foundation.

Bohlen now resides with her husband of almost 47 years, Bob, in Cranston. Her daughter, Nie, and 8-year-old grandson, Sam, along with her youngest son, Patrick, live close by while her older son, Bobby, lives in Portland, Oregon.

There is a real need for this book to find its way to women recently diagnosed with breast cancer and to their families and friends. In 2017, breast cancer will claim the lives of 40,610 women throughout the nation, predicts the American Cancer Society, a nationwide voluntary-health organization dedicated to eliminating cancer. More than 300,000 women in the US will become breast-cancer survivors.

Bosom Buddies has allowed the breast-cancer survivors participating in this unique book project to come to terms with their inner and exterior scars and has enhanced their body image after a mastectomy. Bohlen knows that this healing will take place in readers as well.

At the 2016 National Indie Excellence Awards, Bohlen's book, *Bosom Buddies* was one of three finalists in the Photography division and the winner in the Cancer Books division.

To purchase, call Mary Jane Condon Bohlen at 401-474-8903 or email to **bosombuddies1@verizon.net**.

DAILY GRATITUDE IS ALWAYS GOOD FOR YOUR HEALTH

Published in the *Woonsocket Call* on November 27, 2016

A few days ago we celebrated Thanksgiving, the nation's oldest tradition. More than 48 million Americans traveled a minimum of 50 miles to spend this national holiday with family and friends, and a whopping 46 million turkeys were carved at these gatherings, served with mashed potatoes, gravy, stuffing, green beans, pumpkin and pecan pie.

Thanksgiving always falls on the fourth Thursday of November. It is a leisurely day to catch up with others while centered on eating a traditional Thanksgiving dinner. Many will turn on their TVs to watch National Football League games, the Macy's Thanksgiving Day Parade, or even see the pre-taped Westminster Dog Show.

But with all these outer activities taking place throughout this day, we must not forget that Thanksgiving is a time to be thankful and show gratitude for all our personal and professional blessings.

Being Grateful, Giving Thanks

For this weekly commentary this writer reached out to Rhode Islanders asking them to think about and acknowledge what they were grateful for, and here were their thoughts...

JOHN S. BAXTER, JR., 48, director of constituent services, office of the president of the Senate, is grateful for being able to use professional developed skills to assist in his volunteer work. "Today, I am thankful for being able to make my living helping people through my service in the Rhode Island Senate. I'm also particularly thankful for lessons learned on the job that can be applied when I volunteer in my community; whether it is feeding the hungry, assisting persons with disabilities or supporting the arts," says Baxter, a Pawtucket resident.

JEFFREY BRIER, 63, president of Brier & Brier, is thankful for his family and business clients. This Warren resident says, "I am thankful to sit with my family and enjoy our Thanksgiving meal and each other's presence. Saddened by those who are not with us and for those who have passed on." As an insurance agent, Brier says he finds it gratifying "to meet so many nice people with whom I enjoy working and assisting with their personal and business insurance."

GREG GERRITT, 63, a Providence resident, puts his words into action. Gerritt, founder of Buy Nothing Day Winter Coat Exchange, noted, "I actually skipped when they went around the table asking each to say what they were thankful for. I do not think of it that way. What I did was organize the 20th Buy Nothing Day Winter Coat Exchange. Might be different sides of the same coin."

DENISE PANICHAS, 62, is thankful for the "selfless people" that come into her life. "Being in the nonprofit world, I'm always amazed at how selfless people can be, and no one even knows the good deeds they do...at this time of year, I always take a step back and think to myself: What would the world be without with those willing to sacrifice their time and talents?," says Panichas, a Woonsocket resident who serves as executive director of The Samaritans of Rhode Island.

SCOTT ROTONDO, 43, of Pawtucket, says his "cup truly runneth over" when asked what he is thankful for. The controller at Boston, Massachusetts-based Tivoli Audio, acknowledges, "I'm grateful for my career, my radio show and most of all our newest family addition, my daughter, Jessica, whom we adopted out of foster care. I have made it a point to sincerely thank my family for all the support and love they've shared with me this year."

Finally, **SCOTT WOLF**, 63, a Providence resident, is grateful for positive role models he had while growing up. Wolf, executive director at Grow Smart RI, says, "I thought about how lucky I have been to have so many outstanding role models—my parents first and foremost among them—who are now gone physically but still inspiring me to leave my own positive mark on society."

Being Grateful is Good for Your Health

According to Michael Craig Miller, MD, senior editor, mental-health publishing at Harvard Health Publications, "the simple act of giving thanks is not just good for the community but may also be good for the brain and body."

"By acknowledging the goodness in their lives, expressing gratitude often helps people recognize that the source of that goodness lies at least partially outside themselves. This can connect them to something larger—other people, nature, or a higher power," says Miller, in his blog article entitled, "In Praise of Gratitude," posted on the Harvard health website on October 29, 2015.

In Miller's blog posting, he notes, "In the relatively new field of positive psychology research, gratitude is strongly and consistently linked to greater happiness. Expressing gratitude helps people feel positive emotions, relish good experiences, improve their health, deal with adversity, and build strong relationships."

Adds Robert A. Emmons, Ph.D., on his blog article, "Why Gratitude is Good," posted on November 10, 2015 on the Greater Good Science Center's website, gratitude can allow us to "celebrate the present."

According to Emmons, a professor of psychology at the University of California, Davis, and the founding editor-in-chief of *The Journal of Positive Psychology*, research findings indicate that "gratitude blocks toxic, negative emotions." These findings also show that "grateful people are more stress resistant" and "have a higher sense of self-worth."

So, don't wait until next Thanksgiving to show gratitude for all the good things surrounding you today. Be thankful for everything positive in your life, each and every day. Research tells us that showing gratitude may well be good for your physical and mental well-being.

REVELATIONS BRING TOGETHER HEAVEN AND EARTH

Published in the *Woonsocket Call* on July 17, 2016

A pproaching their twilight years, aging baby boomers might occasionally think about their impending mortality, even contemplating what happens after their last breath is taken, wondering what lies beyond the veil. But a growing number of people who have reported Near Death Experiences (NDE) may just shed some light on this age-old question.

Although some people, diagnosed clinically dead, come back to life after being revived with no conscious memory of this experience, others experiencing an NDE report vivid, personal memories of their out-of-body trip across the veil. During this spiritual experience, the person may meet dead family, friends, and even their spiritual teacher, see a white light or travel through a tunnel.

Critics of NDE may try to explain away this experience as being the result of psychological and physiological causes, but those who come back with direct knowledge of the afterlife don't buy these explanations.

Dozens of books have been published, many being listed on the *New York Times* bestsellers list, detailing the author's clinical death and NDE they strongly believe is evidence of an afterlife.

One book, published by Rodale Books in 2015, details what Tommy Rosa, a Bronx-born plumber learned in 1999 about health and healing during his NDE and coming back to life. Rosa's chance meeting at a conference with Dr. Stephen Sinatra, an integrative cardiologist and psychotherapist, seen on *Dr. Oz* and *The Doctors*, would lead to the publishing of a 247-page book, *Health Revelations from Heaven and Earth*.

A reading of this book reveals two very different approaches of looking at health, one gleaned from a spiritual experience and the other by scientific training, but both lead to the same set of conclusions. The tome offers eight health revelations (being connected with others, faithfulness, your vital force, grounding, being positive, self-love, seeing your body as a temple, and life's purpose) geared to helping you live your best, healthiest life, revitalize yourself and embrace a newfound sense of purpose and spiritual balance—gleaned from Rosa's experience and fully corroborated by four decades of medical expertise and other scientific evidence by Dr. Sinatra, who practices in St. Petersburg, Florida, and Manchester, Connecticut.

Rosa believes experiences described in his book are different from other NDE books published. His eight revelations can be applicable in the reader's daily life.

To date, Rosa has promoted his book and his heavenly revelations in newspapers, radio, and television. More than 20,000 copies of his book have been sold.

Peeking Over the Veil

Eighteen years ago, Rosa was walking across the street to a local convenience store to buy bread when he was hit by a car and became clinically dead for several minutes. Right after he was hit, Rosa felt a tug whisking him off into a tunnel of light [a common NDE]. The 58-year-old was rushed to the hospital and resuscitated, but remained in a coma for weeks. During his NDE, Rosa found himself in "Heaven," where he met a spiritual teacher and was taught the fundamentals about health and healing.

Ultimately, Rosa remembers that he would emerge from his coma not only grateful to be alive, but with a newfound sense of intuition, increased empathy, and more awareness of the connection between Heaven and Earth.

Rosa, a founder of the Stuart, Florida-based Unicorn Foundation whose mission is to bring spiritual awareness and education to everyday people, says that the most important revelation of his NDE was that all living things are connected. "No one's actions are isolated to that specific person, but that every action has a ripple effect throughout the energy of our fellow," he says. In this book. Dr. Sinatra confirms the importance of this revelation, noting how the need for human connection lies at the very heart of human existence. He describes how the practitioner's ability to empathize with his patients is what truly facilitates the healing process, and also touches upon how one's emotions can influence their health and overall well-being.

His perspective of religion and living life has changed, too. Although he was raised a strict Catholic, the diversity of beliefs serves "Heaven" leading a person to a higher divine plane of consciousness. "I know now that everything is a dream and that you don't sweat the small stuff," he says.

Synchronicity Births a Book

At the time of Rosa's NDE, Dr. Stephen Sinatra was dismantling the prevailing ideas of preventive pharmacology with his holistic approach to treatment. When Rosa met the Florida-based cardiologist, he got an intuitive feeling that the physician had an infection in his hip. This insight confirmed Dr. Sinatra's own similar thoughts of infection, and he was later diagnosed with a staph infection. When Rosa shared with Dr. Sinatra the divine revelations of healing that he had learned in his celestial travels, the cardiologist was shocked—the keys to solving the imbalance of energy that he had identified as the cause of most chronic illness were the same as those Rosa was relating. Until this point, Dr. Sinatra hadn't thought about how they were all connected, and now it all made sense.

A dinner conversation would propel Rosa and Dr. Sinatra to write *Health Revelations from Heaven and Earth*, a book covering spiritual revelations from Rosa's NDE and putting a medical slant to it. "I was prepped for this incredible conversation as I had many NDEs in my own cardiac practice," remembers Dr. Sinatra. Once Rosa had discussed how he learned not only the importance of "grounding" during his NDE but other health topics that Dr. Sinatra was espousing in his medical practice and at lectures; it was clear to both that a book project must begin. And it did.

Millions Experience NDE

Over the years, Jeffrey Long, M.D., a leading NDE researcher, has documented more than 3,000 NDEs, posted on the website **http://www.nderf.org.** The practicing radiation oncologist says that this database is by far the largest collection of NDEs, available in 22 languages, that is publicly accessible. Readers from more than 100 foreign countries access Dr. Long's website monthly. Each month more than 300,000 pages are read from this website.

Meanwhile, Dr. Long's website notes that although most people who come near death do not remember anything, about 18 percent [like Rosa] later report that "something happened." That "something" is often a near-death experience NDE, says Long. He notes a 1993 Gallup Poll estimated that 12 to

15 million Americans personally experienced a NDE. As of 2001, almost 600 adults per day across the nation experience an NDE.

In this book Rosa pokes a hole in the veil between the living and dead. He tells it like it is. Because of his NDE, he does not fear death. "Death is only a new beginning," he says.

During his 40 years in medical practice, Dr. Sinatra had been at the bedside of many of his dying patients. "Some I saved. Some I lost," he said, acknowledging that being with his dying patients often frightened him. Rosa's spiritual journey and the lessons learned have brought peace to Dr. Sinatra. "In a heartbeat he literally saved me from my own fear of death," he says.

To purchase a copy of *Health Revelations from Heaven and Earth*, go to **http://amazon.com**.

LOCALS MOURN THE PASSING OF DR. WAYNE W. DYER, ICONIC MOTIVATIONAL SPEAKER

Published in the *Woonsocket Call* on September 6. 2015

On August 30, 2015, the internet was ablaze with the news that Dr. Wayne W. Dyer, one of America's most popular self-help authors and motivational speakers in the field of self-development and spiritual growth, had died one day earlier at his home in Maui, Hawaii. He was 75 years old.

On his popular official Facebook page (with more than 2.5 million likes) Dyer's family announced: "Wayne has left his body, passing away through the night. He always said he couldn't wait for this next adventure to begin and had no fear of dying. Our hearts are broken, but we smile to think of how much our scurvy elephant will enjoy the other side."

Who was this man, raised by an alcoholic father and who lived in orphanages and foster homes as a child, whose books, lectures and workshops, CDs, DVDs, streaming videos and weekly radio show, would strikes a chord with millions all over the world?

A Prolific Writer

According to a statement released by Hay House, over four decades the internationally acclaimed author, born and raised in Detroit, Michigan, penned 42 books, 21 of which became *New York Times* bestsellers. Devoted fans would give him the affectionate moniker "the father of motivation."

After a four-year stint in the United States Navy, Dyer would go on to earn his doctorate in educational counseling from Wayne State University before serving as a professor at St. John's University in New York. Throughout his early years as a college educator and as a clinical psychologist, he realized that there was a need to make the principles of self-discovery and personal growth more accessible to the public.

In 1976, Dr. Dyer began his writing career as an author by traveling the nation selling his first book, *Your Erroneous Zones*, right from the trunk of his car. The self-help book went on to become one of the best-selling books of all time, with more than 60 million copies sold, printings in 47 languages, and 64 weeks spent on the *New York Times* bestseller list. This put Dr. Dyer firmly on America's radar screen, resulting in the bookings on *The Tonight Show Starring Johnny Carson* a whopping total of 37 times.

With the publishing of a number of best-selling books on self-improvement under his belt, Dyer turned his attention to exploring the spiritual aspects of human experience. "My purpose is to help people look at themselves and begin to shift their concepts," Dr. Dyer noted at that time.

"Remember, we are not our country, our race, or religion. We are eternal spirits. Seeing ourselves as spiritual beings without label is a way to transform the world and reach a sacred place for all of humanity," he said. Throughout his life this theme would be woven into all his writings, lectures, and workshops.

In 1993, Dyer began publishing his books with Hay House, founded in 1984, and he quickly became one of its most prolific and popular authors. The company, with its headquarters in Carlsbad, California, with international offices in the United Kingdom, Austria, South Africa, and India, has published more than 300 books and 450 audios from 140 authors.

At Hay House, Dr. Dyer also created several audio programs and videos, and appeared on thousands of television and radio shows over the course of his long career. His books *Manifest Your Destiny*, *Wisdom of the Ages*, *There's a Spiritual Solution to Every Problem*, and the *New York Times* bestsellers *10 Secrets for Success and Inner Peace*, *The Power of Intention*, *Inspiration*, *Change Your Thoughts—Change Your Life*, *Excuses Begone!*, *Wishes Fulfilled*, and *I Can See Clearly Now*, have all been featured as PBS specials, raising more than $200 million for public-television stations nationwide.

Dyer did not even forget his alma mater, Wayne State University. He raised more than $1 million for the educational institution.

Dyer's Death Hits Local Followers

In 1974, Gary Calvino, 62, remembers reading his first Dyer book, the *Erroneous Zones*, one that would totally impact how he would live his life. "It changed my life and got me to think about looking inside my being for my happiness rather than seeking it from others." The author's "authenticity" who lived his principles and "walked his talk" kept Calvino reading more of Dyer's books that ultimately would total 42.

Calvino, setting up a new nonprofit, Mindful Rhode Island, to create an interconnected web of mindfulness throughout the Ocean State, also treasured a chance meeting with Dyer at a lecture in New York City, he says. The Providence resident described a 10-minute private encounter with the motivational speaker, "a gratitude conversation," he says that would ultimately give him a way to communicate in a more "heartfelt way" with his dying father.

"It hit me very hard when I heard of Dyer's death," says Calvino. "I know he had no fear of dying, and he is now in a great place," he adds.

"Reading and watching him on videos over the years actually allowed me to grow with him," says Calvino, stressing that he was able to follow the author through all phases of his personal and spiritual growth. "Every book he wrote was a learning experience for him. With his passing, I will miss his inspirational wisdom."

Wanda Morrison, whose family business, Mind Body Barre is in three locations in southern Massachusetts, has followed the teachings of Dyer since her early teenage days. The 52-year-old says, "I have always known when his books came out, and I probably have read them all."

Morrison's says Dyer had the "most soothing presence and aura about him," adding that people felt his "powerful presence of love and healing."

"'If you change the way you look at things, the things you look at change,' is one of my favorite Dyer quotes," says Morrison, stressing that it's made her more aware that she is a co-creator in her world.

"I was speechless and so sad when I heard of his passing," Morrison says. "There will never be another person like him. His wisdom and way he chose to dedicate his life to help others with writings that were so simple and easy to understand will be hard to duplicate," she noted.

"I will be reading his books and listening or watching his lectures for the rest of my life. He will forever be a part of my world," says Morrison.

Yes, Dyer taught us to overcome both their perceived and real physical limitations to make their dreams come true. If his life mission on Earth was to teach his loyal following to connect with their "Higher Self," he truly succeeded.

Dr. Dyer was married three times, separated from his third wife, and had eight children and nine grandchildren.

To order books, videos, CDs, go to **http://www.drwaynedyer.com**.

15. TRAVEL

"Twenty years from now you will be more disappointed by the things that you didn't do than by the ones you did do. So throw off the bowlines. Sail away from the safe harbor. Catch the trade winds in your sails. Explore. Dream. Discover."

—Mark Twain

SIZING UP BABY BOOMER TRAVEL TRENDS

Published in the *Woonsocket Call* on December 16, 2018

Over a week ago, AARP Travel released the long-awaited results of its annual travel-trend survey, examining travel behaviors across generations, looking at expectations and planning among baby boomers (ages 54 to 72), Gen Xers (38 to 53), and Millennials (ages 21 to 37).

According to the new national AARP survey, boomers, considered to be enthusiastic travelers, expressed an eagerness to travel in 2019, planning to take a total of four to five leisure trips, on which they will spend more than $6,600 (compared to Gen Xers spending $5,400 and Millennials outlaying $4,440.)

Meanwhile, a small number of the AARP survey's respondents say they will travel only internationally (6 percent) while the rest are equally split between traveling throughout the nation (48 percent) or traveling both domestically and internationally (48 percent).

Planning a Trip is Not Last Minute

According to the 47-page *2019 Boomer Travel Trends Report*, released on December 3, 2018, this year's travel planning is taking place earlier as compared to previous years. A significant majority of boomers (88 percent) planning domestic trips in 2019 have already selected their destination, an increase from 72 percent of 2018 domestic travelers. For boomers traveling abroad, 31 percent had booked their 2019 trips by September 2018, up from 23 percent by September of the previous year in 2018 and 17 percent in 2017.

The AARP survey notes that when boomers travel overseas, Europe overall continues to be the most popular choice followed by Italy and France. The findings also indicate that trips to the Caribbean and South and Central America remain popular, but interest in Mexico is waning.

For boomers, domestic travel preferences have not changed in several years; Southern and Western states continue to be popular to most older travelers.

Boomers are most likely to plan summer vacations (13 percent), weekend get-aways (12 percent), and multi-generational trips (11 percent).

Travel destination preferences remain unchanged from last year, with Florida (17 percent) being the top-mentioned location followed by California (11 percent), New York (5 percent), Texas (5 percent), and Las Vegas (5 percent).

"According to this research, boomers' travel plans in 2019 are focused on spending time with family and friends, while getting away from everyday life," said Patty David, director of Consumer Insights and Personal Fulfillment in a statement. "Whether it's a weekend road trip or an international vacation, boomers are eager to travel in 2019 and are planning earlier and spending more than in years past." she says.

The AARP Travel survey results also indicate that when traveling, boomers seek connection with locals for an authentic experience, especially over meals or when taking tours on international trips. Work was not found to be the biggest barrier to travel for older travelers, but cost (40 percent) and health issues/concerns (32 percent) were mentioned most often by the survey respondents.

Boomer respondents also tend to travel to get away from the day-to-day routines (47 percent) to relax (48 percent), and to spend time with family and friends (57 percent). Twenty-four percent of the boomers say they have placed taking an international vacation on their life's bucket list.

Researchers also took a look at intergenerational travel trends, too. Thirty-two percent of grandparents have taken their grandkids on a skip-generation trip, leaving mom and pop at home, and 15 percent of these older travelers are already planning to do so in 2019. Seventy-seven percent of these boomers will do most of the trip planning themselves, and 76 percent will pay for most of the trip.

Working boomers do not feel compelled to stay connected to the office while traveling, but those who choose to will limit contact time, says the AARP survey's finding. A few have even taken the opportunity to extend work trips for pleasure and fun or intend to do so in future trips.

Finally, most of the AARP survey respondents say they travel with a smartphone on domestic trips, but only about half choose to bring them on international trips. The top use for these phones while on vacation is to take photos.

Boomer Travel Trends in the Nation's Smallest State

Lara Salamano, chief marketing officer of the Rhode Island Commerce Corporation, sees tourism as an important industry in the state. "It is the fifth-largest industry in Rhode Island by employment, and in 2017, the total traveler economy reached $6.5 billion," she says.

"Multigenerational vacations featuring extended stays in vacation rentals or weekend family getaways are very popular here in the Ocean State," says Salamano, noting that tourists are taking full advantage of the state's authentic experiences, specifically great food, historic, natural beauty including its beaches, walking and bike trails, and cultural attractions. "We also have a great array of soft adventure activities for the whole family. This is a case where our size works to our advantage as families can easily experience a wide range of different activities in a short period of time," she adds.

Salamano notes that water, sailing, horse-riding on the beach, and golf also attract boomers, too. Rhode Island is playing host to the USGA Senior Open in 2020, she adds.

In addition, boomers are big-shoulder season travelers as they are not tied down by school vacation period. They are free to enjoy midweek and off-peak times of year to avoid higher prices, she says...

While summer remains the state's most popular tourism season, the state's marketing office has identified shoulder seasons as growth opportunities, says Salamano, noting that, "Our most popular trip is domestic travelers living within a three-hour drive."

Salamano sees the Ocean States as quite different from those popular travel destinations chosen by the respondents of this year's AARP's Travel Survey. "Those destinations are also much larger, whereas Rhode Island's small size ensures visitors are spending less time driving in traffic or waiting in lines, and more time actually on vacation. This was the jumping off point for our 'Fun-Sized' ad campaign which we rolled out last year," she said.

To see Fun-Sized videos, go to **http://www.visitrhodeisland.com/press/fun-sized-campaign/**.

Getting the Bang for Your Marketing Dollars

According to Salamano, Rhode Island's public-relations strategy targeting Millennials involves pitching journalists on Rhode Island's latest offerings such as new craft breweries and wineries, restaurants, special events, and hotel accommodations. This has led to placements in national publications (including the *New York Times*, *Washington Post*, *USA Today*, and *Forbes*) as well as more targeted publications such as the *Boston Globe*, the *Milwaukee Journal Sentinel*, and *Time Out New York*.

Digital ads are targeted to both boomers and Millennials. "We have a robust advertising strategy, including digital ad placements to target audiences on websites that include travel planning sites and news publications. Digital advertising allows us to both target audiences and track our performance very effectively. Our 'Fun-Sized' videos feature a wide variety of activities that appeal to both baby boomers and Millennials. This includes rock climbing, horseback riding and bird watching, to music, performances, restaurants, and WaterFire," says Salamano.

To read the full AARP Travel survey results, go to **http://www.aarp.org/ 2019traveltrends**.

LOOKING TO ENHANCE YOUR MENTAL HEALTH AND WELL-BEING? TAKE A TRIP.

Published in the *Woonsocket Call* on October 21, 2018

Just days ago, Washington, DC-based AARP released survey findings tying health and wellness benefits to just planning and taking a leisure trip. According to the 45-page study, authored by Vicki Gelfeld, those who travel reported better emotional and physical health and improved personal relationships and even increased productivity at work. Additionally, overall well-being is one of the biggest advantages of taking a trip, with the benefits starting during the initial planning and extending beyond the trip. The longest-lasting travel benefit reported by the survey respondents is improved relationships with loved ones—lasting six weeks on average.

The AARP Travel Research study, *The Health Outcomes of Travel: Perceptions of Boomers* released October 16, shows four in five boomers experience at least one health benefit during a trip, and 73 percent notice at least one health benefit after coming home. By far, boomers get the greatest boost of health benefits during their trip (56 percent). One in five say they experience health benefits before, during, and after the trip equally. But, Millennials experience a far bigger benefit from planning a trip (23 percent) than boomers (6 percent).

"When it comes to travel, getting away with your buddies or girlfriends is the least stressful type of trip as is Spring Break. On the other hand, family reunions, holiday travel, and/or wedding/graduations tend to have the most stress, although predominately still low stress levels," says the survey's findings.

"This research shows there are many health and wellness benefits during all stages of travel across generations, and seeing those benefits significantly improves their satisfaction with the trip," said Alison Bryant, AARP research senior vice president, in a statement. "Any type of travel, whether it's a weekend getaway or a weeklong trip, can be an effective way to renew and recharge, and the benefits far outweigh the short-lived drawbacks," adds Bryant.

According to the AARP Travel Research's survey findings, 21 percent of the survey respondents say they experience health benefits before, during, and after the trip equally. Of the 73 percent of boomers responding who noticed health benefits post-trip, the most unexpected benefits are better sleep (51 percent), more energy (50 percent) and increased productivity (46 percent).

Additionally, these survey findings also indicated that 72 percent of the boomer respondents credit their travel-health benefits simply to relaxation and fun and 67 percent to spending quality time with loved ones. They also indicate that health benefits that most improve during a trip include improved emotional well-being (54 percent), connection with loved ones (52 percent), amount of energy (35 percent), intellectual curiosity (34 percent) and finally, mental clarity (30 percent).

Additionally, planning a trip completely focused on wellness is not done by many and does not differ by generation. The survey findings reveal that a wellness-focused trip is most likely a result of more intergenerational travel happening within the younger group surveyed. When planning and taking a trip, wellness is not thought of as an underlying reason to travel, but as a byproduct. However, most are open to just letting the feeling of wellness happen. A significant majority of boomers (96 percent) who planned a wellness activity on their trip, but did not exclusively focus on it, said they were "somewhat or very satisfied."

As Others See AARP's Travel Survey Findings …

"This further verifies what we have known for some time," said AARP Rhode Island Communications Director John Martin. "Not to be glib, but for Rhode Islanders, 'travel' can also mean crossing a couple of bridges or driving from, say, Coventry to Newport for a night out."

Martin says, "What I mean to say is that the benefits of travel are not limited to expensive, weeklong vacations to distant destinations. Clearly a week in the Caribbean or a trip to relax and enjoy one's children and grandchildren in San Diego are examples of fulfilling travel. But with so many older Rhode Islanders living on tight retirement budgets, that kind of getaway can be infrequent. When AARP hosts fun events such as a recent vineyard tour and wine-tasting in Middletown, the people we see are active and engaged. They arrive full of energy, and you just know they are making the effort to regularly leave home and that they understand that being active is a big part of their health and well-being."

Adds Dan Sullivan, Jr., CEO of Pawtucket-based Collette, "We're excited to see that the AARP Travel survey closely aligns with Collette strategic thinking in terms of the benefits of travel. For years, we've really looked at the benefits of pre-travel when the anticipation factor sets in. For boomers, having travel as something to really look forward to is invaluable."

The AARP Travel survey results can be found at: **http://www.aarp.org/travelwell**.

AARP Travel, (go to **http://www.aarp.org/travel/**) a valuable resource for Americans age 50 and over, who spend more than $125 billion annually in leisure travel, helps travelers stretch their dollar and itineraries while also stretching their minds and possibilities. AARP Travel provides all interested travelers with vacation ideas, tips, and inspiration for their next getaway.

For details about Collette "one-of-a-kind" tours and vacations, go to **http://www.gocollette.com/en**.

16. VETERANS

"Never was so much owed by so many to so few."   —Winston Churchill

ANALYSIS SAYS THAT AGING VETERANS ARE AT GREATER RISK OF ALZHEIMER'S DISEASE

Published in the *Woonsocket Call* on October 2, 2017

O n Monday, October 2, at a press conference Us Against Alzheimer's, (UsA2), along with veterans' groups, plan to release an issue brief, "Veterans and Alzheimer's Meeting the Crisis Head On," with data indicating that many older veterans will face a unique risk factor for Alzheimer's as a direct result of their military service.

Following the release of this issue brief, on the Tuesday evening reception in Room 106 of the Dirksen Senate Office Building, UsA2, a Washington, DC-based Alzheimer's advocacy group whose mission is to stop Alzheimer's disease by 2020, will launch Veterans Against Alzheimer's (VA2), a national network of veterans and their families, military leaders, veterans' groups, researchers, and clinicians, to focus on raising awareness of the impact of Alzheimer's and other dementias on active and retired military service members.

Dramatic Increase in Veterans with Alzheimer's

Forty-nine percent of those aging veterans age 65 (WW2, Korea, Vietnam and even younger veterans, from the Iraq and Afghanistan conflicts in the coming decades), are at greater risk for Alzheimer's compared to 15 percent of nonveterans over age 65, note the authors of the issue brief. "There is a clear and compelling obligation for greater support to meet the needs of veterans with Alzheimer's," they say.

The issue brief pulls together research-study findings released by the US Department of Veteran's Affairs (VA). One study estimates that more than 750,000 older veterans have Alzheimer's disease and other dementias, another noting that the number of enrollees with Alzheimer's grew 166 percent, from roughly 145,000 in 2004 to 385,000 in 2014.

"Minority communities are at greater risk for Alzheimer's, and minority veterans are predicted to increase from 23.2 percent of the total veteran population in 2017 to 32.8 percent in 2037," says a VA study.

The issue brief also cites study findings that indicate that older veterans who have suffered a traumatic brain injury (TBI) are 60 percent are more likely to develop dementia. Twenty-two percent of all combat wounds in Afghanistan and Iraq were brain injuries, nearly double the rate seen during Vietnam—increasing these younger veterans' lifetime Alzheimer's risk.

Veterans also face a multitude of barriers to effective Alzheimer's diagnosis and care, including a complex Veteran's Administration health system, a lack of understanding about available benefits, and a stigma related to brain and mental health, say issue-brief authors.

George Vradenburg, UsA2's Chairman and Co-Founder, sums up the message to Congress and federal and state policymakers in the released issue brief: "We need to understand so much more about why brain injuries sustained in battle put veterans at greater risk for Alzheimer's. We must encourage veterans to participate in clinical studies to learn about the long-term effects of brain injuries, so we can do everything in our power to mitigate the impact on those who have given so much to this country."

A Call for Funding...

When former Lieutenant Governor Elizabeth Roberts released Rhode's Alzheimer's plan in 2013, to guide and coordinate the state's efforts to care for those with debilitating Alzheimer's and those who care for them, she called the report a "living document," to be continually updated as needed.

With the 5-year update of the State's plan due June 2019, to be submitted to the Rhode Island General Assembly, Lieutenant Governor Dan McKee and the executive board of the Alzheimer's Disease and related disorders working group, will roll up their sleeves to meet that legislative deadline.

McKee and his Alzheimer's plan working group are turning to philanthropic organizations, like the Rhode Island Foundation, to fund their efforts to update the state's Alzheimer's plan. Yes, it costs money to do this and with the incidence of Alzheimer's increasing in the Ocean State, lawmakers and state policymakers need an updated plan to provide them with a road map to effectively utilize state resources and dollars to provide care for those afflicted with the debilitating cognitive disorder.

In 2013, 24,000 Rhode Islanders were afflicted with Alzheimer's disease and other cognitive disorders, and this number will continue to grow each year. With the state being so small, every Rhode Islander is personally touched, either caring for a family member with the cognitive disorder or knowing someone who is a caregiver or patient.

Funding from the Rhode Island General Assembly and philanthropic organizations are needed to get the ball rolling on the state Alzheimer's plan. When updating, don't forget the needs of Rhode Island's aging veterans.

Founded in 2010, Us Against Alzheimer's has worked to secure the national goal of preventing and effectively treating Alzheimer's by 2025 and to assist in securing nearly $500 million in additional public funding for Alzheimer's research over the past few years. The nonprofit's global efforts have influenced the leaders of the world's most powerful nations, the G7, to embrace a similar 2025 goal and to call for greater levels of research investment and collaboration to combat Alzheimer's. Finally, Us Against Alzheimer's works to forge pharmaceutical-industry commitments to improve efficiencies for an expedited drug discovery and approval process.

HONORING THE FALLEN: AUTHOR SALUTES PAWTUCKET RESIDENTS WHO DIED IN VIETNAM WAR

Published in *Senior Digest*, May 2016

For more than 30 years, Terry Nau served as sports editor of the *Pawtucket Times*. When Nau retired in 2012, the seasoned newspaperman did not miss the daily grind of working full-time but soon learned that he missed writing. With free time on his hands, Nau began to write about a part of his life that he had buried for 40 years—his stint in Vietnam as an artilleryman in 1967-68. In his first four years of retirement, the former sports writer would self-publish three books about the Vietnam War.

In 2013, the retiree produced his first book, which dealt with being drafted out of college in 1966 and finding himself in Vietnam by September 1967 for a one-year tour with A Battery, 2/32 Field Artillery. This book, *Reluctant Soldier ... Proud Veteran*, focused on his personal journey towards understanding the role Vietnam played in his life.

A Vietnam Veteran Remembers

For his second book, Nau, a Pennsylvania native, decided to write about the 15 students from his high school who died in Vietnam.

"In 2014, my high-school's 50th reunion committee asked me to try and calculate the number of Vietnam veterans in my Class of 1965," he said, "and from that project came my second book, *We Walked Right Into It: Pennsbury High and the Vietnam War*."

A Pawtucket resident since 1982, Nau said, "It was only natural that I would follow up with a book on Pawtucket and its 21 Vietnam War casualties." His latest book evolved into an oral history, told mostly through the words of surviving family members, friends, and fellow soldiers.

"The courage these families showed became the underlying theme of *They Heard the Bugle's Call: Pawtucket and the Vietnam War*," Nau stated. "It was hard for them to talk about their fallen soldier but after a while, it seemed like they warmed to the idea of remembering these soldiers nearly 50 years after they died," he said.

Celebrating the 50th

Nau's latest book has triggered a movement to honor Pawtucket's "21 Heroes."

"Pawtucket must remember these courageous soldiers, beginning with its first casualty, Marine Corps Lance Corporal Antonio Maciminio, Jr., who died on May 21, 1966," Nau said, noting that the 20-year-old infantry soldier left a pregnant wife who gave birth to their daughter Vicky in October 1966. "Two other soldiers from Pawtucket—Jack Hulme and Michael Dalton—would also die before they ever saw their sons," Nau noted.

On Saturday, May 21, from noon until two o'clock at the pavilion in Slater Memorial Park, the city of Pawtucket will honor its 21 Vietnam War casualties. Antonio J. Pires, director of administration for Mayor Donald Grebien, will speak on behalf of the city. A reading of the city council resolution that declares May 21 as "21 Heroes Day" in Pawtucket will follow.

According to Nau, at least 13 of the 21 families will participate in a Roll Call ceremony that will highlight this event. Each soldier's name will be called out, in the order they fell, beginning with Lance Corporal Maciminio and continuing through Army 1st Lieutenant Michael Dalton, who was the last city resident to die in the war, on June 9, 1971.

The city also plans to honor its surviving Vietnam War veterans with a "Welcome Home" salute from the audience. That will be the final note in an emotional ceremony.

"Vietnam veterans often came home by themselves from the war zone," Nau said. "The welcome they received came from their parents, families and friends. And that was all they wanted. Over the years, our military leaders realized what a mistake it had been to send soldiers home alone, instead of in units. To have the city of Pawtucket honor our Vietnam veterans on the 50th anniversary of the war means a lot to these graying veterans."

"Three of the soldiers' widows will attend, arriving from Florida, California, and New Jersey," Nau said. "Cathy (Maciminio) Dumont is bringing her daughter, Vicky, who turns 50 in October. Vicky will speak her father's name in our Roll Call of heroes. Debbie Dalton and Ellen Hulme will also participate in the Roll Call."

MILITARY RECOGNITION LONG OVERDUE FOR SHEMIN AND JOHNSON

Published in the *Woonsocket Call* on June 7, 2015

Almost a century ago when they fought in the bloody battlefields on Europe's western front, and more than four years after the passing of Frank Buckles, America's last doughboy, in 2011, America's Commander-in-Chief Barack Obama presented the nation's highest military honor to two long-deceased World War I veterans.

At White House ceremony, held on June 2, President Barack Obama recognized the acts of valor of Army Private Henry Johnson, an African-American, and Sergeant William Shemin, who was Jewish. "It's never too late to say thank you," the president told the attendees, including 66 surviving Shemin family members.

"It has taken a long time for Henry Johnson and William Shemin to receive the recognition they deserve," the president said at the formal ceremony to posthumously award the Medal of Honor to the two World War I infantry soldiers for their gallantry and "personal acts of valor above and beyond the call of duty."

Johnson and Shemin fought in France and risked their lives to save others, Obama said, stressing that America "is the country we are today" because they "rose to meet their responsibilities and then went beyond."

The president said, "The least we can do is to say: We know who you are. We know what you did for us. We are forever grateful."

Above and Beyond the Call of Duty

Johnson, an Albany, New York, resident enlisted in the army and was assigned to one of the few units that accepted African-Americans, Company C, 15th New York (Colored) Infantry Regiment—an all-black National Guard unit known as the "Harlem Hellfighters" that later became the 369th Infantry Regiment. Ultimately, the regiment was deployed in 1918, and Johnson's unit brigaded with a French Army colonial unit ending up at the western edge of the Argonne Forest in France's Champagne region.

In the pitch black, pre-dawn hours, in "No Man's Land," Johnson, who had worked before the war as a chauffeur, soda mixer, laborer in a coal yard, and redcap porter at Albany's Union Station, was credited with helping fight off at least 12 soldiers of a German raiding party, despite being wounded, and protecting Sentry Needham Roberts from capture on May 15, 1918.

According to Obama, "Johnson fired until his rifle was empty; he and Roberts threw grenades, and both of them were hit, with Roberts losing consciousness. As the enemy tried to carry away Roberts, Johnson fought back. After his gun jammed, he used it and a Bolo knife to take down the enemy and protect Roberts from capture." Johnson's bravery ultimately would bring a cache of weapons and supplies to the Allies and keep the Germans from gaining valuable intelligence information.

While Johnson was one of the first Americans to receive France's highest award for valor [the Croix de Guerre with Gold Palm] for his bravery in battle "his own nation didn't award him anything—not even the Purple Heart, though he had been wounded 21 times," Obama said.

At the ceremony, Obama also awarded the Medal of Honor to Shemin, a rifleman to Company G, 47th Infantry Regiment, 4th Infantry Division, American Expeditionary Forces, in France.

Shemin, a former semi-pro baseball player and ranger who worked as a forester in Bayonne, New Jersey, repeatedly exposed himself in combat to heavy machine-gun and rifle fire to rescue wounded troops during the Aisne-Marne offensive in France, between August 7 and August 9, 1918.

"After platoon leaders had become casualties, Shemin took command and displayed initiative under fire, until he was wounded by shrapnel and a machine-gun bullet that was lodged behind his left ear," said Obama.

Following three months of hospitalization for his injuries, he was transferred to light duty and served in the army occupation in Germany and Belgium. Shemin received the Purple Heart. He was also awarded the Distinguished Service Cross for battlefield valor on December 29, 1919.

An Act of Congress

It took more than five years to get Shemin's Distinguished Service Cross upgraded to a Medal of Honor, says Colonel Erwin A. Burtnick, (Ret.), who chairs the Awards for Valor Committee, of the Washington, DC-based Jewish War Veterans of the United States (JWV). Elsie Shemin-Roth had approached JWV with her father's records, asking the organization for a review.

Burtnick says Shemin-Ross, a Missouri resident, grew up hearing stories from her father and those who served with him about how anti-Semitism played a role in preventing his recommendation for receiving the Medal of Honor. From the documents submitted and a review of other Distinguished Service Cross and Medal of Honor citations from World War I, the retired colonel felt strongly that if the Jewish soldier had been recommended for the Medal of Honor, he would most likely had received it.

With a federal law required to allow Jewish World War I veterans to receive the Medal of Honor (current law mandates that it must be awarded within five years of when the heroic act being recognized took place), Burtnick asked Shemin-Roth, to help get the ball rolling by contacting Representative Blaine Luekemeyer (R-MO), whose office ultimately drafted the initial legislation, the William Shemin World War I Veterans Act.

Burtnick provided advice in drafting the proposed legislation. Initially introduced in 2010, it was not enacted. However, the legislation along with a companion measure in the Senate introduced by Senator Dean Heller (R-NV) passed and became part of the National Defense Authorization Act (NDAA) of 2012. However, due to a technical requirement, additional legislation was placed in the NDAA of 2015, which allowed the president to award the Medal of Honor to Shemin without regard to the 5-year limitation.

Meanwhile, Senator Charles E. Schumer (D-NY) spearheaded Congressional efforts to get Johnson his Medal of Honor. He knew that the nation's highest military award had long been denied due to racism, but he knew that the African-American deserved recognition for his "bravery and heroism" during World War I.

The New York senator submitted a nearly 1,300-page request to the military in support of Johnson's receiving the Medal of Honor and launched an online petition to build public support. The senator also made a personal call with US Army Secretary John McHugh, met with Under Secretary of Defense for

Personnel and Readiness Jessica Wright—who oversees decisions regarding Medals of Honor—and wrote a letter to Secretary Chuck Hagel, all in an effort to secure the Medal of Honor for Private Johnson.

Senator Schumer, the author of the legislation with the assistance of Senator Ron Wyden (D-OR), successfully pushed for an amendment to be also included in the NDAA of 2015, which also waived the timing restrictions on the Medal of Honor and enabled the president to consider the Medal of Honor request. With Obama's pen stroke, Johnson got his Medal of Honor too.

At the ceremony, Army Command Sergeant Major Louis Wilson, New York National Guard senior enlisted advisor, accepted the medal on Johnson's behalf. Soldiers from the 369th were among the attendees. There were no family members left to accept the prestigious military award.

"It's a blessing; it's an honor; it's a good thing that Henry Johnson is finally being recognized as a hero," Wilson said.

Burtnick came to the White House to see Shemin receive his Medal of Honor and attend a Pentagon enshrinement for the World War I soldier in the Hall of Heroes. "I was elated that our efforts came to fruition. It took over five years to complete," he says, acknowledging that he had fulfilled a pledge to Shemin-Ross when he first contacted her, to meet someday at the White House.

"I was happy to see her, and she was happy to see me," he says.

ABOUT THE AUTHOR

 Herb Weiss has enjoyed a distinguished 40-year career in journalism, earning a national reputation as an expert on aging, health-care and medical issues. More than 790 articles that he has authored or co-authored have appeared in national trade publications and Rhode Island daily, weekly, and monthly newspapers.

The Pawtucket resident writes a weekly senior's commentary covering issues that impact older Rhode Islanders, which is published in *The Pawtucket Times, The Woonsocket Call,* and for *Senior Digest,* a monthly publication. His articles also appear in RINewsToday.com, a statewide news blog.

Herb is a recipient of the 2003 AARP Rhode Island's Vision Award for his weekly newspaper columns. He is a two-time recipient (1994 and 1999) of the American College of Health Care Administrator's National Award for his coverage of long-term care issues. He was also awarded the Distinguished Alumni's Award by the Department of Applied Gerontology at the University of North Texas in 1998, for writings covering senior issues. In 1997, he was selected by the prestigious McKnight's LTC News to be one of its "100 Most Influential People" in Long-Term Care. In 2016, Rhode Island Governor Gina Raimondo appointed him to serve on the Rhode Island Advisory Commission on Aging, and he still sits on this group.

Herb is a 2012 graduate of the Theta II Class of Leadership Rhode Island, Providence, Rhode Island.

In 2014, Weiss co-edited an e-book with Dr. Nancy Carriuolo, then president of Rhode Island College, detailing the emails of Richard Walton, a well-known Rhode Island social activist.

In 2016, Weiss also published a collection of his articles on aging issues, called *Taking Charge: Collected Stories on Aging Boldly.*

Herb and his wife, Patty Zacks, and his chocolate Lab, Molly, reside in Pawtucket, Rhode Island.